OCR AS and A Level Computer Science

P.M. Heathcote

R.S.U. Heathcote

Old Palace *of*
John Whitgift School
Independent Girls' School

If found, please call 020 8688 2027

Date of Issue	Student Name	Form
Oct 23	FAITH A.	12 H

Published by
PG Online Limited
The Old Coach House
35 Main Road
Tolpuddle
Dorset
DT2 7EW
United Kingdom
sales@pgonline.co.uk
www.pgonline.co.uk
2016

PG ONLINE

Acknowledgements

We are grateful to the OCR (Oxford Cambridge and RSA Examinations) for permission to use questions from past papers.

The answers in the Teacher's Supplement are the sole responsibility of the authors and have neither been provided nor approved by the examination board.

We would also like to thank the following for permission to reproduce copyright photographs:
Screenshots of Arriva Bus App © Arriva PLC
Colossus photograph © The National Archives
Google Maps 'StreetView' © Google 2015
Screenshot from Roboform website © Roboform
Alan Turing © By kind permission of the Provost and Fellows, King's College, Cambridge
from Archives Centre, King's College, Cambridge. AMT/K/7/12
Trans-continental Internet connections © Telegeography
Internet registries map © Ripe NCC
thetrainline.com screenshot © by kind permission of thetrainline.com
Other photographic images © Shutterstock

Graphics: PG Online Ltd

Cover picture © 'Away Day' 2015
Mixed media on canvas 61x61cm
Reproduced with the kind permission of Hilary Turnbull
www.hilaryturnbull.co.uk

Cover design and artwork by PG Online Ltd

Typeset by PG Online Ltd

First edition 2016, reprinted April 2017, June 2017, January 2018

Preface

The aim of this book is to provide detailed coverage of the topics in the new OCR AS and A Level Computer Science specification.

The book is divided into twelve sections and within each section, each chapter covers material that can comfortably be taught in one or two lessons. Material that is applicable only to the second year of the full A Level is clearly marked. Sometimes this may include an entire chapter and at other times, just a small part of a chapter.

Each chapter contains exercises and questions, some new and some from past examination questions. Answers to all these are available to teachers only in a free Teacher's Pack which can be ordered from our website **www.pgonline.co.uk**.

This book has been written to cover the topics which will be examined in the written papers at both AS and A Level. Sections 10, 11 and 12 relate principally to problem solving skills, with programming techniques covered in sufficient depth to allow students to answer questions in Component 02. Pseudocode, rather than any specific programming language, is used in the algorithms given in the text. Sample Python programs which implement many of the algorithms are included in a folder with the Teacher's Pack.

Contents

Section 8

Boolean algebra

Section 9

Legal, moral, ethical and cultural issues

Section 10

Computational thinking

Section 11
Programming techniques

Section 12
Algorithms

Section 1

Components of a computer

In this section:

1

Chapter 1 – processor components

Objectives

- Describe the function of the ALU and Control Unit
- Describe the Fetch-Execute cycle and the role of the following registers:
    - Program Counter
    - Accumulator
    - Memory Address Register
    - Memory Data Register
    - Current Instruction Register

The Central Processing Unit (CPU)

The CPU, also known simply as the processor, has a number of different components which enable it to carry out its task of executing instructions.

These components include:

- control unit
- buses
- arithmetic/logic unit (ALU)
- dedicated registers

1-1

Control Unit

The Control Unit controls and coordinates the activities of the CPU, directing the flow of data between the CPU and other devices. It accepts the next instruction, decodes it into several sequential steps such as fetching addresses and data from memory, manages its execution and stores the resulting data back in memory or registers.

Buses

A **bus** is a set of parallel wires connecting two or more components of a computer. It typically consists of 8, 16, 32 or 64 lines.

The processor is connected to main memory by three separate buses. When the CPU wishes to access a particular main memory location, it sends this address to memory on the **address bus**. The data in that location is then returned to the CPU on the **data bus**. Control signals are sent along the **control bus**.

In the figure below, you can see that data, address and control buses connect the processor, memory and I/O controllers. These three buses are known collectively as the **system bus**. Each bus is a shared transmission medium, so that only one device can transmit along a bus at any one time.

Data and control signals travel in both directions between the processor, memory and I/O controllers. Addresses, on the other hand, travel only one way along the address bus: the processor sends the address of an instruction, or of data to be stored or retrieved, **to** memory or **to** an I/O controller.

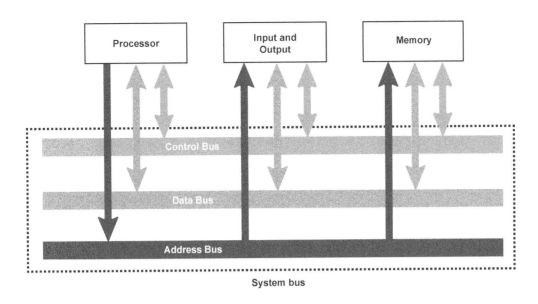

Direction of transmission along the buses

Control bus

The control bus is a bi-directional bus, meaning that signals can be carried in both directions. The data and address buses are shared by all components of the system. Control lines must therefore be provided to ensure that access to and use of the data and address buses by the different components of the system does not lead to conflict.

The purpose of the control bus is to transmit command, timing and specific status information between system components.

Control lines include:

- *Bus Request*: indicates that a device is requesting the use of the data bus

- *Bus Grant*: indicates that the CPU has granted access to the data bus

- *Memory Write*: causes data on the data bus to be written into the addressed location

- *Memory Read*: causes data from the addressed location to be placed on the data bus

- *Interrupt request*: indicates that a device is requesting access to the CPU

- *Clock*: used to synchronise operations

Data bus

The data bus, typically consisting of 8, 16, 32 or 64 separate lines, provides a bi-directional path for moving data and instructions between system components.

Address bus

Memory is divided up internally into units called words. A **word** is a fixed size group of digits, typically 16, 32 or 64 bits, which is handled as a unit by the processor, and different types of processor have different word sizes.

Each word in memory has its own specific address. The address bus transmits the memory addresses of words that are used as operands in program instructions, so that the data can be retrieved and sent back to the processor. When an instruction has been performed and the result is to be stored at a particular memory location, it is transmitted via the data bus.

Arithmetic-Logic Unit (ALU)

The ALU performs arithmetic and logical operations on the data. It can perform instructions such as ADD, SUBTRACT, MULTIPLY, DIVIDE on fixed or floating point numbers. It can also perform shift operations, shifting bits to the left or right within a register. It can carry out Boolean logic operations, comparing two values and using operators such as AND, OR, NOT, XOR.

Registers

Registers are special memory cells that operate at very high speed. Results of all arithmetic, logical or shift operations are temporarily stored in registers and there are typically up to 16 general purpose registers in the CPU.

However, although most modern computers have many registers, some special-purpose processors still use a single **accumulator**, in order to simplify the design. The accumulator takes the place of the general purpose registers. For simplicity, we will assume that results of all operations carried out in the ALU are stored in a single register called the **accumulator**.

Carrying out instructions one after the other requires many different pieces of information to be held. As well as the accumulator, there are several other special-purpose registers:

- the **program counter (PC)**, which holds the address of the next instruction to be executed. This may be the next instruction in a sequence of instructions, or, if the current instruction is a branch or jump instruction, the address to jump to, copied from the current instruction register (CIR) to the PC.

- the **current instruction register (CIR)**, which holds the current instruction being executed, divided into operand and opcode.

- the **memory address register (MAR)**, which holds the **address** of the memory location from which data (or an instruction) is to be fetched or to which data is to be written.

- the **memory data register (MDR)**, which is used to temporarily store the **data** read from or written to memory. It is also sometimes known as the **memory buffer register**.

A simplified diagram showing the connections between these registers is shown below.

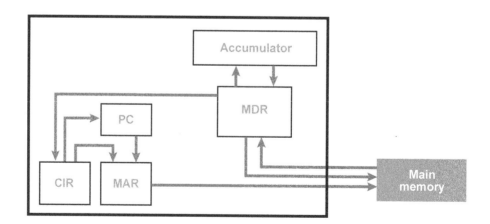

Special-purpose registers in the processor

Q1: Which registers hold and transfer data or instructions? Which registers hold and transfer the memory addresses of data or instructions?

The Fetch-Decode-Execute cycle

The sequence of operations involved in executing an instruction can be divided into three phases – **fetching**, **decoding** and **executing** it. This cycle is repeated over and over as each instruction of the program is executed.

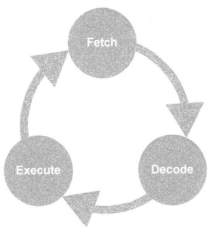

How the registers are used in the Fetch-Execute cycle

(Fetch phase)

1. The address of the next instruction is copied from the program counter (PC) to the memory address register (MAR).

2. The instruction held at that address is copied to the memory data register (MDR). Simultaneously, the content of the PC is incremented so that it holds the address of the next instruction.

3. The contents of the MDR are copied to the current instruction register (CIR).

(Decode phase)

4. The instruction held in the CIR is decoded. The instruction is split into **opcode** and **operand** and the opcode is used to determine the type of instruction and what hardware to use to execute it. The operand holds either:

   - the address of the data to be used with the operation, which is then copied to the MAR, *or*

   - the actual data to be operated on, which will be copied to the MDR

   - the data to be operated on may be passed to the ALU/accumulator

(Execute phase)

5. The appropriate instruction/opcode is carried out on the operand.

Q2: At which stage in this process is the ALU needed? At which stage is the accumulator involved?

1-1

Exercises

1. (a) In the context of computer architecture, explain what is meant by the term **bus**. [2]

   (b) Name three control lines used by the control bus. [3]

   (c) What is the data bus used for? [2]

2. Describe the purpose of each of the following parts of a computer.

   (i) Memory unit [3]

   (ii) ALU [3]

   OCR F451/01 Qu 5 June 2013

3. The figure below shows an incomplete diagram of the components of a processor.

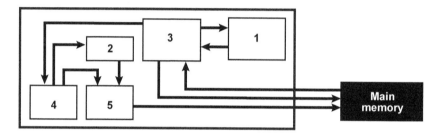

   (a) Provide full names for the components numbered 1 to 5 by completing the table below.

Component number	Component name
1	
2	
3	
4	
5	

   [5]

   (b) The figure below is an incomplete flowchart of the Fetch-Execute cycle.

   Describe the missing steps. [5]

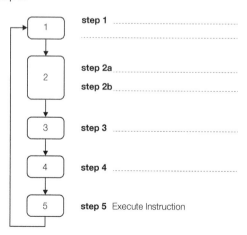

step 1 ....

step 2a ....
step 2b ....

step 3 ....

step 4 ....

step 5 Execute Instruction

Chapter 2 – Processor performance

Objectives

- Describe the factors affecting the performance of the CPU: clock speed, number of cores, cache
- **(A)** • Understand the use of pipelining in a processor to improve efficiency
- Understand how address and data bus size relates to assembly language programs

Factors affecting processor performance

The main factors affecting processor performance are:

- **Clock speed**
- The number of **cores**, or duplicate processors, linked together on a single chip
- The amount and type of **cache memory**

Clock speed

The **system clock** generates a series of signals, switching between 0 and 1 several million times per second and synchronising CPU operations. Each CPU operation starts as the clock changes from 0 to 1 (or in some systems from 1 to 0), and the CPU cannot perform operations faster than the clock cycle (the time the clock takes to go from 0 to 1 and back to 0).

All processor activities begin on a clock pulse, although some activities may take more than one clock cycle to complete. One clock cycle per second = 1 Hertz (Hz), and clock speed is measured in Gigahertz (GHz), about 1 billion cycles per second. Typical speeds for a PC are between 2 and 4 GHz. The greater the clock speed, the faster instructions will be executed.

Number of cores

In a traditional computer (von Neumann machine), instructions are fetched and executed one at a time in a serial manner. However, many computers nowadays have multiple cores. A **dual-core processor** has two processors linked together in the same integrated circuit, and a **quad-core** computer has four linked processors.

Each core is theoretically able to process a different instruction at the same time with its own fetch-execute cycle, making the processor two or even four times faster with a quad-core chip. However, although a dual-core processor has twice the power, it does not always perform twice as fast, because the software may not always be able to take full advantage of both processors.

Amount and type of cache memory

Cache is a small amount of expensive, very fast memory inside the CPU. When an instruction is fetched from main memory it is copied into the cache so if it is needed again soon after, it can be fetched from cache, which is much quicker than going back to main memory. As cache fills up, unused instructions or data still being held are replaced with more recent ones.

> **Q1:** Explain why computers with slower processors but larger cache memory are often found to be faster in system performance tests than computers with faster processors but more limited cache.

1-2

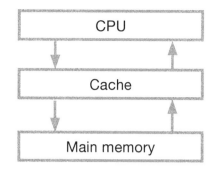

There are different "levels" of cache:

- Level 1 cache is extremely fast but small (between 2-64KB)

- Level 2 cache is fairly fast and medium-sized (256KB-2MB)

- Some CPUs also have Level 3 cache

A-Level only

Pipelining

Pipelining is a technique used by some processors to improve performance. Without pipelining, the steps in the Fetch-Execute cycle take place one after the other. While the next instruction is being fetched, the ALU, the arithmetic part of the processor, is idle.

Using pipelining, the computer architecture allows the next instructions to be fetched at the same time as the processor is performing arithmetic or logic operations, holding them in a buffer close to the processor until the instruction can be performed.

Processor pipelining is sometimes divided into an instruction pipeline and an arithmetic pipeline. The instruction pipeline consists of the stages in which an instruction is moved through the processor, including its being fetched, buffered and then executed. The arithmetic pipeline represents the parts of an arithmetic operation that can be broken down and overlapped as they are performed.

Pipelining is now common in microprocessors used in personal computers. Intel's Pentium chip uses pipelining to execute as many as six instructions simultaneously.

Words and word size

Address bus

Each word, or group of bytes, in memory has its own specific address. When the processor wishes to read a word of data from memory, it first puts the address of the desired word on the address bus. ***The width of the address bus determines the maximum possible memory capacity of the system***. For example, if the address bus consisted of only 8 lines, then the maximum address it could transmit would be (in binary) 11111111 or 255, giving a maximum memory capacity of 256 (including address 0). A system with a 32-bit address bus can address 2^{32} (4,294,967,296) memory locations giving an addressable memory space of 4GiB. (This is the memory capacity of an average PC in 2016.)

Q2: What is a GiB?

Data bus

The data bus transmits the data held in a word of memory, between processor components and memory. The largest operand (which is either an address or an actual value) that can be held in a word is therefore related to the size of the data bus. If the data bus is 16 bits wide, a word cannot hold an integer greater than 2^{16} -1, or more than two characters. A wider data bus can transmit larger values, or more characters at a time, or allow more bits per instruction.

How this relates to assembly language

The basic structure of a machine code instruction in a computer with a 16-bit word may take the format shown below:

Operation code								Operand(s)							
Basic machine operation						Addressing mode									
0	1	0	0	0	1	0	1	0	0	0	0	0	0	1	1

In assembly language, the operation code (opcode) will be expressed as a mnemonic such as ADD, SUB, LDA (load into the accumulator) etc. With only six bits for the opcode, there cannot be more than 2^6 different instructions. The operand has to be held in only 8 bits. This would clearly not be practical in a general purpose computer which is more likely to have a word size of 32, 64 or 128 bits.

Exercises

1-2

1. Name and describe briefly **three** of the main factors affecting processor performance. [9]

2. The program below is written in a low-level language.

```
AB2F  ;Load value 2F into accumulator
BC5D  ;Store contents of accumulator at address 5D
E402  ;Add value 2 to accumulator
BCFF  ;Store contents of accumulator at address FF
AC61  ;Load accumulator with contents of address 61
BC4A  ;Store contents of accumulator at address 4A
```

(a) What is the name of this language? [1]

(b) The machine for which this program is written has limited addressing capability.

   What are the highest and lowest memory addresses that can be addressed by this machine? [2]

(c) What is the width of the address bus in this machine? [1]

Chapter 3 – Types of processor

Objectives

- Describe von Neumann, Harvard and contemporary processor architecture
- Describe the differences between, and uses of, CISC and RISC processors
- Ⓐ Describe GPUs and their uses
- Describe multicore and parallel systems

Memory and the stored program concept

Computers as we know them were first built and developed in the 1940s and 50s, and two of the early pioneers were Alan Turing and John von Neumann. The **von Neumann architecture** specifies the basic components of the computer and processor in which a shared memory and bus is used for both data and instructions.

The **stored progam concept** can be defined as follows: *machine code instructions are fetched and executed serially by a processor that performs arithmetic and logical operations*.

- A program must be resident in main memory to be executed
- The machine code instructions are fetched from memory one at a time, decoded and executed in the processor

Virtually all computers today are built on this principle, and so the general structure as shown in the figure below is sometimes referred to as the **von Neumann machine**.

The von Neumann machine

Memory

0	
1	
2	Instruction
3	Instruction
	. . .
	Data
	Data

The stored program concept

In a von Neumann machine, the same data bus is used to transfer both data and instructions. Similarly, a single address bus is used to transfer the addresses of data and instructions. The same word length is used for all memory, whether it holds data or instructions.

Harvard architecture

The Harvard architecture is a computer architecture with physically separate memories for instructions and data. Harvard architecture is used extensively with embedded **Digital Signal Processing (DSP)** systems. DSP applications include audio and speech signal processing, sonar and radar signal processing, biomedical signal processing, seismic data processing and digital image processing.

- The two different memories can have different characteristics; for example, in **embedded systems** instructions may be held in read-only memory while data memory requires read-write memory

- In some systems, there is much more instruction memory than data memory so a larger word size is used for instructions

- the instruction address bus may be wider than the data bus

Embedded systems include special-purpose computers built into devices often operating in real time, such as those used in navigation systems, traffic lights, aircraft flight control systems and simulators.

Harvard architecture can be faster than von Neumann architecture because data and instructions can be fetched in parallel instead of competing for the same bus.

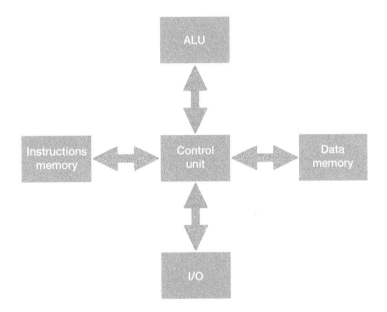

Harvard architecture

Comparison of von Neumann and Harvard architectures

Von Neumann architecture	Harvard architecture
Used in conventional processors in PCs, servers and embedded systems with only control functions	Used in digital signal processing and in embedded systems, mobile communication systems, audio, speech and image processing systems
Data and programs share the same memory	Instructions and data are held in separate memories
One bus is used to transfer data and instructions	Parallel data and instruction buses may be used
Programs can be optimised in size	Programs tend to be large

Contemporary processor architectures

Modern high-performance CPU chips incorporate aspects of both von Neumann and Harvard architecture. In one design, there is one main memory for holding both data and instructions, but CPU cache memory is divided into an instruction cache and a data cache. Harvard architecture is used as the CPU accesses the cache.

Some digital signal processors such as Texas Instruments TMS320 C55x have multiple parallel data buses (two write, three read) and one instruction bus.

Complex Instruction Set Computers (CISC)

In the older CISC architecture used by early generations of computer, a large instruction set is used to accomplish tasks in as few lines of assembly language as possible. The processor hardware is capable of understanding and executing the series of sub-tasks that make up a single instruction. Complex instructions are built into the machine's hardware, and the distinguishing feature of a CISC instruction is that it combines a "load/store" instruction with the instruction that carries out the actual calculation.

For example, to multiply two values held in different memory locations **A** and **B**, storing the result in **A**, a processor using several general purpose registers would load each of the values into a separate register, carry out the multiplication and then store the result back in **A**. The assembly language instruction for a CISC processor might be written something like

```
MULT A, B
```

A CISC processor has in its instruction set a single instruction that will do the loading, multiplication and storing of the result. The instruction is equivalent to the high level instruction a = a * b.

One advantage of CISC architecture is that the compiler has very little work to do to translate a high-level language statement into machine code. Because the code is relatively short, very little RAM is required to store the instructions.

A disadvantage of CISC was that many specialised instructions had to be built into the hardware even though only about 20% of them were used in the average program.

Reduced Instruction Set Computers (RISC)

The opposite approach is adopted in the more modern RISC architecture. Only simple instructions, each taking one clock cycle, can be executed. Thus the multiplication instruction described above might be written:

```
LDA   R1,   A
LDA   R2,   B
MULT  R1,   R2
STO   R1    A
```

The RISC strategy has the disadvantage that the compiler has to do more work to translate high-level code into machine code, and more RAM is required to store the machine code instructions.
However, because each instructions takes the same amount of time, i.e. one clock cycle, pipelining is possible, and the four instructions will execute at least as fast as the single CISC instruction.

RISC has largely replaced CISC as a processor design, but CISC is still used for microcontrollers and embedded systems.

Q1: Which kind of assembly language is generally easier for programmers to code in? An assembly language for a CISC or RISC processor? Why?

Co-processor systems

A **co-processor** is an extra processor used to supplement the functions of the primary processor (the CPU). It may be used to perform floating point arithmetic, graphics processing, digital signal processing and other functions. It may not be a general-purpose processor with the ability to fetch its own instructions, do input and output operations and so on. It generally carries out only a limited range of functions.

Multi-core and parallel systems

Multi-core CPUs are able to distribute workload across multiple CPU cores, thus achieving significantly higher performance.

The IBM Blue Gene supercomputer has 4,098 processors, allowing 560 Teraflops of processing. Supercomputers are used on problems such as weather forecasting, running climate change models, processing Big Data or sequencing DNA.

Many personal computers and mobile devices are dual-core or quad-core, meaning they have two or four processing chips.

The improvement in performance gained by using a multi-core processor is dependent on the software being able to take advantage of the parallel processing capabilities. Maximizing the usage of the computing resources provided by multi-core processors requires adjustments both to the operating system and to existing application software.

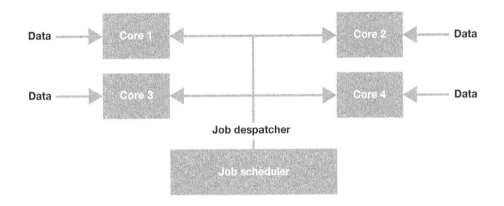

1-3

Some browsers such as Google Chrome and Mozilla Firefox can run several concurrent processes, and a quad-core CPU-based mobile device will deliver higher performance than a single- or dual-core device. All four CPUs may operate when tabbed browsing is used, for example.

A-Level only

Graphics processing unit (GPU)

A GPU is a specialised electronic circuit which is very efficient at manipulating computer graphics and image-processing. Whereas a CPU has a few cores optimised for sequential serial processing, a GPU has a massively parallel architecture consisting of thousands of smaller, more efficient cores designed for handling multiple tasks simultaneously. Its highly parallel structure makes it suitable for tasks where processing of large blocks of visual data is done simultaneously, i.e. in parallel. In a personal computer, a GPU may be present on a graphics card, or embedded on the motherboard. GPUs are now finding more generalised uses in computers used for applications such as machine learning, oil exploration, image processing and financial transactions.

A-Level only

A GPU is a form of **co-processor**, and can be used with a CPU to accelerate scientific, engineering, analytics and other applications, offloading compute-intensive parts of an application to the GPU while the remainder of the code runs on the CPU. From a user perspective, performance is significantly better.

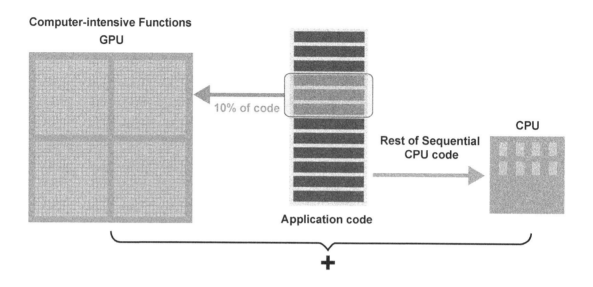

Q2: The image on a computer screen is typically made up of about a million pixels at a common resolution setting. Explain why a graphics card will improve the performance of a computer running a 3-D game.

Case study: DeepMind AlphaGo program

Go is a Chinese game of far greater complexity than chess.

In March 2016 world champion Go player Lee Se-dol from South Korea was defeated by Google's DeepMind AlphaGo program. This was the first time a computer had been able to beat a human

player at the game. DeepMind started by taking a huge database of professional Go matches and training a program to try to predict what move would come next in any given situation.

AlphaGo runs on Google's cloud computer network, using 1,920 processors and a further 280 GPUs.

A simpler version of the program that uses only 48 processors and 8 GPUs has been built to run on one machine.

Ⓐ

Exercises

1. (a) (i) Give the name of the computer architecture that uses the fetch-execute cycle with a single control unit. [1]

   (ii) Registers used during the fetch-execute cycle include the current instruction register (CIR), memory address register (MAR), memory data register (MDR) and program counter (PC).

   Place ticks in the table to show which statements are correct during processing. [4]

	CIR	MDR	PC
Holds a binary value			
Always holds only an address			
May change more than once during a single cycle			
May pass a value to the MAR			

   (b) (i) Compare a Complex Instruction Set Computer (CISC) architecture with a Reduced Instruction Set Computer (RISC) architecture. [4]

   (ii) Explain one advantage, other than cost, of RISC compared with CISC. [2]

   (c) Some computer systems use co-processors.

   Explain the effect of using a co-processor system for each of the following applications.

   (i) Complex calculations for scientific research [2]

   (ii) Printing personalised letters to customers for an advertising campaign [2]

OCR F453/01 June 2014 Qu 3

Chapter 4 – Input devices

Objectives

- Describe different input devices
- Explain how different input devices can be applied as a solution to different problems

Barcodes

Barcodes first started appearing on grocery items in the 1970s, and today they are used for identification in thousands of applications from tracking parcels, shipping cartons, passenger luggage, blood, tissue and organ products around the world to the sale of items in shops and the recording of the details of people attending events. Keeping track of anything accurately is now almost unimaginable without barcodes.

1-4

A handheld barcode scanner used for scanning medical samples

There are two different types of barcode: Linear barcodes such as the one shown above and 2D barcodes such as the Quick Response (QR) code, which can hold more information than the 1D barcode.

A 2D barcode

2D barcodes are used for example in ticketless entry to concerts, or access through gates to board a Eurostar train or passenger airline. They are also used in mobile phone apps that enable the user to take a photo of the code which may then provide them with further information such as a map of their location, product details or a website URL.

Barcode readers

There are four different barcode readers available, each using a slightly different technology for reading and decoding a barcode. The four types are pen-type readers, laser scanners, CCD readers and camera-based readers.

Pen-type readers

In a pen-type reader, a light source and a photo diode are placed next to each other in the tip of a pen. To read a barcode, the tip of the pen is dragged across all the bars at an even speed. The photo diode measures the intensity of the light reflected back from the light source and generates a waveform that is used to measure the widths of the bars and spaces in the barcode.

A pen or wand barcode scanner

Because of their simple design, pen-type scanners are the most durable type of barcode scanner, and can be tightly sealed against dust, dirt, and other environmental hazards. However, their applications are limited because they must come into direct contact with a barcode to read it.

Their small size and low weight makes this type of barcode scanner ideally suited for use with portable (laptop) computers or very low volume scanning applications.

1-4

Laser scanners

Laser scanners work in the same way as pen scanners except they use a laser beam as the light source. They are available in a variety of forms, the most familiar being the in counter units in supermarkets. They are reliable and economical for low-volume applications.

A laser scanner

Camera-based readers

A camera-based **imaging scanner** uses a camera and image processing techniques to decode a 1D or 2D bar code. An imaging scanner can read a barcode on any surface, printed or onscreen, and can also read a code that is damaged or poorly printed. They are used in multiple applications such as:

- age verification by scanning an individual's driving licence

- couponing – a 2D barcode coupon is emailed to a customer, which can be scanned from their phone screen at the POS (Point of Sale). Unique codes for each customer and promotion can be stored in the bar code, so that tracking coupon usage is easy

- event ticketing – tickets can be issued electronically and then scanned off a phone screen

Consumers can use a cell phone to scan a QR code which can, for example:

- display a catalogue of movies or DVDs

- play an MP3 when scanned

- display nutrition information about a product

Digital cameras

A digital camera uses a CCD or CMOS (Complementary Metal Oxide Semiconductor) sensor comprising millions of tiny light sensors arranged in a grid. The binary data from each sensor is recorded onto the camera's memory card so that the image can be reproduced using suitable software at a computer.

A CCD sensor tends to produce higher quality images and they are used in higher end cameras. They are also more reliable since the technology has been around for much longer. This however, is at the cost of power consumption, using up to 100 times that of a CMOS sensor.

1-4

> **Q1:** Suggest a suitable sensor type for use in a mobile phone camera and give a reason why.

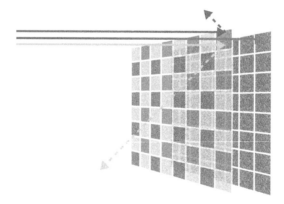

Bayer colour filter applied to a sensor array

Mastercard is testing a new app that allows customers to make purchases online by taking a selfie rather than entering a password. Currently, Mastercard customers enter a password at the point of sale to verify their identity, but these can be forgotten, stolen or intercepted.

Participants in the trial are prompted to take a photograph of their face using the Mastercard app, which is then converted to a binary code using facial recognition technology. This is then compared with a stored code and if the two match up, the purchase is approved.

Q2: Do you see any problems with this procedure?

What other forms of identification could be used for this application rather than entering a password?

Radio Frequency Identification (RFID)

This technology uses both input and output – an input device to read the signal from an RFID chip, and output to transmit a signal from an active tag (see below).

In much the same way as barcodes, RFID tags are increasingly being used to identify and track everything from household products and cars to bank cards and animals. The difference however, is that an RFID tag can be read without line of sight and from up to 300 metres away. They can also pass stored data from the tag to the receiver and vice versa. An RFID chip consists of a small microchip transponder and an antenna. The microchip at the centre of the image below can be manufactured to be less than 1mm in size but the antenna must be larger in order for it to communicate with a base unit. This can increase the size of the smallest tags to about that of a large grain of rice. These can be embedded in special capsules and injected under the skin for the identification of pets.

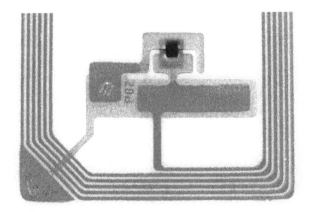 

RFID chip

Passive and active tags

Active tags are physically larger as they include a battery to power the tag so that it actively transmits a signal for a reader to pick up. These are used to track things likely to be read from further away, such as cars as they pass through a motorway toll booth or runners in a marathon as they pass mile markers. Passive tags are much cheaper to produce as they do not have a battery. They rely on the radio waves emitted from a reader up to a metre away to provide sufficient electromagnetic power to the card using its coiled antenna. Once energised, the transponder inside the RFID tag can send its data to the reader nearby. These are most common in tagging items such as some groceries, music CDs, and for smart cards such as Transport for London's Oyster Card or a contactless bank card.

Exercises

1. Describe **three** different input devices that are used by police for crime detection and prevention. [6]

2. Describe **three** different input devices used at a self-checkout in a supermarket, stating for what purpose each of them is used. [6]

Chapter 5 – Output devices

Objectives

- Describe how different output devices can be applied as a solution to different problems

Output devices

Output devices take data produced by the computer and turn it into a form that humans can understand. This could be, for example, written or spoken text, an image on a screen, music or a multimedia presentation. A different type of output device is an actuator, which might respond to an input signal to turn on a sprinkler, open or close windows in a greenhouse, or perform any number of other actions.

Common output devices include screens, printers, multimedia projectors, speakers and actuators.

Screens

There are various different screen technologies used for computers, phones and other devices.

LCD monitors

Liquid crystal display (LCD) monitors contain groups of red, green and blue diodes to form each pixel. The screen is typically back-lit using light-emitting diodes (LEDs). These have several advantages over older technology:

- they reach their maximum brightness almost immediately
- the image is sharper with more realistic and vivid colours
- they produce a brighter light which leads to better picture definition
- since LEDs are very small, screens can be much thinner in construction
- they last almost indefinitely which makes the screens much more reliable
- they consume very little power and therefore produce very little heat as well as reducing running costs

Organic LED (OLED) screens

These are brighter, thinner and lighter than traditional LCD or LED screens. The screen is plastic rather than glass so they are flexible.

OLED screens can be used wherever LCD screens are used, for TV and computer screens, MP3 and cell phone displays. In the future they may be used to make inexpensive animated billboards, super-thin pages for electronic books and magazines, as paintings on a wall that can be updated from a computer or even in clothes – so-called "wearable technology".

They have many advantages over LCDs:

- when made of plastic rather than glass, they are theoretically flexible enough to print onto clothing
- they are much thinner
- they are brighter and need no backlighting, so they consume less power, which translates into longer battery life in a portable device
- LCDs can be slow to refresh (a problem in fast-moving sports or computer games), OLEDs respond up to 200 times faster
- they produce truer colours through a much bigger viewing angle, unlike LCDs where the colours darken and disappear if you look from the side

One drawback is that OLEDs do not last as long, tending to wear out around four times faster than LCDs. They are also very sensitive to water, which is a potential problem in a cellphone.

Printers

Laser printers

Laser printers offer high-quality, high-speed printing. Their function is similar to that of a photocopier, using powdered ink called toner.

This type of printer is becoming increasingly affordable and is frequently used as a home printer, in businesses and in professional printing services. Colour laser printers are far more expensive to run than black and white versions. They contain four toner cartridges (Cyan, Magenta, Yellow and Black or CMYK) and the paper must go through a similar process to the black-only printer four times; once for each colour.

The usage of laser printers for print jobs other than text is limited by the quality of the print produced, which at about 1200 dpi makes photorealistic prints impossible and best left to inkjet printers.

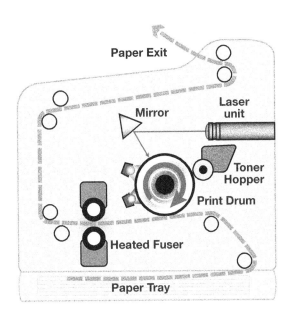

Inkjet printers

Inkjet printers work by spraying minute dots of ink onto paper to create an image. Depending on the **resolution** (dots per inch) of the model, the number of colour cartridges used and the quality of the paper being used, they can produce excellent, photo-realistic images. They are cheaper than laser printers but much slower, and the ink cartridges have to be replaced quite frequently.

Given the choice, it is preferable to use a laser printer when a lot of text needs to be printed, and an inkjet printer to produce high quality photographic images.

Dot matrix printers

These are known as **impact printers**. The print head has a matrix of pins which strike the surface of the paper through an inked ribbon to form letters. These printers are useful when multi-part stationery is required, and they can operate in damp or dirty environments. However, they are noisy, slow and the print quality is poor.

3-D printers

3D printers have been used to create car and aeroplane parts, medical equipment, prosthetic limbs, fashion accessories and a multitude of other items. They have even, controversially, been used to produce working firearms and other weapons.

They are used for creating spare parts for obsolete equipment and to produce prototypes of new products. They can be used in many situations where a one-off item is required, for example to fill in the missing parts of a dinosaur skeleton or a 2000-year old artefact.

1-5

Multimedia projectors

What are the benefits of using a multimedia presentation in a classroom? There are many benefits both to teachers and students:

- in the bad old days 20 or more students would crowd around a desk trying to catch a glimpse of what the teacher was demonstrating on a 16" screen.

- copying down notes written on a chalkboard or whiteboard was a chore

- having an image to focus on while the teacher is explaining something can aid concentration

- watching educational videos or even live webcams adds interest to the lesson

From the teacher's point of view, being able to prepare the lesson in advance and deliver it to several different groups without having to write the same thing on the board every lesson, means the lessons are consistent in quality. With the aid of a projector, the teacher can present text, graphics, audio and video on the screen, display images or videos from the Internet, display PC applications or programs, and use the screen interactively, adding impact to every lesson.

Multimedia projectors are now viewed as essential classroom tools.

Q1: Suggest some other uses and benefits of an LCD projector.

Computer speakers

PCs, smartphones and other portable devices generally have a basic inbuilt speaker which can be used to output music, voice or sound tracks from a video. High quality speakers can be bought separately and when in use, they disable the inbuilt speakers.

Apart from playing music and video soundtracks, uses include giving verbal instructions in a sat-nav system, reading text from the screen for visually impaired people, giving warning beeps and notification alerts (e.g. when you receive an email).

Q2: List some uses of an inbuilt speaker in a smartphone.

Actuators

Actuators are motors that are commonly used in conjunction with sensors to control a mechanism, for example:

- opening a window or valve

- starting or stopping a pump

- turning a wheel

- moving an aircraft aileron

- controlling devices in a "smart home"

Exercises

1. Computer software is used in Geography lessons to teach students about weather systems.

   (a) (i) State the purpose of an input device in a computer system when using
       this software. [1]

   (ii) State the purpose of an output device in a computer system when using this software. [1]

   (b) Describe how the following forms of output will be used by the software.

   (i) Animation [2]

   (ii) Interactive presentation [2]

   OCR June 2014 F451-01 Qu 4

2. State, with reasons, what type of printer you would recommend for the following applications:

   (a) Invoice/delivery note printed on 3-part paper with 2 carbon copies. [3]

   (b) Flyers produced by a small window-cleaning business to be delivered to all homes in a
       particular area. [3]

   (c) Producing high-quality prints of a set of photographs. [3]

1-5

3. What type of screen would you recommend for an in-flight entertainment system?
   Give reasons for your choice. [5]

Chapter 6 – Storage devices

Objectives

- Know the main uses of magnetic, flash and optical storage devices
- Describe the uses of and differences between RAM and ROM
- Describe what is meant by virtual storage

The need for secondary storage

A computer's primary store is Random Access Memory. Unlike RAM, secondary storage is not directly accessible to the processor and has slower access speeds. Secondary storage, however, has the advantage that it retains its contents when the computer's power is turned off. This includes the computer's internal hard disk, optical media and solid state disks.

How storage devices store data

Hard disks, optical disks and solid state disks all use different methods to store data, but in each case, use a technique which allows them to create and maintain a toggle state without power to represent either a 1 or a 0.

Hard disk

A hard disk uses rigid rotating platters coated with magnetic material. Ferrous (iron) particles on the disk are polarised to become either a north or south state. This represents 0 and 1. The disk is divided into tracks in concentric circles, and each track is subdivided into sectors. The disk spins very quickly at speeds of up to 10,000 RPM. Like an old record player, a drive head (like the needle on a record player) moves across the disk to access different tracks and sectors. Data is read from or written to the disk as it passes under the drive head. When the drive head is not in use, it is parked to one side of the disk in order to prevent damage from movement. A hard disk may consist of several platters, each with its own drive head.

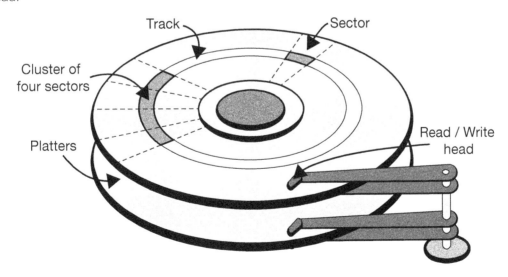

Although hard disks are less portable than optical or solid state media, their huge capacity makes them very suitable for desktop purposes. Smaller, denser surface areas spinning under the read-write heads mean that newer 3.5 inch disks have capacities of up to 640GB.

Optical disk

Optical disks come in three different formats: read-only (e.g. CD-ROM), recordable (e.g. CD-R) and rewritable (e.g. CD-RW. An **optical** disk works by using a high powered laser to "burn" (change the chemical properties of) sections of its surface, making them less reflective. A laser at a lower power is used to read the disk by shining light onto the surface and a sensor is used to measure the amount of light that is reflected back. A read-only CD-ROM disk pressed during manufacture has **pits** in its surface. Those areas that have not been pitted, are called **lands**. At the point where a pit starts or ends, light is scattered and therefore not reflected so well. Reflective and non-reflective areas are read as 1s and 0s. There is only one single track on an optical disk, arranged as a tight spiral.

A **CD-ROM** holds about 700MB of data, whereas a **Blu-Ray** disk (designed to supersede the DVD disk) can hold 50GB. These disks are the same size; their added capacity is owing to the shorter wavelength in the laser they use. This creates much smaller pits, enabling a greater number to fit in the same space along the track and also means that the track can be more tightly wound, and therefore much longer.

Recordable disks use a reflective layer with a transparent dye coating that becomes less reflective when a spot laser "burns" a spot in the track.

Rewriteable compact disks use a laser and a magnet in order to heat a spot on the disk and then set its state to become a 0 or a 1 using the magnet before it cools again. A **DVD-RW** uses a phase change alloy that can change between amorphous and crystalline states by changing the power of the laser beam.

1-6

Pits and Lands   Spiral track

Optical storage is very cheap to produce and easy to send through the post for distribution purposes. It can however be corrupted or damaged easily by excessive sunlight or scratches.

Q1: What type of storage medium is commonly used to hold a feature-length film?

Solid-state disk (SSD)

Solid state disks are packaged to look like hard disk drives, rectangular in shape and sized to match industry-standard dimensions for hard drives, typically 2.5 and 3.5 inches.

A 480 GB solid state drive

Inside, however, instead of platters and a read-write head, there is an array of chips arranged on a board. These components are put into the standard size "housing" so that they fit into existing laptops and desktop PCs. Solid state memory comprises millions of **NAND** flash memory cells, and a controller that manages pages and blocks of memory. Each cell works by delivering a current along the bit and word lines to activate the flow of electrons from the source towards the drain. The current on the word line however is strong enough to force a few electrons across an insulated oxide layer into a floating gate. Once the current is turned off, these electrons are trapped. The state of the NAND cell is determined by measuring the charge in the floating gate. No charge (with no electrons) is considered a 1 and some charge is considered a 0.

Data is stored in pages (typically 4KiB each), grouped into blocks of say, 512KiB. NAND flash memory cannot overwrite existing data. The old data must be erased before data can be written to the same location, and although data can be written in pages, the technology requires the whole block to be erased. As writing to a specific block of NAND cells cannot be done directly, a separate block is created to mirror the data to be transferred to the solid state memory and the data is then written to the new block. The contents of the original block are marked as "invalid" or "stale" and are erased when the user wants to write new data to the drive.

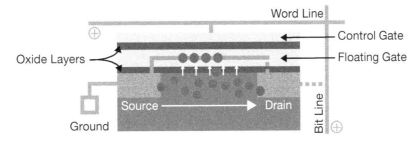

Although capacity is still relatively low, solid state media have faster access speed than hard disks. With no need to move a read-write head across the disk, one piece of data can be accessed just as quickly as any other, even if they are not close together.

SSDs consume far less power than traditional hard drives, meaning that in a laptop, for example, battery life is extended and they stay cooler. In addition, they are less susceptible to damage.

They are also silent in operation, lighter and highly portable – all considerable advantages in personal devices such as mobile phones and MP3 players for example.

Q2: Look up some specifications and prices for hard drives and SSDs.

RAM and ROM

Computers have two kinds of internal memory: **random access memory (RAM)** and **read-only memory (ROM)**.

RAM is used to store programs and data that are currently being used. It is volatile, meaning that its contents are lost when the computer is switched off.

ROM is used to hold information that needs to be permanently in memory. The bootstrap loader, for example, (the small program that starts up as soon as the computer is switched on and causes the operating system to be loaded) has to be held in ROM. In embedded systems such as the software inside a washing machine, vehicle or camera, for example, never changes so is held in ROM.

Virtual storage

In some cases, the computer's RAM may not be not large enough to store all these programs simultaneously, so the hard disk is used as an extension of memory – called **virtual** memory. MS Word may be open on your desktop but if you are not actually using it at a particular time, the operating system may copy the Word software and data to hard disk to free up RAM for the browser software, the VB compiler or whatever you as the user have requested. When you switch back to Word, the operating system will reload it into memory.

Exercises

1. (a) Describe how data is written to and read from a CD-R disk.

   (b) A school has archived all its students' reports on to CD-R. Some years later, a copy of a particular student's reports is requested. Unfortunately it is found that the documents cannot be opened.

      Give **two** reasons why this may be the case. [2]

2. If you are considering purchasing a high-end desktop or laptop you might be offered the option of a solid-state drive (SSD) rather than a traditional hard disk drive.

   (a) Describe briefly how a solid-state drive differs from a hard disk in its operation. [6]

   (b) Ignoring any differences in price and assuming that both drives have the same capacity, state **four** reasons why you might choose the solid-state drive. [4]

1-6

28

Section 2

Systems software

In this section:

2

Chapter 7 – Functions of an operating system

Objectives

- Understand the function and purpose of an operating system

- Describe memory management (paging, segmentation and virtual memory)

- Describe the role of interrupts

- Describe the role of an Interrupt Service Routine (ISR) within the fetch-decode-execute cycle

- Describe the need for processor scheduling algorithms

- Describe scheduling algorithms: round robin, first come first served, multi-level feedback queues, shortest job first and shortest remaining time

What is an operating system?

An operating system is a program or set of programs that manages the operations of the computer for the user. It acts as a bridge between the user and the computer's hardware, since a user cannot communicate with hardware directly.

The operating system is held in permanent storage, for example on a hard disk. A small program called the **loader** is held in ROM. When a computer is switched on, the loader in ROM sends instructions to load the operating system by copying it from storage into RAM.

2-7

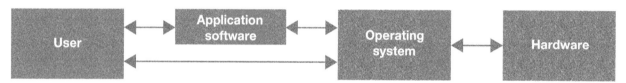

Functions of an operating system

Regardless of whether the operating system is embedded within an mp3 player or is the latest version of Windows installed on a desktop computer, all operating systems share the same basic functions.

An operating system disguises the complexities of managing and communicating with its hardware from the user via a simple interface. Through this interface, a user can naively tap away to complete their tasks, (loading, saving or printing for example), oblivious to the actual operations taking place behind the scenes to support their actions.

Apart from providing a user interface, the operating system has to perform the following functions:

- memory management

- interrupt service routines

- processor scheduling

- backing store management

- management of all input and output

We will look at what each of these functions involves.

Q1: A PC is a multitasking machine. What does this mean? Is it the same thing as multiprocessing?

Memory management

A PC allows a user to be working on several tasks at the same time. You may be listening to music via a streaming site such as Spotify, entering a Python program, checking your emails every so often and running Word so that you can document your program design.

Each program, open file or copied clipboard item, for example, must be allocated a specific area of memory whilst the computer is running. Should a user wish to switch from one application to another in a separate window, each application must be stored in memory simultaneously. The allocation and management of space is controlled by the operating system.

Paging and segmentation

Paging and segmentation are two different techniques for making the optimum use of memory by splitting it into small sections.

Using a paging system, memory is divided into fixed size pages of 4Kb each, and a process currently in memory may be held in several non-contiguous pages. Imagine a program which uses 15K of consecutive memory addresses – these logical memory locations may be physically stored in four separate pages anywhere within the physical memory space. A page table uses mapping to store a link between the **physical** memory address and the **logical** address space of each process.

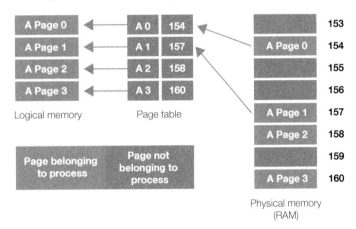

Logical memory   Page table   Physical memory (RAM)

Segmentation is the logical division of address space into varying length segments which depend on the program structure. As with paging, it is possible to load only a part of a program into memory initially.

Virtual memory

Memory is not limitless, so as more and more jobs are loaded into memory, the operating system may swap pages of temporarily inactive jobs out to disk, thus using secondary storage as an extension of memory to make room for the next job which has a share of processor time.

If a large number of jobs are loaded and the computer has insufficient memory, you may notice a deterioration in performance as pages are swapped in and out of RAM, to the point where the operating system is spending most of its time swapping pages in and out and performance slows right down.

On a PC you can look at "System Information" to see how much RAM and virtual memory is available.

Installed Physical Memory (RAM)	4.00GB
Total Physical Memory	3.25GB
Available Physical Memory	1.12GB
Total Virtual Memory	8.12GB
Available Virtual Memory	3.83GB

31

Interrupts

An **interrupt** is a signal from a software program, hardware device or internal clock to the CPU. A software interrupt occurs when an application program terminates or requests certain services from the operating system. A hardware interrupt may occur, for example, when an I/O operation is complete or an error such as 'Printer out of paper' occurs.

Interrupts are also triggered regularly by a timer, to indicate that it is the turn of the next process to have processor time (see 'Processor scheduling' below). It is because a processor can be interrupted that **multi-tasking** can take place.

Interrupt service routines

When the CPU receives an interrupt signal, it suspends execution of the running program or process and disables all interrupts of a lower priority. It then puts the values of the program counter (PC) and of each register onto the system stack, while an **Interrupt Service Routine** is called to deal with the interrupt. Depending on the type of interrupt, a particular routine will be run in order to service it.

Interrupts are assigned priorities, and lower priority interrupts may be disabled while a higher priority interrupt is being serviced. Examples of interrupts in descending order of priority, are given below:

- Power-fail interrupt
- Clock interrupt
- An I/O device sends a signal requesting service or signalling end of I/O operation

Once the interrupt has been serviced, the original values of the registers are retrieved from the stack and the process resumes from the point that it left off.

A test for the presence of interrupts is carried out at the end of each fetch-decode-execute cycle.

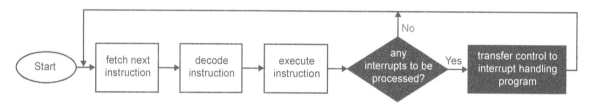

> **Q2:** Do you notice that response time slows down on your PC when you have a lot of programs running? What would be the effect of installing more RAM on your computer? Why?

Processor scheduling

With computers able to run multiple applications simultaneously, the operating system is responsible for allocating processor time to each one as they compete for the CPU. While one application is busy using the CPU for processing, the OS can queue up the next process required by another application to make the most efficient use of the processor. A computer with a single processor can only process one instruction at a time, but by carrying out small parts of multiple larger tasks in turn, the processor can give the appearance of carrying out several tasks simultaneously. This is what is meant by **multi-tasking**.

The **scheduler** is the operating system module responsible for making sure that processor time is used as efficiently as possible. Of course, this is a much more complex task on a large multi-user network where many users may, for example, be accessing the same database or running different applications.

2-7

The objectives of the scheduler are to:

- maximise throughput

- be fair to all users on a multi-user system

- provide acceptable response time to all users

- ensure hardware resources are kept as busy as possible

There are many different scheduling algorithms and some of them are described below.

Round robin

In round robin scheduling, processes are despatched on a first in first out (FIFO) basis, with each process in turn being given a limited amount of CPU time called a **time slice** or quantum. If the process does not complete before its time expires, or before a higher priority interrupt occurs, the despatcher gives the CPU to the next process.

In order to do this, the operating system sets an interrupting clock or **interval timer** to generate interrupts at specific times. This method of scheduling helps to guarantee a reasonable response time to all users of the system. In some systems, a system of priorities may allow a high priority job to have more than one consecutive time slice when their turn comes round

Processor time shared

time slices

First come first served

Jobs are processed in the order in which they arrive, with no system of priorities.

Shortest remaining time

The process with the smallest estimated time to completion is run next. This tends to reduce the number of waiting jobs, and the number of small jobs waiting behind big jobs. Its disadvantage is that it requires knowledge of how long a job will take, so the user has to estimate the job time. This is possible for batch jobs such as payroll, which are performed regularly and usually run overnight, or for any scientific, commercial or other jobs which are run regularly.

Shortest job first

The process with the smallest estimated running time is run next. Its advantages and constraints are much the same as the 'shortest remaining time' algorithm. In a University environment, for example, students will get their short programs run quickly while large research or administration programs which are not time-critical will take longer to complete during busy periods of student activity.

Multi-level feedback queues

This algorithm is designed to:

- give preference to short jobs

- give preference to I/O bound processes

- separate processes into categories based on their need for the processor

The algorithm implements several job queues and jobs can move between queues, depending on how much processor time they use. Since input/output (I/O) is so much slower than processor speed, it is efficient to try and keep the I/O devices as continuously busy as possible, so that a bottleneck does not occur when several programs simultaneously need to send data to the printer, for example. While one job is printing, other jobs can use the processor. The aim is to maximise processor use.

Backing store management

When files and applications are loaded, they are transferred from backing storage into memory. The operating system is required to keep a directory of where files are stored so that they can be quickly accessed. Similarly, it needs to know which areas of storage are free so that new files or applications can be saved. The file management system that comes with your desktop operating system enables a user to move files and folders, delete files and protect others from unauthorised access.

Peripheral management

Different applications will require different input or output devices throughout their operation. If you send a file to print, the operating system will need to communicate with the printer to check that it is switched on and online, check that it is a printer and not, say, the keyboard and begin communication to send it the correct data to print.

The data to be printed will then be transferred to an area of memory called a **buffer**, so that the CPU can continue with another task. The purpose of the buffer is to compensate for the difference in speed between the printer, or other output device, and the CPU.

Exercises

1. (a) An operating system uses interrupts which have priorities.
   Describe the sequence of steps which would be carried out by the interrupt handler when an interrupt is received and handled. [6]

   (b) The operating system of a personal computer supports multi-tasking. One of the operating system functions is memory management.
   Describe **two** different strategies which could be used to manage the available memory. [6]

2. (a) An operating system uses scheduling. One method of scheduling is first come, first served.

   (i) Explain why the first come, first served scheduling method may not be efficient. [2]

   (ii) Describe one other scheduling method. [2]

   (iii) Explain why scheduling is necessary. [4]

   (b) Explain why memory management is necessary. [3]

   (c) Paging may be used in memory management. Describe paging. [3]

   OCR F453/01 Qu 1 June 2014

3. (a) Describe what is meant by

   (i) an interrupt [2]

   (ii) a buffer [2]

   (b) A computer system includes a printer.

   (i) Explain the role of the printer buffer in the transfer of a job from the computer to the printer. [3]

   (ii) Explain why an interrupt is necessary during the transfer of data from the computer to the printer. [3]

   OCR F451/01 Qu 7 June 2013

Chapter 8 – Types of operating system

Objectives

- Describe distributed, embedded, multi-tasking, multi-user and real-time operating systems
- Describe BIOS, device drivers and virtual machines

Distributed operating systems

A distributed operating system is a form of parallel processing system which spreads the load over multiple computer servers. A single job is split up into several tasks and each of these is run on a separate computer, coordinated by the operating system, in such a way that it appears to a user to be a single system. Intranets, for example, may use a distributed system, in which the system is configured as a cluster of servers that share memory and tasks, providing more power than a single large server and resulting in better performance.

Linux, Unix and Windows are all available in distributed versions.

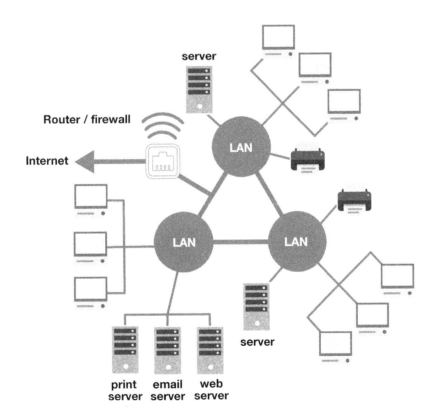

A multi-tasking system

A multi-tasking operating system may run on a standalone computer such as a PC or laptop. The Windows operating system, for example, can run many jobs simultaneously, switching between them so that each one appears to be the only one running. You may be playing music, entering a Python or VB program, and checking your emails occasionally. At any one time if you look at the Task Manager (press **Ctrl-Shift-Esc**) you will probably find it has several programs in memory, most of which are not currently executing.

A multi-user, multi-tasking system

Time-sharing systems are multi-user, multi-tasking systems. A single powerful mainframe or supercomputer is connected to dozens or hundreds of terminals all using the mainframe CPU. Each user gets a slice of processor time according to a scheduling algorithm, as described in the last chapter.

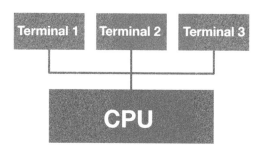

Operating systems used by mobile phones

A mobile phone is a multi-tasking computer that has its own operating system. Operating systems used on smartphones, tablets, PDAs and other mobile devices are termed **mobile operating systems**. They combine the features of a personal computer operating system with their own special features useful for mobile use such as managing cellular and wireless connectivity as well as phone access.

Typically, for example, smartphones respond to the user's touch – the user can tap on the screen to open a program, pinch their fingers together to minimise or enlarge a screen, or swipe across the screen to change pages. They also have features useful for mobile systems such as GPS mobile navigation, camera, video camera, speech recognition, music player.

Most mobile operating systems are tied to specific hardware. Smartphones have two operating systems – the main system operating the user interface and running the application software and a second, low-level proprietary **real-time operating system** which operates the radio and other hardware. These low-level systems have a range of security vulnerabilities permitting others to gain control over a mobile device.

Embedded operating systems

Embedded systems are found in all kinds of hardware from a washing machine or microwave oven, to the control system of a passenger aircraft or a space shuttle. Clearly the requirements will vary accordingly.

First, let's look at the simple case of a basic household appliance in which the application program is held in ROM. The main features of the operating system are:

- it will have a minimal user interface, probably consisting of a few buttons or a dial and maybe a small screen

- it will accept input from sensors, and send output to control devices

- there is a limited amount of RAM so a complex memory management system is not required

- there will not be any permanent data storage devices to be managed

Real-time operating system

What about the operating system in the flight-control system of a "fly-by-wire" airliner such as the Airbus 320? This is a real-time, embedded system.

The operating system on the aircraft or similar safety-critical system must have the following features:

- it must respond very quickly to any inputs or sensors

- it must be able to deal with many inputs simultaneously

- it must have "failsafe" mechanisms designed to detect and take appropriate action if a hardware component fails

- it must incorporate redundancy – that is, if one component fails, it must automatically switch to backup hardware

Q1: Watch the YouTube video "Airbus Fly By Wire Demo" at
https://www.youtube.com/watch?v=MJ2k71Ydwmk and make a list of all the input
and output devices used by the pilots in the cockpit.

2-8

BIOS (Basic Input Output System)

BIOS is the program stored in EPROM (Erasable Programmable Read-Only Memory) that gets your computer started after you turn it on.

The fundamental purpose of BIOS in modern PCs is to initialise and test the system hardware components and to load the operating system (or the key parts of it) from the hard disk into RAM. BIOS was historically used to provide an abstraction layer which allowed a consistent way for application programs and the operating system to interact with input-output devices.

In more modern computers BIOS is not used after loading the operating system.

Device drivers

A device driver is a computer program that provides a software interface to a particular hardware device. This enables operating systems to access hardware functions without needing to know the details of the hardware being used. When you attach a new printer to your computer, for example, you will have to install the device driver program that comes with it before it will work. Sometimes the OS will do this automatically if it detects that the printer is one for which it already has a driver.

Drivers are hardware dependent and operating system specific. A driver typically communicates with the device via the system bus or communications subsystem to which the hardware connects. When a calling program invokes a routine in the driver, the driver issues commands to the device. Once the device sends data back to the driver, the driver may invoke routines in the original calling program.

Virtual machine

2-8

A virtual machine can be defined as any instance where software is used to take on the function of the machine, including executing intermediate code or running an operating system within another to emulate different hardware.

Exercises

1. List **four** features of the user interface which you would expect to find on a smartphone but not on a PC.

    [5]

2. Compare and contrast the functions of operating systems designed for a personal computer and a satellite-navigation system in a car. In this question you will also be assessed on your ability to use good English and to organise your answer clearly in complete sentences, using specialist vocabulary where appropriate.

    [7]

Chapter 9 – The nature of applications

Objectives

- Distinguish between systems software and applications software
- Describe what is meant by a utility program and give examples
- Be able to justify a suitable application for a specific purpose
- Distinguish between open source and closed source software

Categories of software

Software may be grouped into separate categories, illustrated in the figure below.

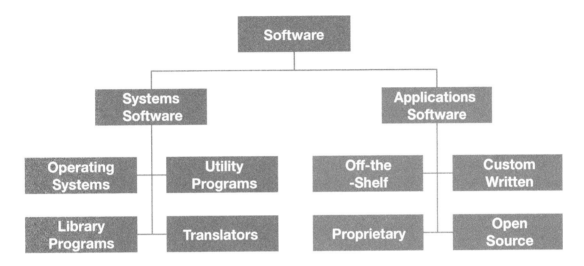

2-9

Classification of software

Software can be broadly classified into **systems software** and **applications software**.

Systems software

System software is the software needed to run the computer's hardware and application programs. This includes the operating system, utility programs, libraries and programming language translators. Libraries and programming language translators will be considered in the next chapter.

Operating system

In the last two chapters we looked at different types of operating system and the function of an operating system. The OS is a set of programs that lies between applications software and the computer hardware, and has many different functions, including:

- resource management – managing all the computer hardware including the CPU, memory, disk drives, keyboard, monitor, printer and other peripheral devices
- provision of a user interface (e.g. Windows) to enable users to perform tasks such as running application software, changing settings on the computer, downloading and installing new software, etc.

Utility programs

Utility software is system software designed to optimise the performance of the computer or perform tasks such as backing up files, restoring corrupted files from backup, compressing or decompressing data, encrypting data before transmission, providing a firewall, etc.

Disk defragmentation

A **disk defragmenter** is a program that will reorganise a magnetic hard disk so that files which have been split up into blocks and stored all over the disk will be recombined in a single series of sequential blocks. This makes reading a file quicker. The software utility *Optimise Drives*, previously called *Disk Defragmenter*, runs automatically on a weekly schedule on the latest versions of Windows. You can also optimise drives on your PC manually.

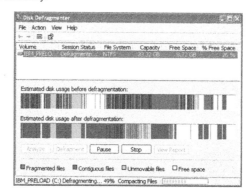

Automatic backup

Several free automatic backup utilities are available for personal and commercial use. An automatic backup utility will allow the user to specify

- **Where** you want to store the backup (the destination)
- **What** you want to backup (the sources)
- **How** you want to run the backup (using full backup that zips the files, or mirror backup that doesn't zip them)
- **When** you want to run the backup (you can schedule it to run automatically or run it manually)

You can then run the backup manually (typically by using a function key) or schedule it to run automatically. (See for example http://www.fbackup.com/)

Automatic updating

An automatic update utility makes sure that any software installed on the computer is up-to-date. For any software already installed on the computer, the automatic update utility will regularly check the Internet for updates. These will be downloaded and installed if they are newer than the version already on the computer.

Firewalls and antivirus software must be updated regularly as new viruses and threats are constantly being devised and discovered.

Application software should also be updated as there will be bug fixes and improvements that become available to people with a licence for that package.

Virus checker

A **virus checker** utility checks your hard drive and, depending on the level of protection offered, incoming emails and internet downloads, for viruses and removes them. Windows 8.1 comes with built-in virus protection called Windows Defender.

Compression software

Several utility programs are supplied as part of the operating system. These include utilities to copy, move and delete files, create, move and delete folders, provide screensavers. Other utility programs such as WinZip for compressing and sharing files have to be purchased from independent suppliers.

Zipped or compressed files can be transmitted much more quickly over the Internet. Sometimes there is a limit to the size of a file which can be transmitted – if you have a 15Mb photograph, you will not be able to email it to a friend if there is a 5Mb limit on the attachments they can receive. Even if they can receive the file, it may take several minutes to download if they do not have a broadband connection.

Applications software

Applications software can be categorised as general-purpose, special-purpose or custom-written (bespoke) software.

General-purpose software such as a word-processor, spreadsheet or graphics package, can be used for many different purposes. For example, a graphics package may be used to produce advertisements or animations, manipulate photographs, draw vector or bitmapped images.

Special-purpose software performs a single specific task or set of tasks. Examples include payroll and accounts packages, hotel booking systems, fingerprint scanning systems, browser software and hundreds of other applications. Software may be bought "**off-the-shelf**", ready to use, or it may be specially written by a team of programmers for a particular organisation. If, say, a hotel wants to buy some visitor booking software, they may be able to find a ready-made package that is quite suitable, or they may want a **bespoke** software package that will satisfy their particular requirements.

"Off–the–shelf" vs bespoke software

Off the shelf	Bespoke software
Less expensive since the cost is shared among all the other people buying the package	More costly and requires expertise to analyse document requirements
May contain a lot of unwanted features, and some desirable but non-essential features may be missing	Features customised to user requirements and other features can be added as needs arise
Ready to be installed immediately	May take a long time to develop
Well documented, well-tested and error-free	May contain errors which do not surface immediately

2-9

Open source vs closed source

Open Source software is governed by the Open Source Initiative that says:

- Software is licensed for use but there is no charge for the licence. Anyone can use it.

- Open Source software must be distributed with the source code so anyone can modify it.

- Developers can sell the software they have created.

- Any new software created from Open Source software must also be "open". This means that it must be distributed or sold in a form that other people can read and also edit.

NB: This is different from **Freeware** (free software) which may be free to use but the user does not get access to the source code. Freeware usually has restrictions on its use as well.

Closed source or proprietary software is sold in the form of a licence to use it.

- There will be restrictions on how the software can be used, for example the licence may specify only one concurrent user, or it may permit up to say, 50 users on one site (site licence).

- The company or person who wrote the software will hold the copyright. The users will not have access to the source code and will not be allowed to modify the package and sell it to other people. This would infringe the copyright (Copyright, Designs and Patents Act).

The benefit of using proprietary software is the support available from the company. There will be regular updates available and technical support lines, training courses and a large user base. Open Source software tends to be more organic – it changes over time as developers modify source code and distribute new versions. There isn't a commercial organisation behind the software so there probably won't be a helpline or regular updates, just a community of enthusiastic developers.

2-9

Q1: Name an open source operating system and open source word processing package

Selecting an application

How would you select suitable software for a particular purpose? You might use some of the following criteria:

- Does it provide all the necessary functionality?

- Does it run on the available hardware?

- Is it available "off the shelf" or will it have to be specially written?

- How much will it cost?

- Is it well-used, tried and tested?

Q2: (a) What criteria would you use when deciding which word-processing software to install on your PC?

(b) What criteria might a school use when deciding on a system for the school library?

Exercises

1. (a) Software can be classified as either **system** or **application software**. What is meant by

    (i) system software? [1]

    (ii) application software? [1]

    (b) Give an example of each type of software. [2]

2. A company sells widgets via an online web store. The process of updating the website and processing sales involves many different types of software.

    Below is a list of software:

    Operating system, Utility software, Special-purpose software, General purpose application software, Bespoke software

    Complete the table below by writing one software category beside each use. You should not use a category more than once. [4]

Software	Category
Firewall software installed on the web server	
Store's own online ordering system designed for their products and systems	
Graphics software to crop product images suitable for uploading to the site	
Online payment verification software	

3. Describe **three** reasons why a company might choose to purchase an "off-the-shelf" special purpose software package rather than a suite of programs written specifically for their needs. [6]

4. A student owns a computer which he uses for:

    -   producing project work in hard copy form

    -   playing games with friends on the internet

    -   downloading video and music files

    He uses a number of pieces of utility software.

    State the purpose of each of the following types of utility software and describe how the student would use them.

    (i)   Compression software [3]

    (ii) Anti-virus software [3]

    (iii) Backup utility [3]

    OCR F451/01 Qu 8 June 2013

2-9

Chapter 10 - Programming language translators

Objectives

- Understand the role of an assembler, compiler and interpreter

- Explain the difference between compilation and interpretation, and describe situations when both would be appropriate

- Explain why an intermediate language such as bytecode is produced as the final output by some compilers and how it is subsequently used

(A) • Describe the stages of compilation: lexical analysis, syntax analysis, code generation and optimisation

(A) • Describe the function of linkers and loaders

(A) • Describe the use of libraries

Assembler

Assembly code is a **low-level language**, with each instruction in assembly code almost always being equivalent to one machine code instruction. The machine code instructions that a particular computer can execute (the **instruction set**) are completely dependent on its hardware, and therefore each different type of processor will have a different instruction set and a different assembly code.

Typically, several lines of low-level code instructions are required to achieve the same result as a single line of high-level code.

Before an assembly code program can be executed, it must be translated into the equivalent machine code, or an intermediate form called **bytecode**. This is done by a program called an **assembler**. The assembler program takes each assembly code instruction and converts it to the 0s and 1s of the corresponding machine code instruction. The input to the assembler is called the **source code** and the output (machine code) the **object code**.

Compiler

A compiler is a program that translates a high-level language such as Visual Basic, Python etc. into machine code. The code written by the programmer, the **source code**, is input as data to the compiler, which scans through it several times, each time performing different checks and building up tables of information needed to produce the final object code. Different hardware platforms will require different compilers, since the resulting object code will be hardware-specific. For example, Windows and the Intel microprocessors comprise one platform, Apple and PowerPC processors another, so separate compilers are required for each.

The object code can then be saved and run whenever needed without the presence of the compiler.

Interpreter

An interpreter is a different type of programming language translator. Once the programmer has written and saved a program, and instructs the computer to run it, the interpreter looks at each line of the source program, analyses it and, if it contains no syntax errors, translates it into machine code and runs it.

For example, the following Python program contains an error at line 5.

```
1  a = 1
2  b = 2
3  c = a + b
4  print("a + b = ", c)
5  e = a - n
6  print("a - b = ", e)
7  print("goodbye")
```

When the program runs, it produces the following output:

```
a + b = 3
Traceback (most recent call last):
  File "C:/Users/A Level sample programs/prog1.py", line 5, in <module>
    e = a - n
NameError: name 'n' is not defined
```

The program produces output at line 4, gets as far as line 5 and then crashes.

However, it is not always quite that simple. If we modify the program to introduce a syntax error at line 6, (missing closing bracket) the interpreter does not attempt to run any of the program until this is fixed.

2-10

```
1  a = 1
2  b = 2
3  c = a + b
4  print("a + b = ", c)
5  e = a - b
6  print("a - b = ", e
7  print("goodbye")
```

When the program runs, it does not execute any of the code but produces the following output:

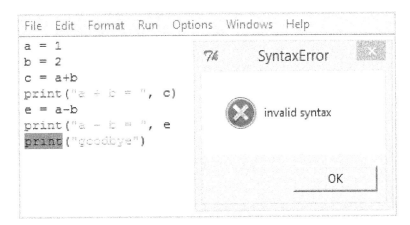

From this we can deduce that the translator has scanned through the whole program checking for certain types of error before executing any of it.

Bytecode

Many languages are not *only* compiled or *only* interpreted – there are various possibilities in between.

Interpreting each line of code just before executing it has become much less common. Most interpreted languages such as Python and Java use an intermediate representation which combines compiling and interpreting. The resulting **bytecode** is then executed by a **bytecode interpreter**.

The bytecode may be compiled once and for all (as in Java) or each time a change in the source code is detected before execution (as in Python).

A big advantage of bytecode is that you can achieve **platform independence**; any computer that can run Java programs has a **Java Virtual Machine (JVM)**, a piece of software which masks inherent differences between different computer architectures and operating systems. The JVM understands bytecode and converts it into the machine code for that particular computer.

A second advantage of using, for example, Java bytecode is that it acts as an extra security layer between your computer and the program. You can download an untrusted program and you then execute the Java bytecode interpreter rather than the program itself, which guards against any malicious programs.

It is also possible to compile from Python into Java bytecode (using the Jython compiler) and then use the Java interpreter to interpret and execute it.

Advantages and uses of compilers and interpreters

A compiler has many advantages over an interpreter:

- the object code can be saved on disk and run whenever required without the need to recompile. However, if an error is discovered in the program, the whole program has to be recompiled
- the object code executes faster than interpreted code
- the object code produced by a compiler can be distributed or executed without having to have the compiler present
- the object code is more secure, as it cannot be read without a great deal of 'reverse engineering'

A compiler would therefore be appropriate when a program is to be run regularly or frequently, with only occasional change. It is also appropriate when the object code produced by the compiler is going to be distributed or sold to users outside the company that produced the software, since the source code is not present and therefore cannot be copied or amended.

Q1: Why would a company or an individual programmer not want to distribute the source code when they sell a software package?

An interpreter has some advantages over a compiler:

- platform independence - the source code can be run on any machine which has the appropriate interpreter available (e.g. Java's byte code)
- it is useful for program development as there is no need for lengthy recompilation each time an error is discovered

Disadvantages of an interpreter

The program may run slower than a compiled program, because each statement has to be translated to machine code each time it is encountered. So if a loop of 10 statements is performed 20 times, all 10 statements are interpreted 20 times.

A-Level only

Stages of compilation

There are three stages of compilation: **lexical analysis**, **syntax analysis**, and **code generation and optimisation**. These stages are described below.

Lexical analysis

Lexical analysis performs the following functions.

1. Superfluous spaces are removed.

   ```
   print (total_mark,   average)   will be converted to
   print(total_mark,average)
   ```

2. All comments, identified for example by # or //, will be removed from the program.

3. Some simple error-checking is performed, for example:

   - an illegal identifier (such as X&Y or ten% in Python) would be flagged as an error

   - the lexical analyser will detect an attempt to assign an illegal value to a constant, such as a value of the wrong type or one that causes overflow or underflow

   (The lexical analyser will not detect misspelt keywords or undeclared variables; this is the job of the **syntax analyser**.)

4. All keywords, constants and identifiers (e.g. variable names) used in the source code are replaced by 'tokens' (unique symbols). For example, numbers will be converted to their run-time representation, and identifiers will be replaced by a pointer to an address in the symbol table. Keywords such as input, print will be replaced by a single item-code.

The symbol table

The symbol table plays a central role in the compilation process. It will contain an entry for every keyword (reserved word) and identifier in the program. The exact format of the entries in the table will vary from compiler to compiler, but typically, entries in the table will show:

- the identifier or keyword
- the **kind** of item (variable, array, procedure, keyword etc.)
- the **type** of item (integer, real, char etc.)
- the **run-time address** of the item, or its **value** if it is a constant

- a pointer to accessing information (e.g. for an array, the bounds of the array, or for a procedure, information about each of the parameters).

Typical entries in a symbol table might be as given below:

	item name	kind of item	type of item	run-time address or value	pointer
1	input	keyword			
2	pi	constant	real	3.14159	
3	radius	variable	real	(?)	
4	=	operator			
5	area	variable	real		
6	numSides	array	integer	(?)	(?)
7	*	operator			
8					

2-10

A-Level only

The statements   `input(radius)`

`area = pi * radius * radius`

could be 'tokenised' and stored as the lexical string   1 3

5 4 2 7 3 7 3

Q2: What further entries to the symbol table will the lexical analyser make on encountering the statement

`circumference = 2 * pi * radius`

Add the entries to the symbol table and then tokenise the statement.

Note that the lexical analyser puts the identifier and its run-time address in the symbol table, so that it can replace them in the source code by 'tokens'. It will not fill in the 'kind of item' and 'type of item'; this is done later by the **syntax analyser**.

Accessing the symbol table

Since the lexical analyser spends a great proportion of its time looking up the symbol table, this activity has a crucial effect on the overall speed of the compiler. The symbol table must therefore be organised in such a way that entries can be found as quickly as possible. The most common way of organising the symbol table is a **hash table**, where the keyword or identifier is 'hashed' to produce an array subscript. As with any hash table, synonyms (collisions) are inevitable, and a common way of handling them is to store the synonym in the next available free space in the table.

Syntax analysis and semantic analysis

Syntax analysis is the process of determining whether the sequence of input characters, symbols, items or tokens form a valid sentence in the language. In order to do this, the language has to be expressed as a set of rules, using for example **syntax diagrams** or **Backus-Naur** form.

Parsing is the task of systematically applying the set of rules to each statement to determine whether it is valid. **Stacks** will be used to check, for example, that brackets are correctly paired. The priorities of arithmetic operators will be determined, and expressions converted into a form (such as **reverse Polish notation**) from which machine code can more easily be generated.

The **semantics** of the program will also be checked in this phase. **Semantics** define the meaning rather than the grammar of the language; it is possible to write a series of syntactically correct statements which nevertheless do not obey the rules for writing a correct program. An example of a semantic error is the use of an undeclared variable in Pascal, or trying to assign a **real** value to an **integer** variable, or using a real number instead of an integer as the counter in a **for ... next** loop.

Q3: Give other examples of a semantic error.

Code generation and optimisation

This is the final phase of compilation, when the machine code is generated. Most high-level language statements will be translated into a number of machine code statements.

Code optimisation techniques attempt to reduce the execution time of the object program by, for example, spotting redundant instructions and producing object code which achieves the same net

2-10

effect as that specified by the source program but not by the same means. The disadvantages of code optimisation are:

- it will increase compilation time, sometimes quite considerably

- it may sometimes produce unexpected results. Consider the following program extract, which is supposed to measure the speed of the object program. Assume `GetTime` is a function which returns the current `time` set in the operating system:

```
start = GetTime;
for count = 1 to 100000
   x = 0
#endfor
finish = GetTime
print(start, finish);
```

The effect of code optimisation may be to detect that it is quite unnecessary to perform the loop 100000 times to set x equal to 0, and optimise the code so that it is only done once!

Linkers and loaders

Once a program has been compiled, any separately compiled subroutines must be linked into the object code. These may be input or output routines, routines such as a random number generator or timer routine which are supplied with the language, or routines written by the programmer and held on disk in a library of subroutines. It is the job of the **linker** to put the appropriate machine addresses in all the external `call` and `return` instructions, so that the modules are linked together correctly.

A relocating loader can load the object code anywhere in memory, provided the programmer has used no absolute addresses and the object code is in relocatable format.

Use of libraries

Library programs are ready-compiled programs, grouped in software libraries, which can be loaded and run when required. In Windows these often have a .dll extension. Most compiled languages have their own libraries of pre-written functions which can be invoked in a defined manner from within the user's program.

Advantages of library routines

Most programming languages have extensive libraries of built-in functions such as chr(), ascii(), sqrt() etc. They also have libraries of modules that provide solutions to common problems in everyday programming, such as mathematical functions, generating random numbers in a specified range, providing a graphical user interface. These libraries can be imported into a user's program and have many advantages including:

- they are tested and error-free

- they save the programmer time in "re-inventing the wheel" to write code themselves to perform common tasks

Q4: What library programs or routines have you used in any of the programs you have written? How is the library invoked by the program?

2-10

A

Exercises

1. A programmer is asked to write a program and can choose between using a low-level language or an imperative high-level language.

   Outline the major differences between these two types of languages, naming an example of each.

   For each language explain:

   - advantages and disadvantages of each one compared to the other

   - what translation software would be used, if applicable

   - a situation when each one would be the most appropriate choice [10]

2. (a) When translating computer languages, intermediate code may be produced.

   Explain the need for intermediate code and its purpose in a virtual machine.

   The quality of written communication will be assessed in your answer to this question. [8]

   (b) State **three** benefits of using library routines when a program is written. [3]

   OCR F453/01 Qu 2 June 2014

A-Level only

2-10

3. The following source code is written in Python. It contains errors.

```
numbers = [9, 5, 4, 15, 3, 8, 11, 2]
numItems = len(numbers)
for i in range(numItems - 1):
    for j in range(numItems - i - 1):
    if numbers[j] > numbers[j + 1]:
        #swap the numbers
        temp = numbers[10]
        numbers[j] = numbers[j + 1]
        numbers[j + 1] = tem
drint (numbers)
```

   Using lines of code from the above program to illustrate your answer, state **two** things that would be done in each of the following stages of compilation:

   (a) Lexical analysis [2]

   (b) Syntax analysis [2]

4. The process of compilation involves a number of stages. Name the stage at which each of the following would be detected.

   (a) An illegal identifier. [1]

   (b) An arithmetic operator is applied to an operator of the data type Boolean. [1]

   (c) An operand is omitted from an arithmetic expression. [1]

A

Section 3

Software development

In this section:

3

Chapter 11 – Systems analysis methods

Objectives

- Describe the waterfall lifecycle model, agile methodologies, extreme programming, the spiral model and rapid application development

- Describe the relative merits and drawbacks of different methodologies and when they might be used

Aspects of software development

There is an infinite variety of different types of problem that can be solved using a computer. Whether you are developing a website for a new company selling goods or services, designing a simulation of a physics experiment, building a control system using a microprocessor, or something else, all software projects have certain aspects in common. Stages of analysis, design, implementation (which includes coding, testing and documentation), installation and evaluation are common to all projects, though they may not easily fall into these categories in some methodologies. The tasks performed at these stages in the old, traditional lifecycle methodology are briefly described below.

Analysis

Before a problem can be solved, it must be defined. The requirements of the system that solves the problem must be established. In the case of a data processing system, or for example the construction of a website, this could cover:

- the **data** – its origin, uses, volumes and characteristics

- the **procedures** – what is done, where, when and how, and how errors and exceptions are handled

- the **future** – development plans and expected growth rates

- **problems** with any existing system

In the case of a different type of problem such as a simulation or game, the requirements will still need to cover a similar set of considerations.

Design

Depending on the type of project, the systems designer may consider some or all of the following:

- **processing:**   the algorithms and appropriate modular structure for the solution, specifying modules with clear documented interfaces

- **data structures:**   how data will be held and how it will be accessed – for example in a dynamic data structure such as a queue or tree, or in a file or database

- **output:**   content, format, sequence, frequency, medium (e.g. screen or hard copy) etc.

- **input:**   volume, frequency, documents used, input methods

- **user interface:**   screens and dialogues, menus, special-purpose requirements

- **security:**   how the data is to be kept secure from accidental corruption or deliberate tampering or hacking

- **hardware:**   selection of an appropriate configuration

Programming and testing

Programming normally involves breaking the problem down into individual modules and further breaking these down until each module performs a single well-defined task. The program code is then written in the chosen programming language.

Obviously a system must be thoroughly tested before being installed to make sure that all errors are discovered and corrected before going 'live'. It is part of the designer's job to come up with a test plan which will ensure that all parts of the system are properly tested.

There are several possible testing strategies.

Black box testing (functional testing)

Black box testing is carried out independently of the code used in the program. It involves looking at the program specification and creating a set of test data that covers all the inputs and outputs and program functions.

White box testing (structural testing)

White box testing is dependent on the code logic, and derives from the program structure rather than its function. The program code is studied and tests are devised which test each possible path at least once. The weakness of white box testing is that it will not detect missing functions – you cannot test what isn't there!

Alpha testing

Alpha testing is carried out by the software developer's in-house testing team. It is essential because it often reveals both errors and omissions in the system requirements definition. The user may discover that the system does not in fact have the required functionality because the requirements were not specified carefully enough, or because the developer has overlooked or misunderstood something in the specification.

Beta testing

When a new package is being developed for release as a software package, beta testing is often used. This involves giving the package to a number of potential users who agree to use the system and report any problems to the developers. Microsoft, for example, delivers beta versions of its products to hundreds of sites for testing. This exposes the product to real use and detects problems and errors that may not have been anticipated by the developers. The product can then be modified and sent out for further beta testing until the developer is confident enough in the product to put it on the market.

Implementation

Coding and testing will be carried out, errors traced and corrected. When all is thought to be satisfactory the software will be installed on the user's system and more testing will be done. At this stage new weaknesses and omissions are almost bound to surface and more work will be carried out.

Evaluation

The evaluation may include a post-implementation review, which is a critical examination of the system three to six months after it has been put into operation. This waiting period allows users and technical staff to learn how to use the system, get used to new ways of working and understand the new procedures required. It allows management a chance to evaluate the usefulness of the reports and on-line queries that they can make, and go through several 'month-end' periods when various routine reports will be produced. Shortcomings of the system, if there are any, will be becoming apparent at all levels of the organisation, and users will want a chance to air their views and discuss improvements. The solution should be evaluated on the basis of **effectiveness**, **usability** and **maintainability**.

3-11

The post-implementation review will focus on the following:

- a comparison of the system's actual performance with the anticipated performance objectives

- an assessment of each aspect of the system against preset criteria

- errors which were made during system development

- unexpected benefits and problems

The waterfall lifecycle model

The **Waterfall Model** illustrates the methodology described above, in which each step is completed one at a time from beginning to end. Each step has specific outputs that lead into the next step. It is possible to return to a previous stage if necessary but the model shows that the developers then have to work back down through the following stages.

The user/customer is involved at the start of the process, in the Analysis stage, but then has little input until the Evaluation stage.

This model was adopted from the manufacturing industry, where changes to hardware made later in the project had high cost implications to work already completed so it was important to get each stage right before moving to the next. Although still popular, it has been now superseded by more effective models.

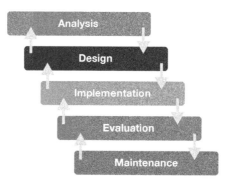

Spiral model

The **Spiral Model** uses the same structured steps but introduces the idea of developing the software in iterative (repeating) stages. At the start of the process the requirements are defined and the developers work towards an initial prototype. Each successive loop around the spiral generates a refined prototype until the product is finished.

Each time around the spiral the following activities are performed:

- **Analyse** the requirements for the next prototype
- **Design** the next version, the new prototype
- **Implement** (code and test) the new prototype
- **Evaluate** the new prototype, which generates a plan for the next iteration

The Spiral Model is mostly used for large scale projects, for example, projects that take years to deliver. Smaller projects use a variation on this called the **Agile Model** (see below).

Agile modelling

At all the stages of analysis, design and implementation, an **agile approach** may be adopted, as the stages of software development may not be completed in a linear sequence. It might be that some analysis is done and then some parts of a system are designed and implemented while other parts are still being analysed and then, for example, implementation and testing may be intermixed. The developer may then go back to design another aspect of the system.

Throughout the process, feedback will be obtained from the user; this is an **iterative process** during which changes made are incremental as the next part of the system is built. Typically the software developers do just enough modelling at the start of the project to make sure that the system is clearly understood by both themselves and the users.

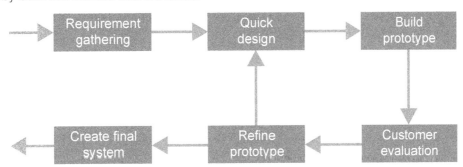

At each stage, a **prototype** is built with user participation to ensure that the system is being developed in line with what the user wants. The success of the software development depends on

- **keeping the model simple**, and not trying to incorporate features which may come in useful at a later date
- **rapid feedback from the user**
- **understanding that user requirements may change** during development as they are forced to consider their needs in detail
- being prepared to make **incremental changes** as the model develops

Extreme programming

Extreme programming (XP) is a software development methodology which is intended to improve software quality and responsiveness to changing customer requirements. It is a type of agile software development in which frequent "releases" of the software are made in short development cycles. This is intended to improve productivity and introduce checkpoints at which new customer requirements can be adopted.

Rapid application development (RAD)

Some very large projects may be developed over a long period of time during which both technology and user requirements change. Major changes at late stages of development can sometimes lead to projects being cancelled or restarted, at considerable cost. In response to this problem the RAD methodology was introduced, offering the promise of much faster completion of major projects. The ideas behind it include:

- workshops and focus groups to gather requirements rather than a formal requirement document

- the use of prototyping to continually refine the system in response to user involvement and feedback

- producing within a strict time limit each part of the system, which may not be perfect but which is good enough

- reusing any software components which have already been used elsewhere

Relative merits and drawbacks of each development methodology

The **waterfall system lifecycle** approach is suitable for very small projects which need careful supervision, such as those undertaken by students or trainees. The absence of user involvement is a serious drawback.

The **spiral model** and the **agile approach** are an improvement in that they acknowledge that users often cannot specify their requirements accurately because they don't understand what is possible. It is much easier to examine a working prototype and figure out what needs to be done to it to turn it into a useful system.

Extreme programming and **rapid application development** are good methodologies for large projects where there is a danger of getting bogged down or sidetracked by suggested improvements, so that developers are continually chasing a moving target.

3-11

Exercises

1. A systems analyst/developer is planning a system for the administration of student courses to be used in an office in a college.

   Describe **three** tasks that may be carried out by the analyst to establish the requirements of the system.   [6]

2. (a) Explain what is meant by the **prototyping/agile approach** to system analysis and design.   [4]

   (b) What are the advantages of this approach?   [4]

   (c) (i) Describe briefly two other approaches to systems development.   [6]

       (ii) Describe the advantages and disadvantages of each of these approaches.   [4]

       (iii) State circumstances in which each of the methods you have described would be appropriate.   [2]

3. Explain the difference between black box testing and white box testing.   [4]

Chapter 12 – Writing and following algorithms

Objectives

- Understand the term 'algorithm'
- Learn how to write and interpret algorithms using pseudocode

Properties of an algorithm

A recipe for chocolate cake, a knitting pattern for a sweater or a set of directions to get from A to B, are all algorithms of a kind.

Computational algorithms

A good algorithm has the following properties:

- It has clear and precisely stated steps that produce the correct output for any set of valid inputs
- It should allow for invalid inputs
- It must always terminate at some point
- it should execute efficiently, in as few steps as possible
- It should be designed in such a way that other people will be able to understand it and modify it if necessary

What kinds of problem are solved by algorithms?

3-12

There are thousands of different practical applications of algorithms. Some of the best-known applications include:

- **Internet-related algorithms.** Algorithms are used to manage and manipulate the huge amount of data stored on the Internet. How does a search engine find all the pages on which particular information resides in a fraction of a second?
- **Route-finding algorithms.** Given two locations, how does a route-finder determine the shortest or best route between the two points? There may be thousands of possible routes. This type of algorithm is used not only for driving a vehicle from A to B, but also for many other applications, for example, finding the best route to transmit packets of data from A to B over a network.
- **Compression algorithms.** These are used to compress data files so that they can be transmitted faster or held in a smaller amount of storage space. For example, MP3 files are compressed so that you can hold thousands of tracks on a mobile phone.
- **Encryption algorithms.** When someone purchases something over the Internet and sends their credit card number and other personal details to the store, the data needs to be encrypted so that even if it is intercepted, it cannot be read.

Q1: Who else uses encryption algorithms?

A simple computational algorithm

Suppose you are given an integer and you need to find its square root. Your calculator can add, subtract, multiply and divide but it does not have a square root function. You know that the answer is an integer.

Here is one way of finding the square root of the integer `number`:

```
1  n = 0              ;initialise n
2  nsquared = n*n
3  Is nsquared = number?
4  If yes, output n. If no, add 1 to n and repeat from step 2
```

When you start to program, it is tempting to get straight to the computer and type in some code to solve a given problem. However, it will generally save time to figure out the steps needed using paper and pencil to write down a **pseudocode** algorithm before you start coding.

Pseudocode is a way of expressing the solution in a way that can easily be translated into a programming language.

Q2: Write pseudocode for the above algorithm to find the square root of an integer, when you know that the answer is an integer. Write and test the program for the integer 19321.

Q3: Which of the properties of a good algorithm, stated at the start of the chapter, does this algorithm not satisfy?

The algorithm described will do the job, but a better solution is based on the well-known binary search algorithm.

A "Divide and Conquer" algorithm

The binary search algorithm uses the "Divide and Conquer" strategy to halve the search area every time a guess is made. It goes like this:

1. `Set low to 1, high to number. Set guess = (low + high)/2` and `nsquared = guess`^{2}

2. `If nsquared > number, set high = guess` to eliminate the top half of the range, otherwise `set low = guess` to eliminate the bottom half of the range

3. `Set guess = (low + high)/2` and `nsquared = guess`^{2}

4. Repeat steps 2 and 3 until `nsquared = number`

We can draw a hierarchy chart to represent these steps:

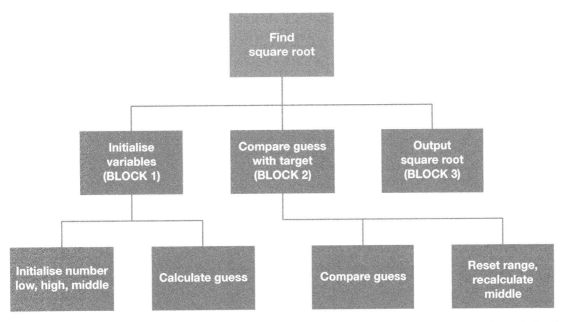

The chart represents the blocks of program code that we will use to solve the problem. The solution is short, so it's not necessary to put each block in a separate subroutine.

```
number = 19321
low = 1
high = number
guess = int((low+high)/2)
nsquared = guess**2              BLOCK 1 SEQUENCE
```

3-12

```
while nsquared != number
   if nsquared > number
      high = guess
   else
      low = guess
   endif
   guess = int((low+high)/2)
   nsquared = guess**2           BLOCK 2 - ITERATION
endwhile
```

```
print("square root is ",guess)  BLOCK 3 - SEQUENCE
```

Q4: Add statements to calculate and print the number of guesses it took to find the answer.

Try writing and running the program for different values of number.

Is there a formula for calculating how many guesses it should take to find the square root?

Interpreting algorithms

A useful skill is to be able to look at someone else's algorithm and decide what it does and how it works. Of course, if the programmer has put in lots of useful comments, used meaningful variable names and split a complicated algorithm into separate modules, that should not be too difficult!

Strategy for interpreting algorithms

Here are some tips, which may seem fairly obvious.

1. Read the comments in the program

2. Look at the variable names to see if they give any clues

3. Follow the steps in the program

4. Try a "dry run" with some test data

Drawing a trace table

A trace table is a useful tool for performing a dry run through a program. As you follow through the logic of the program in the same sequence as the computer does, you note down in the trace table when each variable changes and what its value is.

Q5: Dry run the algorithm below by completing the table.

Assume that x has a value of 7. The MOD operator calculates the remainder resulting from an integer division.

```
answer = True
for count = 2 to (x-1)
    remainder = x MOD count
    if remainder = 0 then
        answer = False
    endif
next count
```

answer	count	remainder
True	-	-
	2	1

What is the purpose of this algorithm?

Exercises

1. In a football league, the results of each match are input to the computer, which updates each team's points.

   In the case of a draw, each team (Team A and Team B) gets one point.

   If Team A wins, then Team A gets 3 points and Team B gets no points.

   The algorithm for updating points in the case of a draw is:

   ```
   if TeamAGoals == TeamBGoals then
      TeamAPoints = TeamAPoints + 1
      TeamBPoints = TeamBPoints + 1
   endif
   ```

   Write an algorithm for updating the points if there is a winner.   [3]

2. Expert jugglers learn new juggling patterns according to certain rules represented by numbers. In this example, the rules for patterns of three numbers are:

   Rule 1: the total value of the numbers in the list must be a multiple of 3

   Rule 2: No number must be one less than the previous number, even if the pattern is repeated indefinitely.

   Here are some valid patterns of three numbers:

   7 4 4

   4 4 1

   Here are some examples of invalid patterns with three numbers:

   4 2 1   (4 + 2 + 1 = 7, which is not a multiple of 3, so does not obey rule 1)

   6 5 1   (5 is one less than the previous number, so this does not obey rule 2)

   6 2 7   (when this is repeated, 6 2 7 6 2 7 6 2 7... 6 is one less than the previous number, so this does not obey rule 2)

   (a) State why the following lists of 3 numbers are not valid patterns of numbers.

      (i) 5 1 6   [1]

      (ii) 4 4 2   [1]

   (b) Write pseudocode for a program which:

      • Prompts the user to enter 3 numbers, one after the other

      • Outputs "INVALID PATTERN" if the sequence of numbers does not obey the two rules.   [7]

3-12

3. José works for a company that provides loans to its customers. When customers take out a loan they decide how much money to borrow and for how many years.

The interest rate is currently 10% but it may change in the future.

José writes the following program to calculate the monthly payment for a loan.

```
01 program loanCalculator
02
03 CONST INTEREST_RATE = 10
04
05 begin
06     amount = input("Enter amount: ")
07     years = input("Enter years: ")
08     annualInterest = amount * interestRate / 100
09     totalToPay = (annualInterest * years) + amount
10     monthlyPayment = totalToPay / (years * 12)
11     print("Monthly Payment:", monthlyPayment)
12 end
```

(a) Using the code above, show the value that will be output if the inputs are:

Amount: 600
Years: 5

You **must** show all your working. [3]

(b) Parentheses have been used in lines 09 and 10.

(i) State why the parentheses in line 09 are **not** essential. [1]

(ii) Explain why the parentheses in line 09 are useful. [2]

(iii) Explain why the parentheses in line 10 are essential. [2]

(c) The algorithm uses a constant.

Identify the constant, and explain why a constant has been used. [3]

(d) The company also offers a savings plan. Customers pay a fixed amount each year into the savings plan. At the end of each year, the company adds the value of the savings plan at the start of the year to the amount paid, and then adds interest of 10% to obtain the final value for the year.

For example, if a customer saves £100 each year, the value of the savings plan for 5 years is shown in the table below

Year	Start	Paid in	Interest	Final
1	0.00	100.00	10.00	110.00
2	110.00	100.00	21.00	231.00
3	231.00	100.00	33.10	364.10
4	364.10	100.00	46.41	510.51
5	510.51	100.00	61.05	671.56

Write an algorithm which allows the user to input the amount saved each year and the number of years, and outputs the growth of the savings plan in the format shown above. [7]

OCR F452/01 Qu 2 2014

3-12

Chapter 13 – Programming paradigms

Objectives

Ⓐ • Understand the need for and characteristics of a variety of programming paradigms

   • Describe the features of procedural languages

Ⓐ • Describe the features of object-oriented languages

A-Level only

Programming paradigms

A programming paradigm is a style of computer programming. Different programming languages support tackling problems in different ways, and there are four major programming paradigms, each supported by a number of different languages. Some languages such as Python, Delphi and Java support more than one programming paradigm.

- **Procedural** programming is supported by languages such as Python or Pascal, which have a series of instructions that tell the computer what to do with the input in order to solve the problem. They are widely used in educational environments, being relatively easy to learn and applicable to a wide variety of problems. **Structured programming** is a type of procedural programming which uses the programming constructs of sequence, selection, iteration and recursion. It uses modular techniques to split large programs into manageable chunks.

- **Object-oriented** programming is supported by languages such as Java, Python and Delphi. OOP was developed to make it possible to abstract details of implementation away from the programmer, make code reusable and programs easy to maintain. It is to a great extent taking over from procedural programming.

- **Declarative** programming is supported by languages such as SQL, where you write statements that describe the problem to be solved, and the language implementation decides the best way of solving it. SQL (covered in more detail in Chapter 18) is used to query databases.

- **Functional** programming is supported by languages such as Haskell, as well as languages such as Python, C# and Java. Functions, not objects or procedures, are used as the fundamental building blocks of a program. Statements are written as a series of functions which accept input data as arguments and return an output. Functional programming is not covered in this course.

Different types of problem require different types of language, and hundreds of different languages have been developed for different types of application. Assembly language was the first language to be developed after machine code, and the next step was the development of procedural languages in the 1960s.

Ⓐ

Procedural languages

A procedural language has built-in data types such as integer, real or floating point numbers, character, Boolean and string. In addition, it typically has **data structures** such as **array** and **record**. Programmers can define their own abstract data types such as queue, stack, tree, or hash table all of which you will study during this course.

Consider an abstract data structure such as a stack. This can be visualised like a stack of plates. You can only add an item to the top of a stack, and you can only remove an item from the top.

The programmer might decide there is a limit to how large the stack is allowed to get, so you can't add to a full stack, and obviously, you can't remove an item from an empty stack.

This abstract data structure can be implemented in different ways. In Python, it could be implemented with the built-in list data structure. In Pascal, you could use an array, with a pointer to the top of the stack. The important thing is, that someone using this data structure should not need to know how it is implemented, any more than they need to know how a square root is worked out when they press the √ (square root) button on a calculator. All the user needs to know is the state and behaviour of the data structure.

Clearly, it is a waste of time for every programmer who needs to use a stack to have to decide how to implement it and write their own subroutines to add and remove items from it. This is where an object-oriented approach comes in.

A-Level only

Object-oriented languages

In an object-oriented language, we define a **class** as the description of what the data looks like (the state) and what the data can do (the behaviour). The user of a class sees only the state and behaviour of a data item. Data items are called **objects**, where an object is an instance of a class.

Programming in an object-oriented language requires thinking in terms of the objects that will carry out the required tasks, rather than thinking about data structures and algorithms. We are familiar with the concept of objects in the physical world – they could be cats, dogs, plates, cars, patients, doctors, students, and so on.

In a hospital system, objects might be patient, ward, doctor, nurse and so on. Each of these objects can be defined as a class, with its own set of behaviours. Each individual ward will be a single instance of the class called ward. The class will have attributes such as `name`, `number_of_beds`, `number_of_patients`, `location`, `type`. A particular instance of the ward may have name *Bramford*, `number_of_beds` 6, `location` *Block E*, `number_of_patients` 5, `type` *Children's*. Its behaviours might include `admit_patient`, `discharge_patient`.

Inheritance

Below is a simple example of a class and its subclasses. Suppose an object-oriented program used by an estate agent defines a class called `Property`. `Property` has attributes including `address`, `owner`, `type`, `number_of_bedrooms`, `price`.

The class `Property` has two subclasses called `Property_For_Rent` and `Property_For_Sale`. The subclasses have the same attributes as the superclass `Property`, and in addition, each has some attributes of its own. The subclasses are said to inherit properties from the superclass, and we can draw an inheritance diagram.

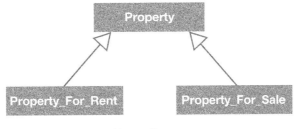

Class diagram

In the class diagram, inheritance is shown using an open-headed arrow.

Example

A class called `DataStructure` is created in an object-oriented language. The `DataStructure` class has two subclasses called `Stack` and `Queue`. Both `Stack` and `Queue` inherit attributes `name`, `size`, `isEmpty` and `isFull` from the superclass. They also inherit methods called `addItem`, `removeItem`.

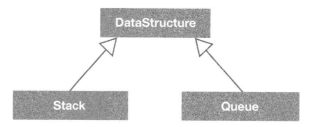

Classes are defined differently in different programming languages, but in the pseudocode that is used on this course, the superclass might be defined like this:

```
class DataStructure
    private size
    private isFull
    private isEmpty
    public procedure new(structureSize)
        size = structureSize
    endprocedure
    public procedure addItem(parameter)
        (instructions to add an item to end of data structure)
    endprocedure
    public function removeItem
        (instructions to remove first item from data structure)
    endfunction
endclass
```

In the definition, attributes are generally described as `private`. This means that users cannot directly access them. They are changed through statements within the various methods. Methods fall into one of two categories – functions, which return a value, and procedures, which do not. For example, when an item is to be added to a data structure, the item which is to be added is passed as a parameter, but nothing is returned. If an item is to be removed, no parameter is needed, and the item removed is returned from the function.

The class `Stack` could be defined as follows:

```
class Stack inherits DataStructure
    public function removeItem
        (instructions to remove item from end of stack)
    endfunction
```

The attributes `size`, `isFull`, `isEmpty` and the methods `new`, `addItem` are inherited from the `DataStructure` class.

3-13

Polymorphism

Polymorphism refers to a programming language's ability to process objects differently depending on their class.

A class of objects has behaviours or **methods**, all of which will be inherited by its subclasses.

In this example the class `Stack` defines its own method `removeItem`. This is because, although there is a method of the same name in the superclass which it could inherit, it will process a `Stack` object differently. In a stack, the *last* item in the stack will be removed. In the superclass, assume that the method `removeItem` removes the *first* item in the data structure. In the case of a queue, this is fine, but it is not what is required for the stack. However, both `Stack` and `Queue` objects carry out the method *addItem* in an identical way, adding the item to the end of the data structure. Hence, the method `addItem` does not need to be redefined in the `Stack` class definition.

This is what is meant by **polymorphism**; the subclass `Stack` redefines the method `removeItem` defined in the superclass `DataStructure` to process objects in the class differently.

The attributes `size`, `isFull`, `isEmpty` are all defined in the superclass `DataStructure`. These attributes cannot be accessed directly if they are declared `private`; they can only be accessed through the class methods. This is known as **encapsulation**.

Constructors and inheritance

Inheritance is denoted by the `inherits` keyword, and superclass methods are defined with the keyword `super`. e.g. `super.new(stackSize)`.

A procedure with the name `new` is a **constructor**. To create a new object called `myStack` of size 20 which belongs to class `Stack`, the following statement would be written:

```
myStack = new Stack(20)
```

More detail on object-oriented programming is given in Section 11, Chapter 58.

Advantages of the object-oriented paradigm

Building code into objects has a number of advantages, including:

- The object-oriented methodology forces designers to go through an extensive planning phase, which makes for better designs with fewer weaknesses

- Encapsulation: the source code for an object can be written, tested and maintained independently of the code for other objects

- Once an object is created, knowledge of how its methods are implemented is not necessary in order for a programmer to use it

- New objects can easily be created with small differences to existing ones

- Reusability: objects that are already defined, coded and tested may be used in many different programs

- OOP provides a good framework for code libraries with a range of software components that can easily be adapted by a programmer

- Software maintenance: an object-oriented program is much easier to maintain than one written in a procedural language because of its modular structure

3-13

A

Exercises

1. A programming paradigm is a style of computer programming. Procedural programming, supported by languages such as Python or Pascal, which have a series of instructions that tell the computer what to do with the input in order to solve the problem, is one example of a paradigm.

    Name and briefly describe **two** other programming paradigms, giving an example of an application of each and a language which supports it. [6]

2. (a) Explain what is meant by the term **class** in object-oriented programming. [2]

    (b) An institution categorises its staff as either **Academic** or **Administration**. Administration staff may be either **Salaried** or **HourlyPaid**.

    Five classes are to be created in an object-oriented programming language.

    (i) Draw a class diagram for the five classes. [3]

    (ii) Describe what is meant by **polymorphism**. [1]

    (iv) Explain how this might apply to a method called **CalculatePay** in the class **Administration**. [2]

3. The system used by a garden centre to store and retrieve details of its products is written in an object-oriented language. Part of the design is shown on the class diagram.

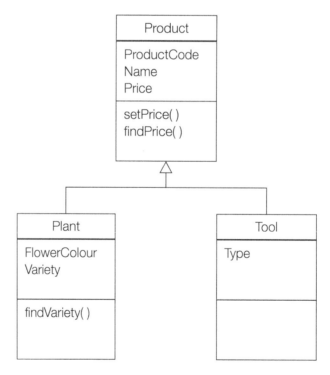

Explain the terms class, derived class, inheritance and encapsulation, using examples from the garden centre.

The quality of written communication will be assessed in your answer to this question. [8]

OCR F453/01 Qu 6 June 2013

Chapter 14 – Assembly language

Objectives

- Be able to write and follow simple assembly language programs

Ⓐ - Understand and apply immediate, direct, indirect and indexed addressing modes

Assembly language instructions

Machine code was the first "language" used to enter programs by early computer programmers. The next advance in programming was to use mnemonics instead of binary codes, and this was called assembly code or assembly language. Each assembly language instruction translates into one machine code instruction.

Assembly code uses mnemonics to represent the operation codes and addresses. Typically, 2-, 3- or 4-character mnemonics are used to represent all the machine code instructions. The **assembler** then translates the assembly language program into machine code for execution.

The following table shows mnemonics for instructions in the instruction set of the Little Man Computer, which is an imaginary computer designed to enable you to easily enter and test assembly language programs.

Mnemonic code	Instruction	Numeric code	Description
ADD	ADD	1xx	Add the contents of the memory address to the Accumulator
SUB	SUBTRACT	2xx	Subtract the contents of the memory address from the Accumulator
STA	STORE	3xx	Store the value in the Accumulator in the memory address given.
LDA	LOAD	5xx	Load the Accumulator with the contents of the memory address given
BRA	BRANCH (unconditional)	6xx	Branch - use the address given as the address of the next instruction
BRZ	BRANCH IF ZERO (conditional)	7xx	Branch to the address given if the Accumulator is zero
BRP	BRANCH IF POSITIVE (conditional)	8xx	Branch to the address given if the Accumulator is zero or positive
INP	INPUT	901	Input into the accumulator
OUT	OUTPUT	902	Output contents of accumulator
HLT	Halt	0	Stops the execution of the program.
DAT	DATA		Used to indicate a location that contains data.

Table 14.1

3-14

You can experiment with the LMC at http://peterhigginson.co.uk/LMC/

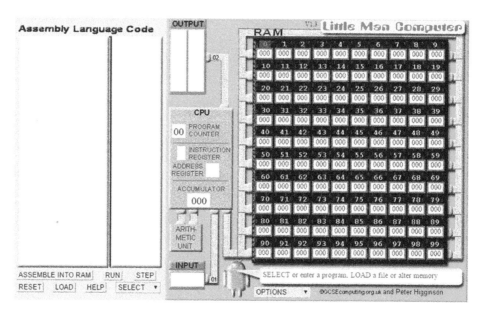

Figure 14.1: The LMC computer simulator

All the examples below use instructions from Table 14.1.

Data transfer and arithmetic operations

Example 1

Input three numbers x, y and z. Calculate and output the value of x + y − z

```
        INP             ;Input y into accumulator ACC)
        STA y           ;Store the number in y
        INP             ;Input x into ACC
        STA z           ;Store the number in z
        INP             ;Input x into ACC
        ADD y           ;Add y to the number in ACC
        SUB z           ;subtract z from the number in ACC
        OUT             ;output the number in ACC
        HLT             ;halt
    x   DAT
    y   DAT
    z   DAT
```

Q1: Write an assembly code program to input a number x and calculate and output 6x – 5.

Branch instructions

The flow of the program can be altered using a **conditional** or **unconditional branch** instruction. The **conditional** branch instructions BRP (Branch if positive), BRZ (Branch if zero) cause a branch to a given label in the program depending on the value held in the accumulator.

An **unconditional** branch instruction, (BRA) will cause a branch whatever the value held in the accumulator.

Example 2

Compare the two numbers held in memory locations num1 and num2, and output the larger. If they are equal, either one can be output.

```
             LDA num1
             SUB num2
             BRP firstmax
             LDA num2
             OUT num2
             HALT
firstmax     LDA num1
             OUT num1
             HLT
```

Q2: Write an assembly code program to input two numbers and output the minimum number.

Example 3

Write an assembly code program which performs integer division. The program inputs two numbers big and small, and outputs the result of big divided by small, ignoring the remainder.

There is no division instruction in this instruction set, so we have to repeatedly subtract small from big, adding 1 to a variable which we will call answer, until big becomes less than zero. Each time we subtract, we add 1 to a variable called answer.

```
          INP              ; Input the number 1
          STA one          ; store in one
          INP              ; Input the number 0
          STA answer       ; Store in answer
          INP              ; Input the divisor
          STA small        ; Store in small
          INP              ; Input the number to be divided
          STA big          ; store value in big
next      SUB small        ; subtract small from ACC which contains big
          STA big          ; Store in big
          BRP more         ; Branch if ACC positive or zero to more
          LDA answer
          OUT              ; Output the answer in ACC
          HLT              ; Halt
more      LDA answer       ; Load answer into ACC
          ADD one          ; Increment ACC
          STA answer       ; Store in answer
          LDA big          ; load what is left of big
          BRA next         ; Branch to next
x         DAT
one       DAT
big       DAT
small     DAT
answer    DAT
```

Q3: Write pseudocode for an equivalent operation in a high-level language

Format of machine code instructions

In Chapter 2, the basic structure of a machine code instruction in a 16-bit word was described as having a format similar to that shown below.

Operation code		Operand(s)							
Basic machine operation			Addressing mode						
0	1	0	0	0	1	0	1	0	0	0	0	0	0	1	1

The LMC instruction set has only 11 instructions, and the imaginary machine has only 100 memory locations. The maximum data value is 999, which can be held in 10 bits. Four bits would be enough to store the operation code, and 7 bits would be enough to store the operand. A word size of 16 bits would be plenty big enough to hold an instruction or a data value.

In a real computer, there will be considerably more than 11 instructions in the instruction set. It will include, for example, multiply and divide in the arithmetic instructions, and shift instructions to shift bits left or right.

There will also normally be up to 16 registers in which calculations can be carried out, rather than a single accumulator.

3-14

A-Level only

Addressing modes

The operation code (**opcode**) consists of binary digits representing the basic operation such as ADD or LOAD, and a 2-digit code representing the **addressing mode**.

There are four different addressing modes, which are indicated by the bit pattern that is the last two bits of the opcode:

using **immediate addressing**, the operand is the **actual value** to be operated on, say 3 or 75

using **direct addressing**, the operand holds the **memory address** of the value to be operated on. This is the only addressing mode used in the LMC assembly language

using **indirect addressing**, the operand is the location (typically a register) which holds the address of the data we want. This enable a larger range of addressable locations.

using **indexed addressing**, the address of the operand is obtained by adding to the contents of a general register (called the **index register**) a constant value. The number of the index register and the constant value are included in the instruction code. Indexed addressing mode is used to access an array whose elements are in successive memory locations.

Examples of the use of each of these are given below.

Suppose contents of accumulator, index register and a section of memory are as follows:

Accumulator ACC holds 25

Index register holds 6

Register 0 (R0) contains 0

Memory location	Contents
1	
2	3
3	
4	8
5	
6	15
7	32
8	27

load immediate 4   will put the value 4 into ACC

load direct 4   will put 8 (the contents of location 4) into ACC

load indirect 4   will put 27 (the contents of the address held in location 4) into ACC

load indexed R0   will put 15 (contents of location (6 + contents of R0)) into ACC

If R0 is now incremented to contain 1,

load indexed R0   will put 32 (contents of location (6+1)) into ACC

By incrementing the value in R0, successive memory locations can be accessed.

3-14

A

Exercises

1. (a) In a particular machine code, the opcode is stored in 6 bits and the operand is stored in 12 bits. What is the maximum number of operations in the machine's instruction set?   [1]

   (b) Explain, with the aid of examples, the difference between immediate, direct and indirect addressing.   [4] **A**

2. Using instructions   ADD x   (Add number stored in x to the accumulator)

   LDA x   (Load into the accumulator the value stored in x

   STA x   (Store the value in the accumulator in location x)

   write an assembly language program that adds together the values stored in memory locations num1 and num2, storing the resulting total in memory location num3.   [3]

3. Write an assembly language program which counts and outputs the number of values entered by the user, and the total of the values input. End of input is signalled by dummy value 0. You may assume that memory locations called increment, total and numvals contain 1, 0 and 0 respectively. (Use LMC assembly language instructions.)   [7]

Section 4

Exchanging data

In this section:

4

Chapter 15 – Compression, encryption and hashing

Objectives

- Know why sound and images are often compressed
- Understand how other files can be compressed
- Understand the difference between lossless and lossy compression
- (A) Explain the advantages and disadvantages of different compression techniques
- (A) Explain run length encoding and dictionary based compression
- (A) Define symmetric and asymmetric encryption
- (A) Understand how and why hashing may be used to encrypt data

Why use compression?

File compression techniques were developed to reduce the storage space of files on disk. With disk storage becoming larger and cheaper, this is less important these days, but the reduction of file size has become even more important in the sharing and transmission of data. Internet Service Providers (ISPs) and mobile phone networks impose limits and charges on bandwidth. Images on websites need to be in a compressed format to enable a web page to load quickly – even on a fast connection, music and video streaming must take advantage of compression in order to reduce buffering. (In streaming audio or video from the Internet, buffering refers to downloading a certain amount of data to a temporary storage area or buffer, before starting to play a section of the music or movie.)

4-15

Compression can be either **lossy**, where unnecessary information is removed from the original file, or lossless. **Lossless** compression retains all information required to replicate the original file exactly.

Lossy compression

Lossy compression works by removing non-essential information. The two **JPG** images below are clearly identifiable as the same thing, but one has been heavily compressed, displaying untidy and blocky compression artefacts as a consequence. Nevertheless, we can make out the subject of the image well, but the degree to which they are compressed comes at the cost of quality.

Original image 310KB

Heavily compressed image 5.7KB

The compression of sound and video works in a similar way. **MP3** files use lossy compression to remove frequencies too high for most of us to hear and to remove quieter sounds that are played at the same time as louder sounds. The resulting file is about 10% of original size, meaning that 1 minute of MP3 audio equates to roughly 1MB in size.

Voice is transmitted over the Internet or mobile telephone networks using lossy compression and although we have no problem in understanding what the other person is saying, we can recognise the difference in quality of a voice over a phone rather than in person. The apparent difference is lost data.

Lossless compression

Lossless compression works by recording patterns in data rather than the actual data. Using these patterns and a set of instructions on how to use them, the computer can reverse the procedure and reassemble an image, sound or text file with exact accuracy and no data is lost. This is most important with the compression of program files, for example, where a single lost character would result in an error in the program code. A pixel with a slightly different colour would not be of huge consequence in most cases. Lossless compression usually results in a much larger file than a lossy file, but one that is still significantly smaller than the original.

Q1: What type of compression is likely to be used for the following: a website image, a zipped file of long text documents and images, a PDF instruction manual?

A-Level only

4-15

Run Length Encoding (RLE)

If you were ordering food from a takeaway restaurant for a group of five friends, it is likely that you might ask for "5 pizzas" rather than "one pizza, and another pizza, and another pizza etc." **Run Length Encoding** exploits the same principle. Rather than recording every pixel in a sequence, it records its value and the number of times it repeats.

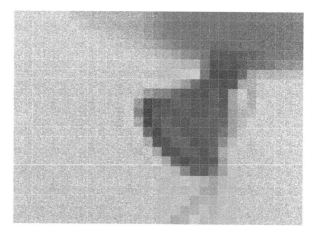

For this section of the balloon image, the encoding for the first row might crudely translate to: 6 green, 8 yellow and 17 orange, using one binary value for the colour value and another for the number of contiguous matching pixels in the run. This would reduce the data necessary to store this row to 6 bytes (00000110 00000001 00001000 00000010 00010001 00000011) rather than 31 bytes assuming a bit depth of 8 and values for each colour of 00000001, 00000010 and 00000011.

6 8 17

Dictionary-based compression techniques

A-Level only

Suppose that instead of sending a complete message, a copy of the Oxford English dictionary was sent alongside a coded message using the page number and the position of the word on that page. The word 'pelican' falls on page 249 as the 7th word on that page. This could be send as 249,7 – using only 2 bytes; considerably fewer than the 7 bytes it would take to send the complete word. (Ignore, for now, the additional space that it would take to send the dictionary with it!)

Dictionary based compression works in a similar way. The compression algorithm searches through the text to find suitable entries in its own dictionary (or it may use a known dictionary) and translates the message accordingly.

Number	Entry	Binary
1	Do	000
2	_unto	001
3	_others	010
4	_as	011
5	_you	100
6	_would	101
7	_have	110
8	_do	111

Using the dictionary table above, the saying **"Do unto others as you would have others do unto you"** would be compressed as **1 2 3 4 5 6 7 3 8 2 5** or in binary using only **33 bits**. This compares to 51 characters or 51 bytes – a reduction of 92%. This still ignores the fact that the dictionary must also be stored with the text, but with a longer body of text to be compressed, a dictionary becomes quite insignificant in size compared with the original, and the original message can still be reassembled perfectly.

4-15

Encryption

Encryption is the transformation of data from one form to another to prevent an unauthorised third party from being able to understand it. The original data or message is known as **plaintext**. The encrypted data is known as **ciphertext**. The encryption method or algorithm is known as the **cipher**, and the secret information to lock or unlock the message is known as a **key**.

The Caesar cipher and the Vernam cipher offer polar opposite examples of security. Where the Vernam offers perfect security, the Caesar cipher is very easy to break with little or no computational power. There are many other methods of encryption – some of which may take many computers many years to break, but almost all of these are still breakable and the principles behind them are similar.

The Caesar cipher

Julius Caesar is said to have used this method to keep messages secure. The **Caesar cipher** (also known as a **shift cipher**) is a type of **substitution cipher** and works by shifting the letters of the alphabet along by a given number of characters; this parameter being the key. Below is an example of a shift cipher using a key of 5.

A	B	C	D	E	F	G	H	I	J	K	L	M	N	O	P	Q	R	S	T	U	V	W	X	Y	Z
↓	↓	↓	↓	↓	↓	↓	↓	↓	↓	↓	↓	↓	↓	↓	↓	↓	↓	↓	↓	↓	↓	↓	↓	↓	↓
F	G	H	I	J	K	L	M	N	O	P	Q	R	S	T	U	V	W	X	Y	Z	A	B	C	D	E

Q2: Using the table above, what is the ciphertext for 'JULIUS CAESAR' using a shift of 5?

Q3: What word can be translated from the following ciphertext using a key of -2: ZYBECP

You will no doubt be able to see the ease with which you can decrypt a message using this system.

DGYDQFH WR ERUGHU DQG DWWDFN DW GDZQ

Even if you had to attempt a brute force attack on the message above, there are only 26 different possibilities. Otherwise you might begin by guessing the likelihood of certain characters first and go from there. Using cryptanalysis on longer messages, you would quickly find the most common ciphertext letter and could start by assuming this was an E, for example; or perhaps an A. (*Hint.*)

The Vernam cipher

The **Vernam** cipher, invented in 1917 by the American scientist Gilbert Vernam, is the only cipher still proven to be unbreakable. All others are based on **computational security** and are theoretically discoverable given enough time, ciphertext and computational power.

One-time pad

The encryption key or **one-time pad** must be equal to or longer in characters than the plaintext, be truly random and be used only once. One-time pads are used in pairs where the sender and recipient are both party to the key. Both must meet in person to securely share the key and destroy it after encryption or decryption. Since the key is random, so will be the distribution of the characters meaning that no amount of cryptanalysis will produce any meaningful results.

The bitwise exclusive or XOR

An **XOR** operation is carried out between the binary character value of the first character of the plaintext and the first character of the one-time pad. Use the ASCII chart on page 160 for reference.

Plaintext: M	Key: +	XOR: f
1	0	1
0	1	1
0	0	0
1	1	0
1	0	1
0	1	1
1	1	0

Q4: Using the ASCII chart and the XOR operator, what ciphertext character will be produced from the letter **E** with the key **w**?

Using this method, the message "**Meet on the bridge at 0300 hours**" encrypted using a one-time pad of **+tkiGeMxGvnhoQ0xQDlllVdT4slJm9qf** will produce the ciphertext:

f◀♫g#X3♂H#Y6!i(=vTg⌐Ci"⌐L ⌐⌐

The encryption process will often produce strange symbols or unprintable ASCII characters as in the above example, but in practice it is not necessary to translate the encrypted code back into character form, as it is transmitted in binary. To decrypt the message, the XOR operation is carried out on the ciphertext using the same one-time pad, which restores it to plaintext.

Cryptanalysis and perfect security

Other ciphers that use non-random keys are open to a cryptanalytic attack and can be solved given enough time and resources. Even ciphers that use a computer generated random key can be broken since mathematically generated random numbers are not actually random; they just appear to be random. A truly random sequence must be collected from a physical and unpredictable phenomenon such as white noise, the timing of a hard disk read/write head or radioactive decay. Only a truly random key can be used with a Vernam cipher to ensure it is mathematically impossible to break.

Symmetric (private key) encryption

Symmetric encryption, also known as **private key** encryption, uses the same key to encrypt and decrypt data. This means that the key must also be transferred (known as **key exchange**) to the same destination as the ciphertext, which causes obvious security problems. The key can be intercepted as easily as the ciphertext message to decrypt the data. For this reason **asymmetric** encryption can be used instead.

Asymmetric (public key) encryption

Asymmetric encryption uses two separate, but related keys. One key, known as the **public key**, is made public so that others wishing to send you data can use this to encrypt the data. This public key cannot decrypt data. Another **private key** is known only by you and only this can be used to decrypt the data. It is virtually impossible to deduce the private key from the public key. It is possible that a message could be encrypted using your own public key and sent to you by a malicious third party impersonating a trusted individual. To prevent this, a message can be digitally 'signed' to authenticate the sender.

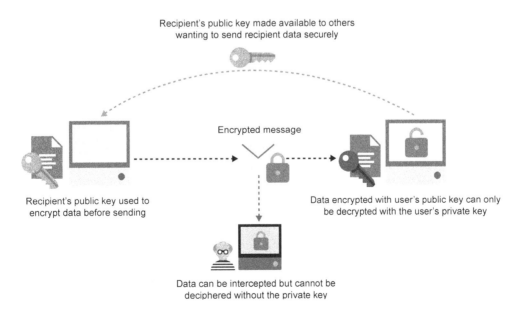

Recipient's public key made available to others
wanting to send recipient data securely

Encrypted message

Recipient's public key used to
encrypt data before sending

Data encrypted with user's public key can only
be decrypted with the user's private key

Data can be intercepted but cannot be
deciphered without the private key

Q5: Governments sometimes demand copies of encryption keys in order to decrypt messages if necessary. What reasons are there for and against governments doing this?

A-Level only

Hashing

A hashing function provides a mapping between an arbitrary length input and a usually fixed length or smaller output. Unlike the encryption techniques described above, it is one-way; you cannot get back to the original. This is useful for storing encrypted PINs and passwords so that they cannot be read by a hacker. To verify a user's password, the software applies the hash function to the user input and compares it with the one stored.

Methods of hashing are discussed in Section 7, Chapter 37.

Cryptographic hash functions

A **hash total** is a mathematical value calculated from unencrypted message data. This value is also referred to as a **checksum** or **digest**. The process is irreversible and impossible to crack other than by trying all of the possible inputs until a match is found. Since the hash total is generated from the entire message, even the slightest change in the message will produce a different total.

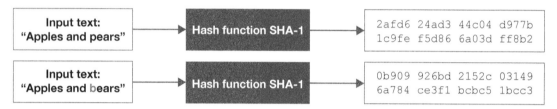

Digital signatures

A **digital signature** or hash value is the equivalent of a handwritten signature or security stamp, but offers even greater security. The sender of the message uses their own private key to encrypt the hash total. The encrypted total becomes the digital signature since only the holder of the **private key** could have encrypted it. The signature is attached to the message to be sent and the whole message including the digital signature is encrypted using the recipient's **public key** before being sent. The recipient decrypts the message using their private key, and decrypts the digital signature using the sender's public key. The hash total is then reproduced based on the message data and if this matches the total in the digital signature, it is certain that the message genuinely came from the sender and that no parts of the message were changed during transmission. To ensure that the message could not be copied and resent at a later date, the time and date can be included in the original message, which if altered, would cause a different hash total to be generated.

Digital signatures can be used with any kind of message regardless of whether encryption has also been used. They can be used with most email clients or browsers making it easy to sign outgoing communications and validate signed incoming messages. If set up to use digital signatures, your browser should warn you if you download something that does not have a digital signature. This would also mean that anything sent by you, including online commercial and banking transactions, can be verified as your own.

> **Q6:** Assuming their private key has not been compromised, a digital signature authenticates the sender beyond legal doubt. How might this help protect against viruses?

Hoax digital signatures could be created using a bogus private key claiming to be that of a trusted individual. In order to mitigate against this, a **digital certificate** verifies that a sender's public key is formally registered to that particular sender.

Digital certificates

While digital signatures verify the trustworthiness of message content, a **digital certificate** is issued by official **Certificate Authorities** (CAs) such as Symantec or Verisign and verifies the trustworthiness of a message sender or website. This certificate allows the holder to use the **Public Key Infrastructure** or PKI. The certificate contains the certificate's serial number, the expiry date, the name of the holder, a copy of their public key, and the digital signature of the CA so that the recipient can authenticate the certificate as real. Digital certificates operate within the Transport layer of the TCP/IP protocol stack. TCP/IP is covered in Chapter 22.

A

Exercises

1. (a) Explain why compression is considered necessary for images on the web. [2]

   (b) Explain why lossy compression techniques would not be suitable for use with files containing large bodies of text. [1]

   (c) Suggest a suitable lossless method for compressing text. [1]

2. (a) Explain the difference between lossy and lossless data compression. [2]

   (b) Run-length encoding (RLE) is a pattern substitution compression algorithm. Data is stored in the format (colour,run), where 0 = White and 1 = Black.

```
a. (0,1),(1,5),(0,1),
b. (1,7),
c. (1,1),(0,2),(1,1),(0,2),(1,1),
d. (1,7),
e. (0,1),(1,1),(0,1),(1,1),(0,1),(1,1),(0,1),
f. (0,1),(1,1),(0,1),(1,1),(0,1),(1,1),(0,1),
g. (0,1),(1,1),(0,3),(1,1),(0,1)
```

4-15

   Reassemble the encoded sequence above to form a 7x7 web icon image in the grid below. [3]

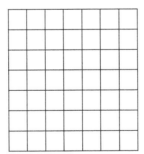

   (c) RLE encoding is a lossless compression method. Give **one** disadvantage of lossless compression over lossy methods for the compression of images. [1]

3. (a) State what is meant by **symmetric encryption** and explain with the aid of an example how it can be implemented. [4]

   (b) (i) Explain what is meant by **asymmetric encryption**. [4]

      (ii) Explain why this form is more secure than symmetric encryption. [2]

   A

Chapter 16 – Database concepts

Objectives

- Explain the concept of a relational database
- Define the terms: flat file, entity, attribute, primary key, foreign key, secondary key, entity relationship modelling, referential integrity
- Produce an entity relationship model for a simple scenario involving multiple entities

Modelling data requirements

When a systems designer begins work on a new proposed computer system, one of the first things they need to do is to examine the data that needs to be input, processed and stored and determine what the data **entities** are.

Definition: An **entity** is a category of object, person, event or thing of interest to an organisation about which data is to be recorded.

Examples of entities are: Employee, Film, Actor, Product, Recipe, Ingredient. Each entity in a database system has **attributes**.

A flat file database

A flat file database consists of a single file. It might be a suitable structure to hold the names and addresses of all members of a sports club, or information about all the DVDs in your personal collection.

Most databases, however, are concerned with more than one entity, and the relationships between the entities. In a collection of DVDs, you might want to keep a record of which main actors starred in each film. **Actor** would be a second entity in its own right.

Example 1

A dentist's surgery employs several dentists, and an appointments system is required to allow patients to make appointments with a particular dentist.

Entities in this system include **Dentist**, **Patient** and **Appointment**. The attributes of **Dentist** may include Title, Firstname, Surname, Qualification.

Attributes of **Patient** may include Title, Firstname, Surname, Address, Telephone.

Q1: Can you suggest any more attributes for **Patient**?

Q2: What attributes might the entity **Appointment** have?

Entity descriptions

An entity description is normally written using the format

Entity1 (Attribute1, Attribute2...)

The entity description for **Dentist** is therefore written

Dentist (Title, Firstname, Surname, Qualification)

Entity identifier and primary key

Each entity needs to have an **identifier** which uniquely identifies the entity. In a relational database, the entity identifier is known as the **primary key** and it will be referred to as such in this section. Clearly none of the attributes so far identified for **Dentist** and **Patient** is suitable as a primary key. A numeric or string ID such as D13649 could be used. In the entity description, the primary key is underlined.

Dentist (<u>DentistID</u>, Title, Firstname, Surname, Qualification)

Q3: Is National Insurance Number a suitable primary key for Patient? If not, why not?

Secondary key

A database needs to be set up so that it can be searched quickly. An **index** of all the primary keys in the database, and where the record is held, is automatically maintained by the database software. However, more than one index may be needed.

If for example a patient rings up to make an appointment with the dentist, they are unlikely to know their patient ID, A **secondary index** on surname is likely to be held.

Relationships between entities

The different entities in a system may be linked in some way, and the two entities are said to be related.

There are only three different 'degrees' of relationship between two entities. A relationship may be

- **One-to-one**   Examples of such a relationship include the relationship between Husband and Wife, Country and Prime Minister.

- **One-to-many**   Examples include the relationship between Mother and Child, Customer and Order, Borrower and Library Book.

- **Many-to-many**   Examples include the relationship between Student and Course, Stock Item and Supplier, Film and Actor.

Entity relationship modelling

The relationship between entities can be modelled graphically. An **entity relationship diagram** is a diagrammatic way of representing the relationships between the entities in a database. To show the relationship between two entities, both the degree and the name of the relationship need to be specified. E.g. In the first relationship shown below, the degree is one-to-one, the name of the relationship is *in charge of*.

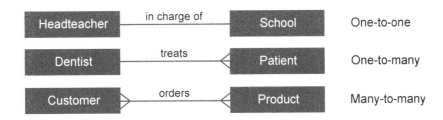

The concept of a relational database

In a relational database, a separate **table** is created for each entity identified in the system. Where a relationship exists between entities, an extra field called a **foreign key** links the two tables.

Foreign key

A foreign key is an attribute that creates a join between two tables. It is the attribute that is common to both tables, and the primary key in one table is the foreign key in the table to which it is linked.

Example: In the one-to-many relationship between Dentist and Patient, the entity on the 'many' side of the relationship will have **DentistID** as an extra attribute. This is the foreign key.

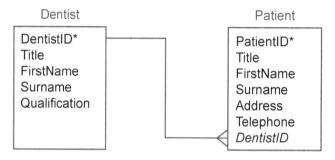

Note that the primary key is indicated by an asterisk, and the foreign key is shown in italics.

Linking tables in a many-to-many relationship

When there is a many-to-many relationship between two entities, tables cannot be directly linked in this way. For example, consider the relationship between **Student** and **Course**. A student takes many courses, and the same course is taken by many students.

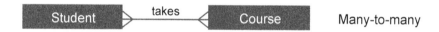

In this case, an extra table is needed to link the **Student** and **Course** tables. We could call this StudentCourse, or Enrolment, for example.

The three tables will now have attributes something like those shown below:

Student (<u>StudentID</u>, Name, Address)

Enrolment (<u>*StudentID*</u>, <u>*CourseID*</u>)

Course (<u>CourseID</u>, Subject, Level)

Composite key

In this data model, the table linking **Student** and **Course** has two foreign keys, each linking to one of the two main tables. The two foreign keys also act as the primary key of this table. A primary key which consists of more than one attribute is called a **composite primary key**.

Drawing an entity relationship diagram

A database system will frequently involve many different entities linked to each other, and an entity relationship diagram can be drawn to show all the relationships.

Example 2

A hospital inpatient system may involve entities **Ward**, **Nurse**, **Patient** and **Consultant**. A ward is staffed by many nurses, but each nurse works on only one ward. A patient is in a ward and has many nurses looking after them, as well as a consultant, who sees many patients on different wards.

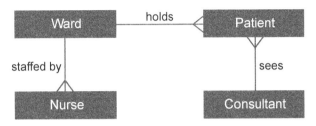

Q4: Is there a relationship between **Patient** and **Nurse**?

Q5: Draw entity relationship diagrams to illustrate the relationships between

(a) **Product** and **Component**

(b) **Customer**, **Order** and **Product** (An order may be for several different products.)

4-16

Referential integrity

When tables are linked in a relational database, it is important to ensure that, for example, a particular component is not deleted if it is used in a product in the Product table. This is known as referential integrity.

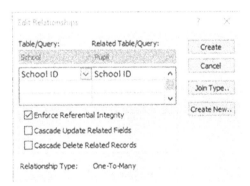

Enforcing referential integrity, linked by School ID

The screenshot above shows a relationship being created in MS Access between two tables linked by School ID.

Exercises

1. An estate agent keeps a database of all the properties it has for sale, the owners of the properties, and all the prospective buyers.

    Details about the properties for sale, including address, number of bedrooms, type of property, asking price are held in a table called **Property**.

    (a) Suggest a suitable primary key for the **Property** table.   [1]

    (b) Suggest two attributes in the **Property** table that may be defined as secondary keys, justifying why each should be defined in this way.   [4]

    Data on prospective buyers include name, telephone, address, type of property required, lower and upper limit for price.

    Data on vendors include name, address, telephone.

    A fourth entity, **Viewing** holds data about all viewings.

    (c) Suggest **three** attributes for the entity **Viewing**.   [3]

    (d) Write entity descriptions for each of the entities **Property**, **Vendor**, **Buyer** and **Viewing**. In each case, identify any primary and foreign keys.   [8]

    (e) Draw an entity relationship diagram showing relationships between these four entities.   [4]

2. A library plans to set up a database to keep track of its members, books and loans. Entities are defined as follows:

    Member (MemberID, Surname, FirstName, Address)

    Book (BookID, ISBN, Title, Author)

    Loan (MemberID, BookID, LoanDate, DueDate)

    When the book is returned the loan record is deleted.

    (a) Draw an entity relationship diagram showing the relationships between the entities.   [3]

    (b) A relational database is created with tables for each of these entities. The key in the Loan table is made up of two fields.

    What is the name given to a key that is made up of multiple attributes?   [1]

    (c) What is meant by a **foreign** key? Identify a foreign key in one of the tables.   [3]

3. An exam board wants to set up a database to hold data about its courses, exam papers, exam entries, candidates and results. For the purpose of this exercise, assume that each candidate can sit each exam once only. A course may have several exam papers (Comp 1, Comp 2, etc.).

   The data to be stored for the candidate are CandidateNumber, FirstName, Surname, DateOfBirth.

   The data to be stored for the course are CourseID, Subject, Level.

   The data held for each individual exam paper includes CourseID, ExamPaperID, DateOfExam, Title, TotalMarks, ExamPaperWeighting.

   (a) State an identifier for the entity **ExamPaper**.　　　　　　　　　　　　　　[1]

   (b) Draw an entity-relationship diagram showing the relationships between the entities.　[3]

   (c) Write an entity description for a **Results** entity which will store the exam mark that candidates receive for each exam paper.　　　　　　　　　　　　　　　　　　[2]

4. (a) Discuss the suitability of flat files and relational databases for use by a family at home and for use in a large mail order company.

   The quality of written communication will be assessed in your answer to this question.　[8]

   (b) In any relational database, primary and foreign keys are used.

   　(i) What is a primary key?　　　　　　　　　　　　　　　　　　　　　　　[1]

   　(ii) Explain the use of a primary key as a foreign key.　　　　　　　　　　　[3]

   OCR F453/01 Qu 9 June 2014

4-16

Chapter 17 – Relational databases and normalisation

Objectives

- Describe the use of secondary keys and indexing
- (A) Normalise relations to third normal form
- (A) Understand why databases are normalised

Relational database design

In a relational database, data is held in tables (also called **relations**) and the tables are linked by means of common attributes.

A **relational database** is a collection of tables in which relationships are modelled by shared attributes.

Conceptually then, one row of a table holds one record. Each column in the table represents one attribute.

e.g. A table holding data about an entity **Book** may have the following rows and columns:

Book

BookID	DeweyCode	Title	Author	DatePublished
88	121.9	Mary Berry Cooks the Perfect	Berry, M	2014
123	345.440	The Paying Guests	Waters, S	2014
300	345.440	Fragile Lies	Elliot, L	2015
657	200.00	Learn French with stories	Bibard, F	2014
777	001.602	GCSE ICT	Barber, A	2010
etc				

To describe the table shown above, you would write

Book (BookID, DeweyCode, Title, Author, DatePublished)

Note that:

The **entity name** is shown outside the brackets

The **attributes** are listed inside the brackets

The **primary key** is underlined

The primary key is composed of one or more attributes that will uniquely identify a particular record in the table. (When describing an entity this is called an **entity identifier**.)

Indexing

In order that a record with a particular primary key can be quickly located in a database, an **index** of primary keys will be automatically maintained by the database software, giving the position of each record according to its primary key.

One or more secondary indexes may be defined when the database is created, for any attribute that is often used as a search criterion. For example, in the above table both Author and Title might be defined as secondary keys. This would speed up searches on either of these fields, which would otherwise have to be searched sequentially.

Linking database tables

Tables may be linked through the use of a common attribute. This attribute must be a primary key of one of the tables, and is known as a **foreign key** in the second table.

We saw in the last chapter that there are three possible types of relationship between entities: one-to-one, one-to-many and many-to-many.

Normalisation

Normalisation is a process used to come up with the best possible design for a relational database. Tables should be organised in such a way that:

- no data is unnecessarily duplicated (i.e. the same data item held in more than one table)

- data is consistent throughout the database (e.g. a customer is not recorded as having different addresses in different tables of the database). Consistency should be an automatic consequence of not holding any duplicated data. This means that anomalies will not arise when data is inserted, amended or deleted.

- the structure of each table is flexible enough to allow you to enter as many or as few items (for example, components making up a product) as required

- the structure should enable a user to make all kinds of complex queries relating data from different tables

There are three basic stages of normalisation known as first, second and third normal form.

First normal form

A table is in **first normal form (1NF)** if it contains no repeating attribute or groups of attributes.

Example 1

A company manufacturing soft toys buys the component parts (fake fur, glass eyes, stuffing, growl etc.) from different suppliers. Each component may be used in the manufacture of several different toys (teddy bear, dog, duck etc.) Each component comes from a sole supplier.

Sample data to be held in the database is shown in the table:

ProductID	ProductName	Cost Price	Selling Price	Comp ID	CompName	Comp Qty	Supplier ID	SupplierName
123	Small monkey	2.50	5.95	ST01	Stuffing	30	ABC	ABC Ltd
				G56	Eye (small)	2	BH Glass	Brown & Hill
				FF77	Brown Fur	0.3	FineFur	Fine Toys Ltd
156	Pink kitten	3.10	6.00	ST01	Stuffing	45	ABC	ABC Ltd
				G120	Eye (medium)	2	XYZ Glass	XYZ Ltd
				FF88	Pink Fur	0.35	FineFur	Fine Toys Ltd
				S34	Soundbox	1	Ping Toys	Ping & Co

Table 17.1

4-17

A-Level only

As the first stage in normalization, we need to note that there are repeating groups of attributes in this table; for example, ProductID 123 has three components with IDs ST01, G56 and FF77. We need to split the data into two tables to get rid of the repeating groups.

Note that a table in a relational database may be referred to as a **relation**.

Two entities, **Product** and **Component**, can be identified. These have the following relationship:

These two entities could be represented in standard notation:

> Product (ProductID, ProductName, CostPrice, SellingPrice)
>
> Component (CompID, CompName, SupplierID, SupplierName)

We have not yet put CompQty (the amount or number of each component that is needed to make a particular product) in either table, but we will come to that.

The two tables need to be linked by means of a common attribute, but the problem is that because this is a many-to-many relationship, whichever table we put the link attribute into, there needs to be *more than one* attribute.

e.g.   Product (ProductID, ProductName, CostPrice, SellingPrice, CompQty, ComponentID)

is no good because each toy has several components, so which one would be mentioned?

Similarly, Component (CompID, CompName, SupplierID, SupplierDetails, ProductID)

is no good either because each component is used in a number of different products.

One obvious solution (and unfortunately a bad one) springs to mind. How about allowing space for four components in the record for each product?

> Product (ProductID, ProductName, CostPrice, SellingPrice, CompID1, CompQty1, CompID2, CompQty2, CompID3, CompQty3, CompID4, CompQty4)

Q1:   Why is this not a good idea?

This table contains repeating attributes, which are not allowed in first normal form. The attributes ComponentID and CompQty are repeated four times. The table is therefore NOT in first normal form.

It would be represented in standard notation with a line over the repeating attributes:

> Product (ProductID, ProductName, CostPrice, SellingPrice, $\overline{\text{CompID, CompQty}}$)

To put the data into first normal form, the repeating attributes must be removed.

Introducing the link table

At this stage it becomes clear why we need a third table to link the two tables **Product** and **Component**.

The three tables now have attributes as follows:

> Product (*ProductID*, ProductName, CostPrice, SellingPrice)
>
> ProductComp (*ProductID*, *CompID*, CompQty)
>
> Component (*CompID*, CompName, SupplierID, SupplierName)

4-17

The design is now in 1NF because it contains no repeating attribute or groups of attributes.

Q2: Draw three tables representing these three entities and put the test data from Table 1 in the correct tables.

Q3: Which of the primary keys is a composite key?

Dealing with a Many-to-Many relationship

As you get more practice in database design, you will notice that *whenever* two entities have a many-to-many relationship, you will *always* need a link table 'in the middle'. Thus:

will become:

Second normal form - Partial key dependence test

A table is in **second normal form (2NF)** if it is in first normal form and contains no **partial dependencies**. A partial dependency would mean that one or more of the attributes depends on only part of the primary key, which can only occur if the primary key is a composite key.

The only table in which this could arise is **ProductComp** as this is the only table with a composite primary key. However, the only attribute in this table apart from the primary key is CompQty, which depends both on both parts of the primary key – which product and which particular component in that product.

The tables are therefore now in second normal form.

(To demonstrate tables which are not in second normal form, we'll look at Example 2 shortly.)

Third normal form - Non-key dependence test

A table is in **third normal form (3NF)** if it is in second normal form and contains no 'non-key dependencies'. A non-key dependency is one where the value of an attribute is determined by the value of another attribute which is not part of the key. 3NF means that:

All attributes are dependent on the key, the whole key, and nothing but the key.

Looking at the **Component** table, the SupplierName attribute is dependent on CompID and not on the SupplierID. It therefore needs to be removed from this relation and a new relation created.

The database, now in third normal form, consists of the following tables:

Product (<u>ProductID</u>, ProductName, CostPrice, SellingPrice)

ProductComp (*<u>ProductID</u>, <u>CompID</u>*, CompQty)

Component (<u>CompID</u>, CompName, *SupplierID*)

Supplier (<u>SupplierID</u>, SupplierName)

The entity relationship diagram showing the relationships between these four tables in third normal form is shown below. Each entity has its own table.

Example 2

A school plans to keep records of Sports Day events for different years in a database. The data that needs to be held for each event in a particular year is illustrated in the following table:

EventID	Year	EventName	Winner	TimeOrDistance
GA100	2015	Girls Under 14 100m	Claire Gordon	16.1
BJ100	2015	Junior Boys 100m	Marc Harris	13.1

The entity description is:

Event (EventID, Year, EventName, Winner, TimeOrDistance)

The composite primary key is composed of EventID and Year. Winner and TimeOrDistance depend on the whole key.

However, EventName depends only on EventID, not on Year, so this is a partial dependency. This table is therefore not normalised. It does not satisfy the requirement of a table in second normal form, namely that there are no partial dependencies.

> **Q4:** Show how the database may be normalised by writing entity descriptions for each relation. Draw an entity relationship diagram.

The importance of normalisation

A normalised database has major advantages over an un-normalised one.

No data redundancy

One of the aims of normalising a database design is to remove the possibility of redundant data from any of the tables. Redundant data is data that appears in more than one database table, which can cause inefficiencies and inconsistencies in the data, as explained in the next paragraph.

Maintaining and modifying the database

It is easier to maintain and change a normalised database.

Data integrity is maintained since there is no unnecessary duplication of data. For example, a customer with a particular customer ID will have their personal details stored only once. If the customer changes address, the update needs only to be made to a single table, so there is no possibility of inconsistencies arising with different addresses for the customer being held on different files.

It will also be impossible to insert transactions such as details of an order, for a customer who is not recorded in the database.

4-17

A-Level only

Faster sorting and searching

Normalisation will produce smaller tables with fewer fields. This results in faster searching, sorting and indexing operations as there is less data involved.

A further advantage is that holding data only once saves storage space.

Deleting records

A normalised database with correctly defined relationships between tables will not allow records in a table on the 'one' side of a one-to-many relationship to be deleted accidentally. For example, a customer who still has unresolved transactions on file cannot be deleted. This will prevent accidental deletion of a customer who has an unpaid invoice recorded, for example.

A

Exercises

1. The publisher of several magazines has a relational database in which the details of each magazine are held. One of the tables in the database holds details of all the major articles in each magazine.

    (a) Write a description for entities **Magazine** and **Article**, showing for each table the primary key, a foreign key if applicable, and at least two other attributes, using the format

        EntityName (<u>primary key</u>, attribute1, attribute2, attribute3… $\overline{\text{foreign key}}$) [6]

    (b) Suggest, with a reason, an attribute in either table which it would be useful to define as a secondary key. [2]

A-Level only

4-17

2. A college department wishes to create a database to hold information about students and the courses they take. The relationship between students and courses is shown in the following entity relationship diagram.

Each course has a tutor who is in charge of the course.

Sample data held on the database is shown in the table below.

Student Number	Student Name	DateOfBirth	Gender	Course Number	CourseName	TeacherID	Teacher Name
1111	Bell, K	14-01-1998	M	COMP23	Java1	8563	Davey,A
2222	Cope, F	12-08-1997	F	COMP23 COMP16 G101	Java1 Intro to OOP Animation	8563 2299 1567	Davey,A Ross,M Day,S
3333	Behr,K	31-07-1996	M	COMP16 COMP34	Intro to OOP Database Design	2299 3370	Ross,M Blaine, N

    (a) Show how the data may be rearranged into relations which are in third normal form. [6]

    (b) State **two** properties that the tables in a fully normalised database must have. [2]

A-Level only

3. A museum has permanent displays but also runs a programme of special events. People may pay an annual fee to become Friends of the Museum. Friends can attend events, which they must book in advance. This, and other data about the museum, is stored in a relational database. Part of the entity-relationship (E-R) diagram is shown.

(a) (i)   State the type of relationship between FRIEND and TICKET.   [1]

   (ii) Explain the use of primary and foreign keys in FRIEND and TICKET.   [4]

(b) When the database was being designed, an initial version of the diagram showed a direct relationship between FRIEND and EVENT.

   Draw this initial E-R diagram with FRIEND and EVENT only.   [1]

   Explain why TICKET was inserted.   [3]

OCR F453-01 Qu 9 June 2013

A

4-18

Chapter 18 – Introduction to SQL

Objectives

Ⓐ • Be able to use SQL to retrieve data from multiple tables of a relational database

Ⓐ • Be able to interpret and modify SQL

SQL

SQL, or **Structured Query Language** (pronounced either as S-Q-L or Sequel) is a **declarative language** used for querying and updating tables in a relational database. It can also be used to create tables. In this chapter, we will look at SQL statements used in querying a database.

The tables shown in Tables 18.1, 18.2 and 18.3 below will be used to demonstrate some SQL statements. The tables are part of a database used by a retailer to store details of CDs in a database that will allow information about the CDs to be extracted. The four entities **CD**, **CDSong**, **Song** and **Artist** are connected by the following relationships:

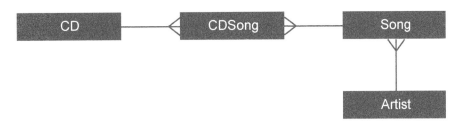

Figure 18.1

The **CD** table is shown below.

CDNumber	CDTitle	RecordCompany	DatePublished
CD14356	Shadows	ABC	06/05/2014
CD19998	Night Turned Day	GHK	24/03/2015
CD25364	Autumn	ABC	11/10/2015
CD34512	Basic Poetry	GHK	01/02/2016
CD56666	The Lucky Ones	DEF	16/02/2016
CD77233	Lucky Me	ABC	24/05/2014
CD77665	Flying High	DEF	31/07/2015

*Table 18.1: **CD** table*

SELECT .. FROM .. WHERE

The SELECT statement is used to extract a collection of fields from a given table. The basic syntax of this statement is

SELECT   *list the fields to be displayed*

FROM   *list the table or tables the data will come from*

WHERE   *list the search criteria*

ORDER BY   *list the fields that the results are to be sorted on (default is Ascending order)*

Example 1

```
SELECT     CDTitle, RecordCompany, DatePublished
FROM       CD
WHERE      DatePublished BETWEEN #01/01/2015# AND #31/12/2015#
ORDER BY   CDTitle
```

This will return the following records:

CDTitle	RecordCompany	DatePublished
Autumn	ABC	11/10/2015
Flying High	DEF	31/07/2015
Night Turned Day	GHK	24/03/2015

Conditions

Conditions in SQL are constructed from the following operators:

Symbol	Meaning	Example	Notes
=	Equal to	CDTitle = "Autumn"	Different implementations use single or double quotes
>	Greater than	DatePublished > #01/01/2015#	The date is enclosed in quote marks or, in Access, # symbols.
<	Less than	DatePublished < #01/01/2015#	
!=	Not equal to	RecordCompany != "ABC"	
>=	Greater than or equal to	DatePublished >= #01/01/2015#	
<=	Less than or equal to	DatePublished <= #01/01/2015#	
IN	Equal to a value within a set of values	RecordCompany IN ("ABC", "DEF")	
LIKE	Similar to	CDTitle LIKE "S%"	Finds Shadows (wildcard operator varies and can be *)
BETWEEN... AND	Within a range, including the two values which define the limits	DatePublished BETWEEN #01/01/2015# AND #31/12/2015#	
IS NULL	Field does not contain a value	RecordCompany IS NULL	
AND	Both expressions must be true for the entire expression to be judged true	DatePublished > #01/01/2015# AND RecordCompany = "ABC"	
OR	If either or both of the expressions are true, the entire expression is judged true.	RecordCompany = "ABC" OR RecordCompany = "DEF"	Equivalent to RecordCompany IN ("ABC", "DEF")
NOT	Inverts truth	RecordCompany NOT IN ("ABC", "DEF")	

Q1: SQL statements are written in the format

```
SELECT  *
FROM    table
WHERE   condition
```

Write a query which will display all fields of records in the CD table published by the ABC or GHK record company in 2014-2015. (Note that the * means 'Display all fields in the record'.) Referring to the data in *Table 1*, what are the CDNumbers of the records returned by this query?

Specifying a sort order

ORDER BY gives you control over the order in which records appear in the Answer table. If for example you want the records to be displayed in ascending order of RecordCompany and within that, descending order of DatePublished, you would write, for example:

```
SELECT *
FROM CD
WHERE DatePublished < #31/12/2015#
ORDER BY RecordCompany, DatePublished Desc
```

This would produce the following results:

CDNumber	CDTitle	RecordCompany	DatePublished
CD25364	Autumn	ABC	11/10/2015
CD77233	Lucky Me	ABC	24/05/2014
CD14356	Shadows	ABC	06/05/2014
CD77665	Flying High	DEF	31/07/2015
CD19998	Night Turned Day	GHK	24/03/2015

Extracting data from several tables

So far we have only taken data from one table. The **Song** and **Artist** tables have the following contents:

SongID	SongTitle	ArtistID	MusicType
S1234	Waterfall	A318	Americana
S1256	Shake it	A123	Heavy Metal
S1258	Come Away	A154	Americana
S1344	Volcano	A134	Art Pop
S1389	Complicated Game	A318	Americana
S1392	Ghost Town	A123	Heavy Metal
S1399	Gentle Waves	A134	Art Pop
S1415	Right Here	A134	Art Pop
S1423	Clouds	A315	Art Pop
S1444	Sheet Steel	A334	Heavy Metal
S1456	Here with you	A154	Art Pop

*Table 18.2: **Song** table*

4-18

ArtistID	ArtistName
A123	Fred Bates
A134	Maria Okello
A154	Bobby Harris
A315	Jo Morris
A318	JJ
A334	Rapport

Table 18.3: **Artist** *table*

Using SQL you can combine data from two or more tables, by specifying which table the data is held in. For example, suppose you wanted SongTitle, ArtistName and MusicType for all *Art Pop* music. When more than one table is involved, SQL uses the syntax `tablename.fieldname.` (The table name is optional unless the field name appears in more than one table.)

```
SELECT Song.SongTitle, Artist.ArtistName, Song.MusicType
FROM Song, Artist
WHERE (Song.ArtistID = Artist.ArtistID) AND (Song.MusicType = "Art Pop")
```

The condition `Song.ArtistID = Artist.ArtistID` provides the link between the **Song** and **Artist** tables so that the artist's name corresponding to the ArtistID in the **Song** table can be found in the **Artist** table. This will produce the following results:

SongTitle	ArtistName	MusicType
Volcano	Maria Okello	Art Pop
Gentle Waves	Maria Okello	Art Pop
Right Here	Maria Okello	Art Pop
Clouds	Jo Morris	Art Pop
Here with you	Bobby Harris	Art Pop

SQL JOIN

`JOIN` provides an alternative method of combining rows from two or more tables, based on a common field between them. The query above could be written as follows:

```
SELECT Song.SongTitle, Artist.ArtistName, Song.MusicType
FROM Song
JOIN Artist
ON Song.ArtistID = Artist.ArtistID
WHERE Song.MusicType = "Art Pop"
```

Q2: Write an SQL query which will give the SongTitle, ArtistName, MusicType of all songs by *JJ* or *Rapport*, sorted by ArtistName and SongTitle.

The fourth table in the database is the table **CDSong** which links the songs to one or more of the CDs.

CDNumber	SongID
CD14356	S1234
CD14356	S1258
CD14356	S1415
CD19998	S1234
CD19998	S1389
CD19998	S1423
CD19998	S1456
CD25364	S1256
CD25364	S1392
CD34512	S1392
CD34512	S1234
CD34512	S1389
CD34512	S1444
CD77233	S1256
CD77233	S1344
CD77233	S1399
CD77233	S1456

*Table 18.4: **CDSong** table*

4-18

Example 2

We can make a search to find the CDNumbers and titles all the CDs containing the song *Waterfall*, sung by JJ.

```
SELECT Song.SongID, Song.SongTitle, Artist.ArtistName, CDSong.CDNumber,
CD.CDTitle
FROM Song, Artist, CDSong, CD
WHERE CDSong.CDNumber = CD.CDNumber
    AND CDSong.SongID = Song.SongID
    AND Artist.ArtistID = Song.ArtistID
    AND Song.SongTitle = "Waterfall"
```

This will produce the following results:

SongID	SongTitle	ArtistName	CDNumber	CDTitle
S1234	Waterfall	JJ	CD14356	Shadows
S1234	Waterfall	JJ	CD19998	Night Turned Day
S1234	Waterfall	JJ	CD34512	Basic Poetry

Note that in the SELECT statement, it does not matter whether you specify `Song.SongID` or `CDSong.SongID` since they are connected. The same is true of `CDSong.CDNumber` and `CD.CDNumber`. The Boolean conditions `CDSong.SongID = Song.SongID` and `Artist.ArtistID = Song.ArtistID` are required to specify the relationships between the data tables. (See the entity relationship diagram in Figure 18.1.)

A-Level only

Exercises

1. A school keeps records of school trips on a database. There are four tables on the database named PUPIL, TRIP, TEACHER, PUPILTRIP, defined as follows:

    PUPIL (PupilID, PupilSurname, PupilFirstName)

    TRIP (TripID, Description, StartDate, EndDate, Destination, NumberOfStudents, TeacherID)

    TEACHER (TeacherID, Title, FirstName, Surname)

    PUPILTRIP (PupilID, TripID)

    (a) Draw an entity relationship diagram showing the relationship between the entities.   [4]

    (b) Write SQL statements for each of the following operations:

    (i) find the first name and surname of all pupils who went on a trip with TripID 14.   [4]

    (ii) find all the trips for which the teacher with surname "Black" has been in charge, giving teacher's title and surname, trip description and start date, sorted in descending order of start date.   [4]

    (iii) find the firstnames and surnames of all the pupils who went on any trip with "Year 7" in the description (e.g. "Year 7 Geography field trip" in May 2015, showing the firstname and surname of the teacher in charge.   [6]

A-Level only

Chapter 19 – Defining and updating tables using SQL

Objectives

A • Be able to use SQL to define a database table

A • Be able to use SQL to update, insert and delete data from multiple tables of a relational database

Defining a database table

The following example shows how to create a new database table.

Example 1

Use SQL to create a table named **Employee**, which has four columns: EmpID (a compulsory *int* field which is the primary key), EmpName (a compulsory *character* field of length 10), HireDate (an optional *date* field) and Salary (an optional *real number* field).

```
CREATE TABLE Employee
(
EmpID      INTEGER NOT NULL, PRIMARY KEY,
EmpName    VARCHAR(20) NOT NULL,
HireDate   DATE,
Salary     CURRENCY
)
```

4-19

Data types

Some of the most commonly used data types are described in the table below. (The data types vary depending on the specific implementation.)

Data type	Description	Example
CHAR(n)	Character string of fixed length n	ProductCode CHAR(6)
VARCHAR(n)	Character string variable length, max. n	Surname VARCHAR(25)
BOOLEAN	TRUE or FALSE	ReviewComplete BOOLEAN
INTEGER, INT	Integer	Quantity INTEGER
FLOAT	Number with a floating decimal point	Length FLOAT (10,2) (maximum number of digits is 10 and maximum number after decimal point is 2)
DATE	Stores Day, Month, Year values	HireDate DATE
TIME	Stores Hour, Minute, Second values	RaceTime TIME
CURRENCY	Formats numbers in the currency used in your region	EntryFee £23.50

Altering a table structure

The ALTER TABLE statement is used to add, delete or modify columns (i.e. fields) in an existing table.

To add a column (field):

```
ALTER TABLE Employee
ADD Department VARCHAR(10)
```

To delete a column:

```
ALTER TABLE Employee
DROP COLUMN HireDate
```

To change the data type of a column:

```
ALTER TABLE Employee
MODIFY COLUMN EmpName VARCHAR(30)NOT NULL
```

Q1: Use SQL to create a table called Student which is defined as follows:

StudentID	6 characters	(Primary key)
Surname	20 characters	
FirstName	15 characters	
DateOfBirth Date		

Q2: Write an SQL statement to add a new column named YearGroup, of type Integer.

Defining linked tables

If you set up several tables, you can link tables by creating foreign keys.

Example 2

Suppose that an extra table is to be added to the Employee database which lists the training courses offered by the company. A third table shows which date an employee attended a particular course.

The structure of the **Employee** table is:

EmpID	Integer (Primary key)
Name	30 characters maximum
HireDate	Date
Salary	Currency
Department	30 characters maximum

The structure of the **Course** table is:

CourseID	6 characters, fixed length (Primary key)
CourseTitle	30 characters maximum (must be entered)
OnSite	Boolean

The structure of the **CourseAttendance** table is:

CourseID	6 characters, fixed length (foreign key)
EmpID	Integer (foreign key) Course ID and EmpID form a composite primary key
CourseDate	Date (note that the same course may be run several times on different dates)

The **CourseAttendance** table is created using the SQL statements:

```
CREATE TABLE CourseAttendance
(
CourseID    CHARACTER(6)NOT NULL,
EmpID       INTEGER NOT NULL,
CourseDate  DATE,
FOREIGN KEY CourseID REFERENCES Course(CourseID),
FOREIGN KEY EmpID REFERENCES Employee(EmpID)
PRIMARY KEY (CourseID, EmpID)
)
```

Q3: Write the SQL statements to create the Course table.

4-19

Inserting, updating, and deleting data using SQL

The SQL INSERT INTO statement

This statement is used to insert a new record in a database table. The syntax is:

```
INSERT INTO tableName (column1, column2, …)
VALUES (value1, value2, …)
```

Example: add a record for employee number 1122, Bloggs, who was hired on 1/1/2001 for the technical department at a salary of £18000.

```
INSERT INTO Employee (EmpID, Name, HireDate, Salary, Department)
VALUES ("1122", "Bloggs", #1/1/2001#, 18000, "Technical")
```

Note that if all the fields are being added in the correct order you would not need the field names in the brackets above to be specified. INSERT INTO Employee would be sufficient

Example: add a record for employee number 1125, Cully, who was hired on 1/1/2001. Salary and Department are not known.

```
INSERT INTO Employee (EmpID, Name, HireDate)
VALUES ("1125", "Cully", #1/1/2001#)
```

A-Level only

The SQL UPDATE statement

This statement is used to update a record in a database table. The syntax is:

```
UPDATE tableName
SET column1 = value1, column2 = value2, …
WHERE columnX = value
```

Example: increase all salaries of members of the Technical department by 10%

```
UPDATE Employee
SET Salary = Salary*1.1
WHERE Department = "Technical"
```

Example: Update the record for Bloggs, who has moved to Administration.

```
UPDATE Employee
SET Department = "Administration"
WHERE EmpID = "1122"
```

The SQL DELETE statement

This statement is used to delete a record from a database table. The syntax is:

```
DELETE FROM tableName
WHERE columnX = value
```

Example: Delete the record for Bloggs.

```
DELETE FROM Employee
WHERE EmpID = "1122"
```

Q4: The table Student is defined below:

StudentID	6 characters	(Primary key)
Surname	20 characters	
FirstName	15 characters	
DateOfBirth	Date	

(a)   Use SQL to add a record for Jennifer Daley, StudentID AB1234, Date of Birth 23/06/2005.

(b)   Update this record, the student's name is Jane, not Jennifer.

(c)   Add a new column DateStarted to the table, of type DATE.

A

Exercises

1. A car dealer accepts orders for new vehicles from its customers, and puts in an order to the manufacturer for the customised vehicle(s). There may be more than one vehicle on the customer order if for example a company is replacing its fleet of hire cars. When a car arrives, a member of staff telephones or emails the customer to inform them that it is ready for collection.

   Details of the vehicles, customers and orders are to be stored in a relational database using the following four relations:

   Vehicle (<u>VehicleID</u>, VehicleName, Model, Price, SupplierName)

   CustomerOrder (<u>OrderID</u>, CustomerID, Date)

   CustomerOrderLine (<u>OrderID</u>, <u>VehicleID</u>)

   Customer (<u>CustomerID</u>, CustomerName, EmailAddress, TelephoneNumber)

   (a) These relations are in Third Normal Form (3NF).

      (i) What does this mean?   [2]

      (ii) Why is it important that the relations in a relational database are in Third Normal Form?   [2]

   (b) On the incomplete entity relationship diagram below show the degree of any **three** relationships that exist between the entities.   [3]

Vehicle	CustomerOrder

Customer	CustomerOrderLine

   (c) Complete the following SQL statement to create the Vehicle relation, including the key field.

   ```
   CREATE TABLE Vehicle (
   ```
                                                                                  [3]

   (d) A fault has been identified with all cars of Model 10765. The manager needs a list of the names and telephone numbers of all the customers who have purchased this type of car so that they can be contacted and the car recalled for modification. This list should contain no additional details and must be presented in alphabetical order of the names of the customers.

   Write an SQL query that will produce this list.   [6]

4-19

Chapter 20 – Transaction processing

Objectives

- Describe methods of capturing, selecting, managing and exchanging data
- **A** • Describe what is meant by transaction processing and ACID (Atomicity, Consistency, Isolation, Durability)
- **A** • Describe what is meant by record locking and why it is necessary in a multi-user database
- **A** • Describe what is meant by redundancy

Capturing data

Before data is added to a database, it has to be captured or input by some means or other. Manual methods include transcribing data from a form that has been filled in, for example by a customer ordering items from a catalogue or a market researcher filling in forms on the High Street.

Cheques paid in at a bank are scanned using magnetic ink character recognition (MICR); the bank number, customer account number and cheque number are printed in special magnetic ink along the bottom of the cheque. The amount of the cheque has to be manually entered by the bank clerk.

Some forms such as lottery tickets, multiple choice questionnaires or exams may be read using optical mark recognition (OMR), and other types of form using OCR Optical Character Recognition.)

Other automated methods include smart card readers, scanners such as those used at airports to scan passports and barcode readers or scanners.

Q1: Describe some other automated methods of capturing data to be stored on a database.

Selecting and managing data

Data may be selected before it is even added to a database, depending on whether or not it matches specified criteria. For example, a speed camera may automatically photograph only those vehicles which are exceeding the speed limit.

Once in the database, SQL may be used to select data from different tables which match required criteria. Using the selected data, reports may be produced, letters sent out by post or email, new stock items automatically re-ordered, records added, updated or deleted.

Exchanging data

A common method of transferring data between one computer system and another (usually via the Internet) without the need for human intervention is EDI (Electronic Data Interchange). Using standardised message formatting, documents can be exchanged electronically. Transaction software processes the information and the software on the receiving end looks up details of, for example, items to be purchased, price, buyer's name and address etc. in an order processing system.

EDI can be used in countless different applications, such as by Exam Boards to send results to schools, or by insurance companies to check that an applicant has a driver's licence.

Transaction processing and ACID   A-Level only

In the context of databases, a single logical operation on data is defined as a transaction. For example, a customer booking a cinema ticket, and making an online payment using a credit card, is a single transaction even though it involves multiple actions.

The database system has to ensure that it is not possible to complete only part of a transaction, for example booking the cinema ticket without paying for it. **ACID (Atomicity, Consistency, Isolation, Durability)** is a set of properties that guarantees that transactions are processed reliably.

4-20

Atomicity

Atomicity requires that a transaction must be processed in its entirety or not at all. Atomicity must guarantee that in any situation, including power cuts or hard disk crashes, it is not possible to process only part of a transaction.

Consistency

The **consistency** property ensures that no transaction can violate any of the defined validation rules for maintaining the integrity of the database. When a database is created, **referential integrity** rules will be specified between linked tables (see Chapter 16). Thus it will not be possible, for example, to record a mark in a RESULTS table for a student who is not in the STUDENT table in the database. Similarly, it will not be possible to delete a record from the STUDENT table if they have marks on the RESULTS table.

Isolation

The **isolation** property ensures that concurrent execution of transactions leads to the same results as if transactions were processed one after the other.

Durability

The **durability** property ensures that once a transaction has been committed, it will remain so, even in the event of a power cut. For example, if the online sale of a cinema ticket is in the process of being completed, it should not be possible for the number of seats sold to be updated but the customer's debit card not processed. As each part of the transaction is completed, it is held in a buffer on disk until all elements of the transaction are completed. Only then will the changes to the database tables be made.

Potential problems with multi-user databases

Allowing multiple users to simultaneously update a database table may cause one of the updates to be lost unless measures are taken to prevent this.

When an item is updated, the entire record (indeed the whole **block** in which the record is physically held) will be copied into the user's own local memory area at the workstation. When the record is saved, the block is rewritten to the file server. Imagine the following situation:

User A accesses a customer record, thereby causing it to be copied into the memory at his/her workstation, and starts to type in a new address for the customer.

User B accesses the same customer record, and alters the credit limit and then saves the record and calls up the next record that needs updating.

User A completes the address change, and saves the record.

Q2: What state will the record be in? (i.e. which address and credit limit will it hold?)

There are several methods which may be employed to avoid updates being lost.

Record locks

Record locking is the technique of preventing simultaneous access to objects in a database in order to prevent updates being lost or inconsistencies in the data arising. In its simplest form, a record is locked whenever a user retrieves it for editing or updating. Anyone else attempting to retrieve the same record is denied access until the transaction is completed or cancelled.

Problems with record locking

If two users are attempting to update two records, a situation can arise in which neither can proceed, known as **deadlock**. Suppose a bank clerk is updating Customer A's record with a transfer to Customer B's account. Meanwhile a second bank clerk is trying to update Customer B's record, as he needs to transfer money to Customer A's account.

User1	User2
locks Customer A's record	locks Customer B's record
tries to access Customer B's record	tries to access Customer A's record
waits ..	waits ..

DEADLOCK!

The DBMS must recognise when this situation has occurred and take action. **Serialisation, timestamp ordering** or **commitment ordering** may be used.

Serialisation

This is a technique which ensures that transactions do not overlap in time and therefore cannot interfere with each other or lead to updates being lost. A transaction cannot start until the previous one has finished. It can be implemented using **timestamp ordering**.

Timestamp ordering

Whenever a transaction starts, it is given a timestamp, so that if two transactions affect the same object (for example record or table), the transaction with the earlier timestamp should be applied first.

In order to ensure that transactions are not lost, every object in the database has a **read timestamp** and a **write timestamp**, which are updated whenever an object in a database is read or written.

When a transaction starts, it reads the data from a record causing the read timestamp to be set. When it writes the updated data back to the record it will check the read timestamp. If this is not the same as the value that was saved when this transaction started, it will know that another transaction is also taking place on the record. A range of potential problems can thus be identified and avoided.

Commitment ordering

This is another serialisation technique used to ensure that transactions are not lost when two or more users are simultaneously trying to access the same database object. Transactions are ordered in terms of their dependencies on each other as well as the time they were initiated. It can be used to prevent deadlock by blocking one request until another is completed.

Redundancy

Very many organisations such as banks, airport systems, hospitals, and others cannot afford to have their computer systems go down even for a few seconds, with consequent loss of transaction data. These organisations maintain two or even three identical systems in different geographical locations, so that every transaction is written to two or three different storage facilities. This built-in hardware redundancy protects agianst loss of data in the event of power failure or other disasters.

If one system fails, the backup system automatically takes over and processing can continue.

4-20

Exercises

1. (a) Explain how, in a client-server database with multiple users, an update made by one user may not be recorded if the database management system does not have measures in place to ensure the integrity of the database. [3]

    (b) Explain what is meant by deadlock and how this can arise. [2]

    (b) Name and describe briefly a method of preventing this from happening. [2]

2. (a) Describe what is meant by referential integrity in a database. [2]

    (b) Describe what is meant by the ACID model in database theory. [6]

Section 5

Networks and web technologies

In this section:

5

Chapter 21 – Structure of the Internet

Objectives

- Understand the structure of the Internet
- Describe the term 'Uniform Resource Locator' in the context of networking
- Understand the purpose and function of the Domain Name Server (DNS) system
- Explain the terms 'domain name' and 'IP address'
- Describe how domain names are organised
- Describe the characteristics of LANs and WANs

A short history of the Internet and the World Wide Web

The Internet is a network of networks set up to allow computers to communicate with each other globally. A United States defence project in the 1960s (ARPA) created **ARPANET** to enable distant departments working on the same project to communicate without the need for physical travel. The project developed, as did their means of communication and the Internet idea was born. In 1995 the Internet became a public hit when the World Wide Web emerged and user numbers began to climb, reaching 2.5 billion users worldwide in 2015 – roughly one third of the world's population. The **World Wide Web** (WWW) is a collection of web pages that reside on computers connected to the Internet. It uses the Internet as a service to communicate the information contained within these pages. The concept of the WWW and using a browser to search the information contained within it was first developed by **Sir Tim Berners-Lee**, a British scientist working at CERN in Geneva, Switzerland. The World Wide Web is not the same as the Internet and even today, the Internet is frequently used without using the WWW.

5-21

Q1: Give one example of where the Internet can be used without the World Wide Web.

Global Internet users (1995 - 2015)

Global Internet users (1995 - 2015). Legend: Internet users (Millions); Percentage of the world's population. Data points: 1995 — 16 (0.4%); 2000 — 361 (5.8%); 2005 — 1018 (15.7%); 2010 — 2040 (28.1%); 2015 — 2500 (33%).

The physical structure of the Internet

Each continent uses backbone cables connected by trans-continental leased lines fed across the sea beds. National **Internet Service Providers** (ISPs) connect directly to this backbone and distribute the Internet connection to smaller providers who in turn provide access to individual homes and businesses.

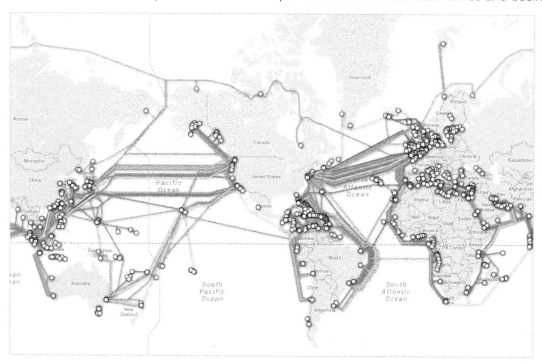

Trans-continental Internet connections, TeleGeography

Uniform Resource Locators (URLs)

A **Uniform Resource Locator** is the full address of an Internet resource. It specifies the location of a resource on the Internet, including the resource name and usually the file type, so that a browser can request it from the website server.

Internet registries and registrars

Internet registrars hold records of all existing website names and the details of those domains that are currently available to purchase. These are companies that act as resellers for domain names and allow people and companies to purchase them. All registrars must be accredited by their governing registry.

Internet registries are five global organisations governed by the **Internet Corporation for Assigned Names and Numbers** (ICANN) with worldwide databases that hold records of all the domain names currently issued to individuals and companies, and their details. These details include the registrant's name, type (company or individual), registered mailing address, the registrar that sold the domain name and the date of registry. The registries also allocate IP addresses and keep track of which address(es) a domain name is associated with as part of the **Domain Name System** (DNS).

5-21

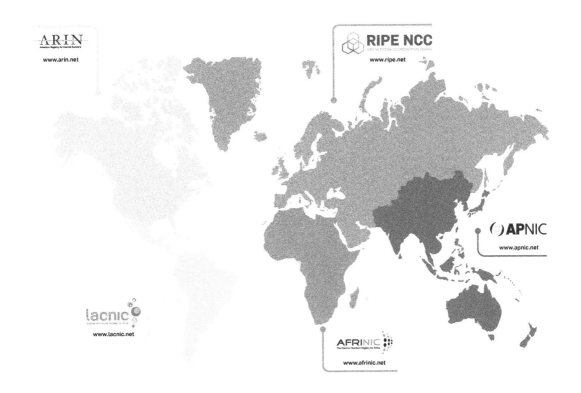

Domain names and the Domain Name System (DNS)

A domain name identifies the area or domain that an Internet resource resides in. These are structured into a hierarchy of smaller domains and written as a string separated by full stops as dictated by the rules of the **Domain Name System** (DNS).

5-21

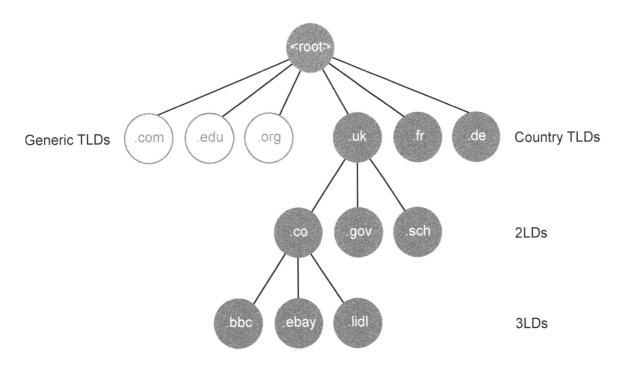

A hierarchical domain system from Top Level Domains (TLDs) to 3rd Level Domains (3LDs)

Each domain name has one or more equivalent **IP addresses**. The DNS catalogues all domain names and IP addresses in a series of global directories that domain name servers can access in order to find the correct IP address location for a resource. When a webpage is requested using the URL a user enters, the browser requests the corresponding IP address from a local DNS. If that DNS does not have the correct IP address, the search is extended up the hierarchy to another larger DNS database. The IP address is located and a data request is sent by the user's computer to that location to find the web page data. A webpage can be accessed within a browser by entering the IP address if it is known. Try entering 74.125.227.176 into a browser.

Q2: Why are IP addresses not used to access websites instead of alphanumeric addresses?

Fully Qualified Domain Name (FQDN)

A **fully qualified domain name** is one that includes the host server name, for example **www**, **mail** or **ftp** depending on whether the resource being requested is hosted on the web, mail or ftp server. This would be written as www.websitename.co.uk or **mail**.website.co.uk for example.

IP addresses

An IP or **Internet Protocol** address is a unique address that is assigned to a network device. An IP address performs a similar function to a home mailing address.

130.142.37.108

The **IP address** indicates where a packet of data is to be sent or has been sent from. **Routers** can use this address to direct the data **packet** accordingly. If a domain name is associated with a specific IP address, the IP address is the address of the server that the website resides on.

Wide Area Networks (WANs)

As a network of **inter**-connected **net**works, the Internet comprises millions, if not billions of **Local Area Networks** and individual users to form the world's largest **Wide Area Network**.

A **Wide Area Network** is generally defined to be one that relies on third party carriers or connections such as those provided by British Telecom. WANs are typically spread over a large geographical area, even across continents.

Local Area Networks (LANs)

A **Local Area Network** consists of a number of computing devices on a single site or in a single building, connected together by cables. The network may consist of a number of PCs, other devices such as printers and scanners, and a central server. Users on the network can communicate with each other, as well as sharing data and hardware devices such as printers and scanners.

LANs can transmit data very fast but only over a short distance.

5-21

Physical bus topology

A LAN can use different layouts or topologies. In a bus topology, all computers are connected to a single cable. The ends of the cable are plugged into a terminator.

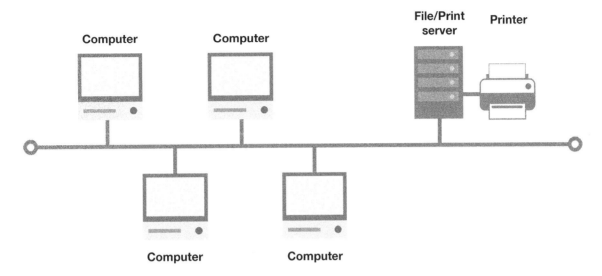

Advantage of a bus topology

- Inexpensive to install as it requires less cable than a star topology and does not require any additional hardware

Disadvantages of a bus topology

- If the main cable fails, network data can no longer be transmitted to any of the nodes

- Performance degrades with heavy traffic

- Low security – all computers on the network can see all data transmissions

5-21

Physical star topology

A **star** network has a central node, which may be a switch or computer which acts as a router to transmit messages. A **switch** keeps a record of the unique MAC address (see chapter 22) of each device on the network and can identify which particular computer on the network it should send the data to.

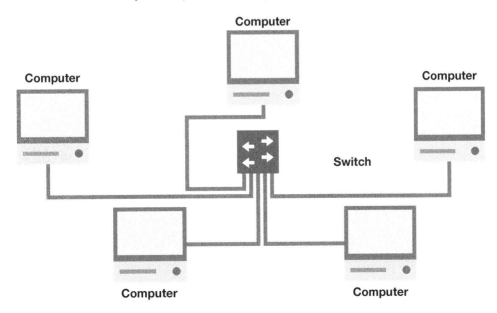

Advantages of a star topology

- If one cable fails, only one station is affected, so it is simple to isolate faults

- Consistent performance even when the network is being heavily used

- Higher transmission speeds can give better performance than a bus network

- No problems with 'collisions' of data since each station has its own cable to the server

- The system is more secure as messages are sent directly to the central computer and cannot be intercepted by other stations

- Easy to add new stations without disrupting the network

Disadvantages of a star network

- May be costly to install because of the length of cable required

- If the central device goes down, network data can no longer be transmitted to any of the nodes

Physical vs logical topology

The **physical topology** of a network is its actual design layout, which is important when you select a wiring scheme and design the wiring for a new network.

The **logical topology** is the shape of the path the data travels in, and describes how components communicate across the physical topology. The physical and logical topologies are independent of each other, so that a network physically wired in star topology can behave logically as a bus network by using a bus protocol and appropriate physical switching.

For example, any variety of **Ethernet** uses a logical bus topology when components communicate, regardless of the physical layout of the cable.

5-21

> **Q3:** (a) What topology does your school use? It may be a hybrid of different topologies.
> (b) Can you tell whether the physical layout differs from the logical layout?

Wi-Fi

Wi-Fi is a local area wireless technology that enables you to connect a device such as a PC, smartphone, digital audio player, laptop or tablet computer to a network resource or to the Internet via a **wireless network access point (WAP)**. An access point has a range of about 20 metres indoors, and more outdoors.

In 1999, the Wi-Fi Alliance was formed to establish international standards for interoperability and backward compatibility. The Alliance consists of a group of several hundred companies around the world, and enforces the use of standards for device connectivity and network connections.

A-Level only

Wireless Access Point (WAP)

In order to connect to a wireless network, a computer device needs a **wireless network adaptor**. The combination of computer and interface controller is called a **station**. All stations share a single radio frequency communication channel, and each station is constantly tuned in on this frequency to pick up transmissions. Transmissions are received by all the stations within range of the wireless access point.

To connect to the Internet, the WAP usually connects to a **router**, but it can also be an integral part of the router itself.

Laptop computer   **Wireless access point**   **Printer**

A laptop connected wirelessly to a printer

Ⓐ

Mesh network topologies

Mesh networks are becoming more common with the widespread use of wireless technology. Each node in a mesh network has a connection to every other node, by transmitting data across any intermediate nodes. Only one node requires a connection to the Internet and all others can share this connection. Mesh networks can quickly become big enough to cover entire cities.

5-21

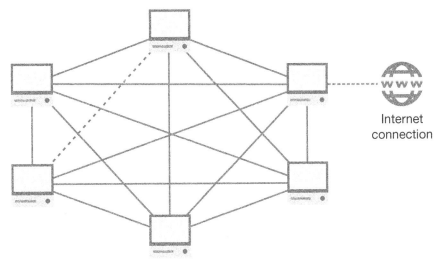

Internet connection

Advantages of a wireless mesh network

- The advantages of a mesh network include:
- No cabling costs
- The more nodes that are installed, the faster and more reliable the network becomes, since one blocked or broken connection (as shown above) can easily be circumvented by another route. In this respect, the mesh topology can be described as '**self healing**'.
- New nodes are automatically incorporated into the network
- Faster communication since data packets do not need to travel via a central switch

Exercises

1. A Uniform Resource Locator (URL) is the address of a resource on the Internet. For example, http://www.pgonline.co.uk/courses/alevel/computing_test.html.

   Explain the different parts of the address.

   (a) www. [1]

   (b) pgonline.co.uk [1]

   (c) /courses/alevel/computing_test.html [1]

2. A village hall committee is considering purchasing a lease on a web domain to set up a new website to advertise their events. They have been advised to contact an Internet registrar.

   (a) Explain the role of an Internet registrar. [3]

   (b) What is the primary role of an Internet Service Provider (ISP)? [1]

3. Mahmood wants to create a small office network for a home enterprise.

   (a) Describe what is meant by a LAN. [2]

   (b) Suggest **two** items of hardware that would be required to create a wireless LAN. [2]

Chapter 22 – Internet communication

Objectives

- Describe circuit switching and packet switching
- Understand the role of packet switching and routers
(A) - Understand the function of network hardware devices
- Understand the importance of protocols and standards
- Describe the roles of the four layers in the TCP/IP protocol stack
- Be familiar with transferring files using FTP as an anonymous and non-anonymous user
- Explain the role of an email server in sending and retrieving email

Circuit switching

Circuit switching creates a direct link between two devices for the duration of the communication. The public telephone system is an example of a circuit switched network. When a caller dials a number, various switches in telephone exchanges set up a path between the caller and the recipient. The connection is set up for the entire duration of the call including periods of silence and pauses. This enables two people to hold a call without any delay in the delivery of speech.

If two computers use the circuit switching principle, bandwidth is wasted during the periods when no data is being sent. The two devices must also transmit and receive data at the same rate, so circuit switched networks can only connect computers or devices that operate at the same transfer rate. On the other hand, since this is an exclusive connection between the two devices for the duration of the communication, data segments (or packets) arrive in the same order that they are sent, simplifying the process of reconstructing the message at the recipient end.

Because switches are used to connect and disconnect the circuits, electrical interference is produced and although this is not a serious problem for speech, it may produce corrupt or lost data if the path is being used to transmit data. If this is likely to be a problem, a leased line may be used instead.

Packet switching

Packet switching is a method of communicating packets of data across a network on which other similar communications are happening simultaneously. Website data that you receive arrives as a series of packets and an email will leave you in a series of **packets**.

Data packets

Data that is to be transmitted across a network is broken down into more manageable chunks called **packets**. The size of each packet in a transmission can be fixed or variable, but most are between 500 and 1500 bytes. Each packet contains a **header** and a **payload** containing the body of data being sent. Some packets may also use a trailer section with a **checksum** or **Cyclical Redundancy Check** (CRC) to detect transmission errors by creating and attaching a hash total calculated from the data contained in the packets. In essence, this hash total commonly involves adding up the total number of 1s in the transmission. The CRC checksum is recalculated for each packet upon receipt and matched to help verify that the payload data has not changed during transmission. If the CRC totals differ, the packet is refused with suspected data corruption and a new copy is requested from the sender.

5-22

The header (much like the box(es) of a consignment you might send or receive through the post) includes the sender's and the recipient's IP addresses, the protocol being used with this type of packet and the number of the packet in the sequence being sent, e.g. packet 1 of 8. They also include the **Time To Live** (TTL) or **hop limit**, after which point the data packet expires and is discarded.

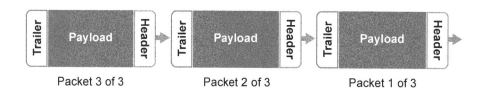

Packet 3 of 3   Packet 2 of 3   Packet 1 of 3

Data packets queueing to be sent

Q1: Why is the sender's IP address included in the packet header?

The payload of the packet contains the actual data being sent. Upon receipt, the packets are reassembled in the correct order and the data is extracted.

Routing packets across the Internet

The success of packet switching relies on the ability of packets to be sent from sender to recipient along entirely separate routes from each other. At the moment that a packet leaves the sender's computer, the fastest or least congested route is taken to the recipient's computer. They can be easily reassembled in the correct order at the receiving end and any packets that don't make it can be requested again.

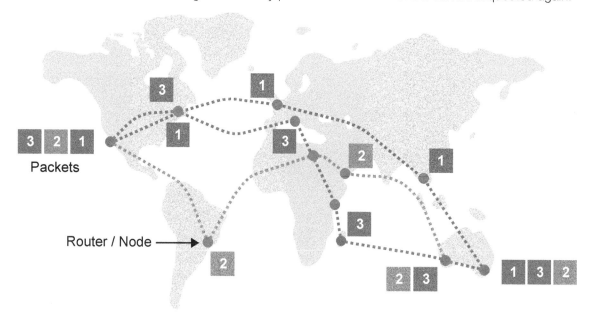

Packets

Router / Node

Q2: What information is included in the packet header to enable the receiving computer to reassemble packets in the correct order?

5-22

Routers

Each node in the diagram above represents a **router**. Routers are used to connect at least two networks, commonly two LANs or WANs, or to connect a LAN and its ISP's network. The act of traversing between one router and another across a network is referred to as a **hop**. The job of a router is to read the recipient's IP address in each packet and forward it on to the recipient via the fastest and least congested route to the next router, which will do the same until the packet reaches its destination. Routers use routing tables to store and update the locations of other network devices and the most efficient routes to them. A routing algorithm is used to find the optimum route. The routing algorithm used to decide the best route can become a bottleneck in network traffic since the decision making process can be complicated. A common shortest path algorithm used in routing is **Dijkstra's algorithm**. (See Chapter 64.)

When a router is connected to the Internet, the IP address of the port connecting it must be registered with the Internet registry because this IP address must be unique over the whole Internet.

Gateways

Routing packets from one network to another requires a router if the networks share the same protocols, for example TCP/IP. Where these protocols differ between networks, a **gateway** is used rather than a router to translate between them. All of the header data is stripped from the packet leaving only the raw data and new data is added in the format of the new network before the gateway sends the packet on its way again. Gateways otherwise perform a similar job to routers in moving data packets towards their destination.

Media Access Control (MAC) addresses

Every computer device, whether it's a PC, smartphone, laptop, printer or other device which is capable of being part of a network, must have a wired or wireless Network Interface Card (NIC). Each NIC has a unique **Media Access Control** address (**MAC** address), which is assigned and hard-coded into the card by the manufacturer and which uniquely identifies the device. The address is 48 bits long, and is written as 12 hex digits, for example:

00-09-5D-E3-F7-62

You can find out the MAC address of your PC by selecting **Command Prompt** from the **Start** menu in Windows, and then typing `ipconfig /all`. This will display the physical address, i.e. MAC address.

Displaying your computer's MAC address

Q3: Do some research to find out whether you can change the MAC address of your PC. Why might someone want to do this?

The importance of protocols and standards

A protocol is a set of rules defining common methods of data communication. These rules need to be standard across all devices in order for them to communicate with each other. **HTTP (HyperText Transfer Protocol)** has become the standard protocol for browsers to render web pages. **TCP/IP** is also used worldwide and enables communication with any other computer connected to the Internet regardless of its location.

The TCP/IP protocol stack

The **Transmission Control Protocol / Internet Protocol (TCP/IP)** protocol stack is set of networking protocols that work together as four connected layers, passing incoming and outgoing data packets up and down the layers during network communication.

There are four layers:

- Application layer
- Transport layer
- Internet layer
- Link layer

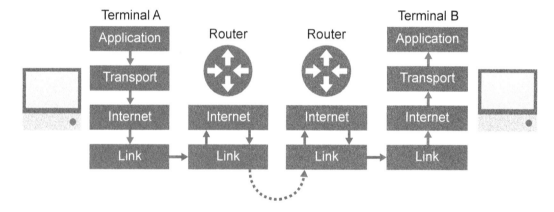

Figure 22.1 The TCP/IP protocol stack

The role of the four layers in the stack

Various protocols operate at each layer of the stack, each with different roles. In each layer, the data to be sent is wrapped, or encapsulated in an envelope containing new packet data as it descends the layers and is unwrapped again at the receiving end in a networking equivalent of a game of pass the parcel.

The application layer

The **application layer** sits at the top of the stack and uses protocols relating to the application being used to transmit data over a network, usually the Internet. If this application is a browser, for example, it would select an appropriate higher-level protocol for the communication such as HTTP, POP3 or FTP.

Imagine the following text data is to be sent via a browser using the **Hypertext Transfer Protocol** (HTTP):

"Only two things are infinite, the universe and human stupidity, and I'm not sure about the former."
Albert Einstein

5-22

The transport layer

The **transport layer** uses the **Transmission Control Protocol (TCP)** to establish an **end-to-end connection** with the recipient computer. The data is then split into packets and labelled with the packet number, the total number of packets and the **port** number through which the packet should route. This ensures it is handled by the correct application on the recipient computer. In the example below, port 80 is used as this is a common port used by the HTTP protocol, called upon by the destination browser.

If any packets go astray during the connection, the transport layer requests retransmission of lost packets. Receipt of packets is also acknowledged.

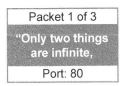 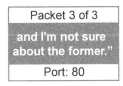

The Internet layer

The **Internet layer** adds the source and destination **IP addresses**. **Routers** operate on the network layer and will use these IP addresses to forward the packets on to the destination. The addition of an **IP address** to the **port** number forms a **socket**, e.g. 42.205.110.140:80, in the same way that the addition of a person's name is added to a street address on an envelope in order to direct the letter to the correct person within a building. A socket specifies which device the packet must be sent to and the application being used on that device.

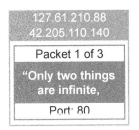  

5-22

The link layer

The link layer is the physical connection between network nodes and adds the unique **Media Access Control (MAC)** addresses identifying the **Network Interface Cards (NICs)** of the source and destination computers. These means that once the packet finds the correct network using the IP address, it can then locate the correct piece of hardware. The destination MAC address is that of the device that the packet is being sent to next. Unless the two computers are on the same network, the destination MAC address will initially be the MAC address of the first router that the packet will be sent to.

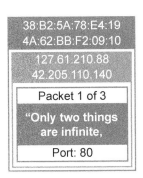 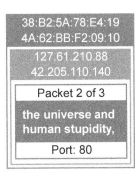 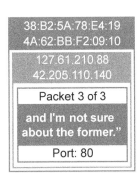

At the receiving end, the MAC address is stripped off by the link layer, which passes the packets on to the Internet layer. The IP addresses are then removed by the Internet layer which passes them on to the transport layer to remove the port numbers and reassemble the packets in the correct order. The resulting data is then passed to the application which presents the data for the user. Since routers operate on the Internet layer, source and destination MAC addresses are changed at each router node. Packets, therefore, move up and down the lower layers in the stack as they pass through each router or switch between the client and the server as shown in Figure 22.1.

Q4: Imagine you are sending a friend a consignment of 5000 widgets in five boxes via a shipping agent. What information would you, the shipping agent, an intermediary depot and the delivery drivers write on the boxes or on a cover note inside? How does this relate to the TCP/IP stack?

Transferring files with FTP

File Transfer Protocol (FTP) is a very efficient method used to transfer data across a network, often the Internet. FTP works as a high level protocol in the Application layer using appropriate software. The user is presented with a file management screen showing the file and folder structure in both the local computer and the remote website. Files are transferred simply by dragging them from one area to the other. FTP sites may also be used by software companies offering large updates, or by press photographers to upload their latest photographs to a remote newspaper headquarters, for example. Most FTP sites require a username and password to authenticate the user, but some sites could be configured to allow **anonymous use** without the need for any login information.

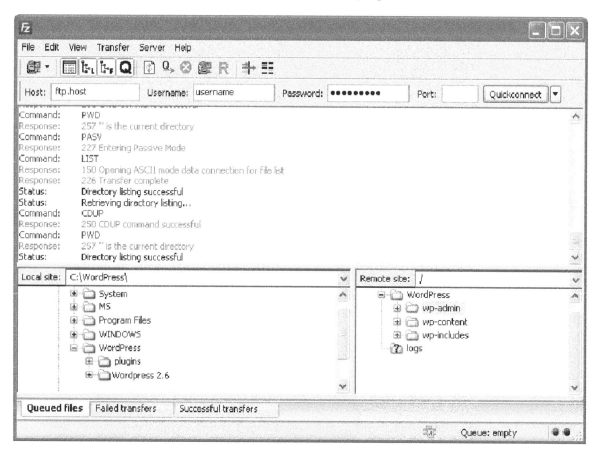

FileZilla – Open source FTP software

5-22

The role of a mail server in retrieving and sending email

A **mail server** acts as a virtual post office for all incoming and outgoing emails. These servers route mail according to its database of local network user's email addresses as it comes and goes, and store it until it can be retrieved. **Post Office Protocol (v3) (POP3)** is responsible for retrieving emails from a mail server that temporarily stores your incoming mail. When emails are retrieved, they are transferred to your local computer, be it a desktop or mobile phone, and deleted from the server. As a result, if you are using different devices to access email via POP3, you will find that they don't synchronise the same emails on each device. **Internet Message Access Protocol (IMAP)** is another email protocol that is designed to keep emails on the server, thus maintaining synchronicity between devices. **Simple Mail Transfer Protocol (SMTP)** is used to transfer outgoing emails from one server to another or from an email client to the server when sending an email.

| Computer | Mail server | Internet | Mail server | Mail server | Computer |

Q5: Georgina is trying to contact her brother Nick, who is currently travelling overseas. Georgina has no idea where Nick is exactly and sends an email to his webmail account. Explain, with reference to the protocols involved, how Nick is able to pick up Georgina's message.

Exercises

5-22

1. All Internet connected devices communicate via the TCP/IP protocol stack. This has four layers – the application, transport, Internet and link layers.

    (a) Describe the roles of each layer when two devices are communicating over the Internet. [8]

    (b) (i) Give the names of **one** piece of network hardware that operates on the Internet layer. [1]

    (ii) Give the names of **one** piece of network hardware that operates on the Link layer. [1]

2. Major parts of the Internet run on a packet switched network that relies on routers and gateways to communicate.

    (a) What is meant by the term *packet switching*? [2]

    (b) A data packet contains a header and a payload. The header contains data that it used to route the packet to its destination.

    State **three** data items that might be contained in a data packet's header. [3]

    (c) Explain the difference between a *router* and a *gateway*. [2]

Chapter 23 – Network security and threats

Objectives

Ⓐ • Discuss network security and threats

Ⓐ • Discuss use of firewalls, proxies and encryption

Ⓐ • Discuss worms, Trojans and viruses and the vulnerabilities that they exploit

Firewalls

A **firewall** is a security checkpoint designed to prevent unauthorised access between two networks, usually an internal trusted network and an external, deemed untrusted, network; often the Internet. Firewalls can be implemented in both hardware and/or software. A router may contain a firewall.

A typical firewall consists of a separate computer containing two **Network Interface Cards** (NICs), with one connected to the internal network, and the other connected to the external network. Using special firewall software, each data packet that attempts to pass between the two NICs is analysed against preconfigured rules (**packet filters**), then accepted or rejected. A firewall may also act as a **proxy server**.

Packet filtering

Packet filtering, also referred to as **static filtering**, controls network access according to network administrator rules and policies by examining the source and destination IP addresses in packet headers. If the IP addresses match those recorded on the administrator's 'permitted' list, they are accepted. Static filtering can also block packets based on the protocols being used and the port numbers they are trying to access. A **port** is similar to an airport gate, where an incoming aircraft reaches the correct airport (the computer or network at a particular IP address) and is directed to a particular gate to allow passengers into the airport, or in this case to download the packet's payload data to the computer.

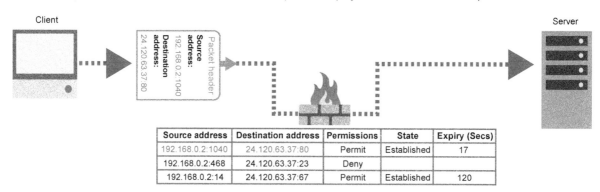

Source address	Destination address	Permissions	State	Expiry (Secs)
192.168.0.2:1040	24.120.63.37:80	Permit	Established	17
192.168.0.2:468	24.120.63.37:23	Deny		
192.168.0.2:14	24.120.63.37:67	Permit	Established	120

Certain protocols use particular ports. Telnet, for example, is used to remotely access computers and uses port 23. If Telnet is disallowed by a network administrator, any packets attempting to connect through port 23 will be dropped or rejected to deny access. A dropped packet is quietly removed, whereas a rejected packet will cause a rejection notice to be sent back to the sender.

A-Level only

Proxy servers

A **proxy server** intercepts all packets entering and leaving a network, hiding the true network addresses of the source from the recipient. This enables privacy and anonymous surfing. A proxy can also maintain a cache of websites commonly visited and return the web page data to the user immediately without the need to reconnect to the Internet and re-request the page from the website server. This speeds up user access to web page data and reduces web traffic. If a web page is not in the cache, then the proxy will make a request of its own on behalf of the user to the web server using its own IP address and forward the returned data to the user, adding the page to its cache for other users going through the same proxy server to access. A proxy server may serve hundreds, if not thousands of users.

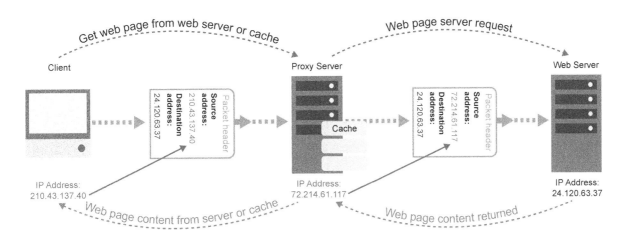

Proxy servers are often used to filter requests providing administrative control over the content that users may demand. A common example is a school web-proxy that filters undesirable or potentially unsafe online content in accordance with the school usage policies. Such proxies may also log user data with their requests.

Encryption

Encryption is one way of making messages travelling over the Internet secure. Different encryption methods are covered in Section 4, Chapter 15.

Worms, Trojans and viruses

Worms, Trojans and viruses are all types of **malware** or **malicious software**. They are all designed to cause inconvenience, loss or damage to programs, data or computer systems.

Viruses and worm subclasses

Viruses and **worms** have the ability to self-replicate by spreading copies of themselves. A worm is a sub-class of virus, but the difference between the two is that viruses rely on other host files (usually executable programs) to be opened in order to spread themselves, whereas worms do not. A worm is standalone software that can replicate itself without any user intervention. Viruses come in various types but most become memory resident when their host file is executed. Once the virus is in memory, any other uninfected file that runs becomes infected when it is copied into memory. Other common viruses reside in macro files usually attached to word processing and spreadsheet data files. When the data file is opened, the virus spreads to infect the template and subsequently other files that you create. Macro viruses are usually less harmful than other viruses but can still be very annoying.

5-23

```
READF X C  M      E MAKERS NE    MEMMAKER      M MMA ER  N    M    C M
FA OU B  OM        E.COM.E       MOVE E   H      OO     L    P   . X
HE   C  3          DR VE.S S     SE      E E       E          S          E
LO   I  L 6P       R   N.E E     M       H                    S
MON  M   X           O .C M      F      X                     A
QBASIC.              U B        O     6                       H
SMARTDR.    I ( M      X4,300     .    .                    A H C .
TREE.CO.          M M        Y9 0 4  TUER  .       N   S       ABEL E .
COMMANDH          ROR      X        ARTMXEX      E  K  .       ODE. 0 E
C:\DOS>V 8        SAM  I T  O       INTD.N.     MST LS..       OWER E E
C:\DOS>M.P E      UMA TMAC. M     S NFIG038 L   SHAR .EXDE     IZER.EXEE
C:\DOS>.CEME      ANFORME3,01     Vbytes.UMBLP  SORT.EXEEI     UBST.EXEPRO
```

The Cascade virus caused text characters to fall from the top of the screen

A worm can reside within a data file of another application and will usually enter the computer through a vulnerability or by tricking the user into opening a file; often an attachment in an email. Rather than simply infecting other files like a virus on your own machine, a worm can replicate itself and send copies to other users from your computer; commonly by emailing others in your electronic address book.

Owing to the ability of a worm to copy itself, worms are often responsible for using up bandwidth, system memory or network resources, causing computers to slow and servers to stop responding.

> **Q1:** Look up the ILOVEYOU, Melissa, Blaster and Cascade viruses or worms. Why should you exercise caution in opening attachments in emails or data files containing macro code?

Trojans

A Trojan is so-called after the story of the great horse of Troy, according to which soldiers hid inside a large wooden horse offered as a gift to an opposition castle. The castle guards wheeled the wooden horse inside their castle walls, and the enemy soldiers jumped out from inside the horse to attack. A Trojan is every bit as cunning and frequently manifests itself inside a seemingly useful file, game or utility that you want to install on your computer. When installed, the payload is released, often without any obvious irritation. A common use for a Trojan is to open a back door to your computer system that the Trojan creator can exploit. This can be in order to harvest your personal information, or to use your computer power and network bandwidth to send thousands of spam emails to others. Groups of Internet-enabled computers used like this are called botnets. Unlike viruses and worms, Trojans cannot self-replicate.

Giovanni Domenico Tiepolo - The Procession of the Trojan Horse in Troy, c.1760

5-23

System vulnerabilities

Malware exploits vulnerabilities in our systems, be they human error or software bugs. People may switch off their firewalls or fail to renew virus protection which will create obvious weaknesses in their systems. Administrative rights can also fail to prevent access to certain file areas which may otherwise be breached by viral threats. Otherwise cracks in software where data is passed from one function, module or application to another, (which is often deemed to have been checked and trusted somehow by the source) may open opportunities for attackers.

People are often the weakest point in security. **Passwords** are no guarantee of protection against unauthorised access since these are sometimes written down, guessed or dishonestly 'blagged' using **social engineering** techniques to persuade the password holder to divulge their authentication credentials.

Protection against threats

Code quality is a primary vulnerability of systems. Many malware attacks exploit a phenomenon called 'buffer overflow' which occurs where a program accidentally writes values to memory locations too small to handle them, and inadvertently overwrites the values in neighbouring locations that it is not supposed to have access to. As a result of a buffer overflow attack, overflow data is often interpreted as instructions. The virus could be written to take advantage of this by forcing the program to write something to memory which may consequently alter its behaviour in a way that benefits the attacker.

Social engineering, including phishing, is a confidence trick used to persuade individuals to open files, Internet links and emails containing malware. Spam filtering and education in the use of caution is the most effective method against this sort of vulnerability.

> **Q2:** In what ways are social engineering methods used to fraudulently elicit a password or authentication details from a user?

Regular operating system and antivirus software updates will also help to reduce the risk of attack. Virus checkers usually scan for all other malware types and not just viruses, and since new variants are created all the time to exploit vulnerabilities in systems software, it is vital that your system has the latest protection. In the worst cases, a lack of monitoring and protection within a company can make national headlines.

Exercises

1. A large company network uses a firewall as part of its security.

   (a) What is meant by a 'firewall'? [2]

   (b) The company also uses anti-virus software as protection against worms, viruses and Trojans.

      (i) Give **one** reason why the anti-virus software should be kept up-to-date. [1]

      (ii) State the difference between worms, viruses and Trojans. [3]

2. Malicious attacks on systems are frequently identified and blocked by various systems.

   (a) How might a proxy server reduce the risks of malware attacks on a network? [1]

   (b) Give **three** methods that school systems administrators can use to reduce the threat of malware. [3]

   (c) Explain how the use of a proxy server may make access to websites faster for users. [2]

Chapter 24 – HTML and CSS

Objectives

- Understand HTML and the role of HTML on the World Wide Web

- Understand CSS and the role of CSS in web pages

- Be familiar with various HTML and CSS tags and their functions

- Use inline CSS directly within HTML files using the <style> tag, and with external style sheets

HyperText Markup Language (HTML)

HTML is the language or script that web pages are written in. It describes the content and structure of a web page so that a browser is able to interpret and render the page for the viewer. HTML is usually used in conjunction with **Cascade Style Sheets** (**CSS**) which dictate the style and formatting of a web page rather than its content.

HTML and CSS

The effects of HTML and CSS on a webpage can be seen left, without CSS styles, and with styles on the right:

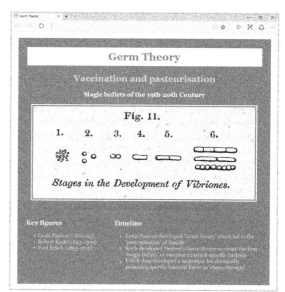

HTML only, without CSS   *HTML with CSS formatting*

HTML Tags

HTML is made up of **tags** written in angle brackets, often in opening and closing pairs, e.g. <html> and </html>.

A standard web page comprises two sections – a **head** and a **body**. The head contains the title of the webpage that may appear in a window header or browser tab, and any script that may enrich your page content. The body contains the main content of the page, defining text, images and hyperlinks. An HTML file can be created using a text editor such as Notepad, or using software such as Adobe Dreamweaver.

The **<head>** section contains the page title and any scripts or styles.

```
Web Page - Notepad                    –   □   ×
File  Edit  Format  View  Help
<html>
<head>
              <title> Page Title </title>
</head>

<body>

</body>
</html>
```

The **<body>** section contains the main HTML page content.

Q1: Create a simple HTML file in Notepad as shown above. Change the `<title>` text and add text to the `<body>` section. What effect does this have when viewed in a browser?

A table of common tags and their function is given below:

HTML Tag	Definition
`<html>`	All code enclosed within these tags is interpreted as HTML
`<body>`	Defines the content in the main browser content area
`<head>`	Defines the browser tab or window heading area
`<title>`	Defines the text that appears with the tab or window heading area
`<h1>, <h2>, <h3>`	Heading styles in decreasing sizes
`<p>`	A paragraph separated with a line space above and below
`<img>`	Self closing image tag with parameters: `<img src = `**`location, height=x, width=y`**`>`
`<a>`	Anchor tag defining a hyperlink with location parameter: `<a href="`**`location`**`">` Link text `</a>`
`<ol>, <ul>`	Defines an ordered (numbered) or unordered (bulleted) list
`<li>`	Defines an individual list item within either a numbered or bulleted list

5-24

The HTML <div> tag

The `<div>` tag facilitates the **division** of a page into separate areas, each of which may be referred to uniquely by name, and styled differently using CSS.

CSS Script

CSS is a scripting language similar to HTML that is used to describe the layout and styles of a web page. Styles can be applied to existing HTML elements such as `<h1>`, `<p>` or `<div>`.

Embedded, inline and external CSS

CSS script can be inserted directly into the HTML document `<head>` as **internal** or **embedded** CSS between its own `<style></style>` tags. It can also be entered directly within the HTML body, known as **inline** CSS, as shown in lines 15 and 19 of the example HTML script overleaf. Either of these methods enable styles to be kept within the HTML document, and inline CSS can help make one-off style adjustments that are unlikely to affect any other part of the website. By far the most common technique, however, is to make style declarations in an **external style sheet.** A link to the external sheet can be placed in the HTML file using the `<link>` tag, for example see line 4 of the HTML script on the following page. Linking to an external style sheet has the advantage that multiple HTML or webpage files within the same site can each link to the same style sheet so that formatting can be applied consistently without the need to duplicate CSS styles.

Identifiers and classes

Identifier and class **selectors** are named 'hooks' onto which you can hang styles. You can then apply these grouped styles to an HTML element such as a `<div>` element by adding the class or id name as a parameter, e.g.

```
<div id="page">.
```

The styles for the id selector called page are listed within curly brackets within the CSS document:

```
#page{max-width:800px; margin: 20px auto; padding: 30px;
                        background-color: #cc6633;}
```

(Refer to line 8 of the HTML script on the next page, and lines 13-19 of the CSS script overleaf.) Any HTML content within the page divider will be styled accordingly.

Identifiers

Identifiers are defined with a hash tag (#) preceding the id name, e.g. **#header** (CSS lines 21-26). Identifiers must be unique to every webpage. In this 'Germ theory' example, #header is a good example of a unique element since a webpage is likely only to contain one header.

Classes

Classes work in a similar way to an identifier but use a full stop as a prefix to the class name e.g. `.list` (CSS Script lines 35-38). Classes can be used multiple times on a webpage. In the example within this chapter, there are two lists which share common formatting unique to the list element such as the font colour. This can be defined in the CSS and applied to all list `<div>` regions on the page. See HTML Script lines 22 and 32.

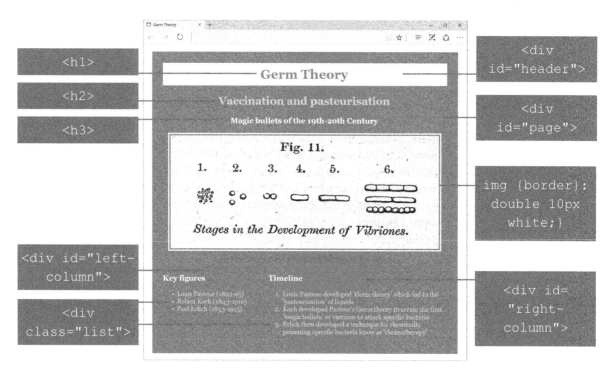

HTML Script

```
1   <html>
2   <head>
3       <title>Germ Theory</title>
4       <link href="styles.css" rel="stylesheet" type="text/css">
5   </head>
6
7   <body>
8       <div id="page"> <!--Opening page-->
9           <div id="header">
10              <h1>Germ Theory</h1>
11          </div>
12          <h2>Vaccination and pasteurisation</h2>
13          <h3>Magic bullets of the 19th-20th Century</h3>
14          <img src="germ_theory.jpg" width="750" height="300" alt="The atmospheric
    germ theory">
15          <p style="margin: 10px 0px;">
16              <a href="https://archive.org/details/b21480308">The atmospheric germ
    theory, 1868 Edinburgh Medical Journal</a>
17          </p>
18
19          <div id="left-column" style="float:left; text-align: left;
20          width:300px;">
21              <h3>Key figures</h3>
22              <div class="list">
23              <ul>
24                  <li>Louis Pasteur (1822-1895)</li>
25                  <li>Robert Koch (1843-1910)</li>
26                  <li>Paul Erlich (1853-1915)</li>
27              </ul>
28              </div>
29          </div> <!--Closing left-column div-->
30          <div id="right-column">
31              <h3>Timeline</h3>
32              <div class="list">
33              <ol>
34                  <li>Louis Pasteur developed 'Germ theory' which led to the
    'pasteurisation' of liquids</li>
35                  <li>Koch developed Pasteur's Germ theory to create the first
    'magic bullets' or vaccines to attack specific bacteria</li>
36                  <li>Erlich then developed a technique for chemically poisoning
    specific bacteria know as 'chemotherapy'</li>
37              </ol>
38              </div>
39          </div> <!--Closing right-column div-->
40          <div style="clear:both;"></div>
41      </div> <!--Closing page div-->
42  </body>
43  </html>
```

5-24

Q2: Explain the function of the HTML code on lines 14 and 16.

Q3: The webpage owners would like to change the font colour of the numbered and bulleted text to white. Explain what change needs to made in order to achieve this.

CSS script

```
1   @charset "utf-8";
2
3   body
4   {
5       margin: 0px;
6       padding: 0px;
7       background-color:white;
8       font-family: Georgia, Times New Roman, "serif";
9       font-size: 18px;
10      text-align: center;
11  }
12
13  #page /* Styles for Page */
14  {
15      max-width:800px;
16      margin: 20px auto;
17      padding: 30px;
18      background-color: #cc6633;
19  }
20
21  #header /* Styles for Heading */
22  {
23      padding: 5px;
24      background-color: white;
25      text-align: center;
26  }
27
28  #right-column
29  {
30      float: right; /* Moves the container to the right */
31      width: 500px; /* Adjust width to fit content */
32      text-align: left;
33  }
34
35  .list
36  {
37      color: #ffcc66;
38  }
39
40  img
41  {   border: double 10px white;}
42
43  h1
44  {   font-size:36px; color: #cc6633; margin: 0px; padding: 5px;}
45
46  h2
47  {   font-size:30px; color: #ffcc66;}
48
49  h3
50  {   color:white;}
```

5-24

Exercises

1. A website has the following HTML code.

```
<html>
    <head>
        <title>Garden Roses</title>
    </head>

    <body>
        <h1 style="font-family:Arial; color:red">Species</h1>
        <p>There are over 100 species of rose.</p>

        <!-Part b -->

        <ul>
            <li>Climbing roses</li>
            <li>Shrub roses</li>
            <li>Rambling roses</li>
        </ul>
    </body>
</html>
```

(a) Sketch and annotate the website as it would appear in a browser. [4]

5-24

(b) The site owner would like to add a hyperlinked image rose.jpg in place of the comment `<!-- Part b -->`. The image would link to the website http://www.roses.com. Write the code to enable this. [3]

(c) Heading 1 <h1> has had some styles applied using inline CSS.

   (i) Give **one** advantage of using CSS styles within the HTML document. [1]

   (ii) Give **two** advantages of using an external CSS style sheet. [2]

(d) An external CSS style sheet is added to the web page. This contains three rules. Describe what effect if any these rules will have on the appearance of the web page. Where there is no effect, this should be stated.

   (i) `body {background-color: lightGreen}` [1]

   (ii) `p.bold {font-weight: bold}` [1]

   (i) `h1 {text-align: center}` [1]

(e) The text within the <ul> tags needs to be styled in green with the intention that any other lists added to the page share the same style. Explain how this can be achieved. [3]

2. Cascade Style Sheets (CSS) make use of **.classes** and **#identifiers**.

(a) Explain the difference between them giving an example of when each might be used. [2]

(b) Explain how a CSS style defined as a class or identifier may be applied to a specific section of HTML content. [2]

Chapter 25 – Web forms and JavaScript

Objectives

- Be able to add HTML form controls to a web page

- Explain the role of JavaScript inside web pages

- Understand and follow JavaScript syntax

- Write basic JavaScript code for a given scenario

- Use JavaScript to change the content of HTML elements

- Create output, including alert boxes, using JavaScript

Web forms

Web forms enable websites to collect user input data and selections. Input types include textboxes, check boxes and radio buttons, for example.

Input can be validated and submitted to the website owner's database or processed as part of a search query to find, for example, train times or your nearest shop branch when you enter a postcode.

Creating a web form using basic HTML form controls

A simple, unformatted web form that uses basic text boxes for input and a pair of buttons to **submit** and **reset** the page can be created very quickly. It will remain functionless however until actions are applied to it. JavaScript can be used to add **behaviours** to a web page, and included in that, active web forms.

The HTML script below should be compared with the screenshot of the page below.

```
<h1>Register</h1>
<form action="process.php" method="post">
    <label>Enter your email to register:</label>
    <input type="text" id="email" value="" size="40" />
    <button type="submit">Submit</button>
    <button type="reset">Reset</button>
</form>
```

Q1: The buttons are created in the browser window using built-in formatting. How might customised styling be applied?

Form handling with submit and reset actions

The button type is specified as an attribute of the button, e.g. `type="reset"`. This will provide some basic functionality in the case of the **reset** button which clears the form data. A **submit** button type will send data to a **form handler** specified in the **action** attribute of the `<form>` tag. The form handler on the server will then process the form data – in this case, an email address.

5-25

Q2: What is the form handler called in the example above?

JavaScript

JavaScript is a **script** language that uses all of the same programming constructs that are familiar in languages such as Python and VB. It should not be confused with the language Java. JavaScript is commonly used to add interactivity to websites, including the manipulation of page objects, animations, navigation tools and form validation. JavaScript is **interpreted** rather than compiled. **Compilers** produce **object code** which is specific to a particular type of processor. JavaScript needs to be translated into the object code for whichever computer the browser is running on, and will be translated by the interpreter when the web page is displayed. An interpreter in the browser reads the JavaScript code, interprets each line and runs it. Some of the latest browsers however, use 'Just-In-Time' compilation which compiles JavaScript into executable **bytecode** just before execution.

Input

JavaScript can be used to process input data on the client's computer. This may change the local page interactively or post data to a server. The advantages of processing input data before it is posted to a server are that:

- the local computer can validate erroneous data before submission to a database

- a busy server is relieved from having to process everything itself.

Output

JavaScript can reference and interact with HTML elements to edit, style or move them. For example, a **validation** script may change a 'postcode' input label to become red if a user has entered invalid data:

```
document.getElementById("postcode").style.color="red";
```

Using JavaScript to control webpage functions

Building on the example of a basic web form above, JavaScript can be used to create a simulated Captcha form shown below.

The HTML form elements are given ids in order for the JavaScript to reference them. (See lines 16-19 of the HTML form script below.) Buttons are given onClick **attributes** in order to execute JavaScript functions when they are pressed. Their type has also been changed to become "`button`" rather than `submit` or `reset` actions. (See lines 20-21.)

HTML form script

```
1    <!DOCTYPE html>
2    <html>
3    <head>
4       <title>Register with Captcha</title>
5       <style>
6          body, input { font-family: Arial, Helvetica, "sans-serif"; font-size: 15px; }
7       </style>
8    </head>
9
10   <body>
11
12   <h1>Register with Captcha</h1>
13
14   <form>
15      <div id="captchaImage"> </div> <!-- Empty div to contain random Captcha image -->
16      <label id="captchaPrompt">Enter the word shown above:</label><br />
17      <input type="text" id="captchaResponse" value="" size="40" /><br /><br />
18      <label id="emailPrompt">Enter your email to register:</label><br />
19      <input type="text" id="email" value="" size="40" /><br /><br />
20      <button type="button" onClick="validateForm();">Submit</button>
21      <button type="button" onClick="setupForm();">Reset</button>
22      <input type="hidden" id="captchaAnswer" value="" />
23   </form>
24
```

5-25

JavaScript code

JavaScript functions and commands are added to HTML documents within <script> tags.

```
25   <script type="text/javascript">
26   // needs to run when page loads or refreshes
27   function setupForm() {
28       document.getElementById("captchaPrompt").innerHTML='Enter the word shown above:';
29       document.getElementById("captchaPrompt").style.color="black";
30       document.getElementById("captchaResponse").value="";
31       document.getElementById("emailPrompt").innerHTML='Enter your email to register:';
32       document.getElementById("emailPrompt").style.color="black";
33       var captcha=["captcha1.jpg","captcha2.jpg","captcha3.jpg"];
34       var captchaAnswer=["weasel","moose","polecat"];
35       var j=Math.ceil(Math.random() * captcha.length);
36       j--; // Javascript indexes start at 0 - the count is 3 items, so subtract 1 to get item in
     range 0-2
37       document.getElementById("captchaImage").innerHTML="<img src='"+captcha[j]+"' width='305'
     height='100' />";
38       document.getElementById("captchaAnswer").value=captchaAnswer[j];
39   }
40
41   function validateForm() {
42       // validates the captcha
43       if (document.getElementById("captchaResponse").value != document.getElementById(
     "captchaAnswer").value) {
44           document.getElementById("captchaPrompt").style.color="red";
45       } else {
46           // validates the email for an @ character within the string
47           var valid=false;
48           var email=document.getElementById("email").value;
49           //var emailLength=email.length;
50           if(email.indexOf("@") >= 1) {
51               valid=true;
52           }
53           if(valid==true){
54               alert('Thank you for registering with address: \n' + email);
55               document.getElementById("emailPrompt").style.color="black";
56           } else {
57               document.getElementById("emailPrompt").innerHTML='Enter a valid email to register:';
58               document.getElementById("emailPrompt").style.color="red";
59           }
60
61       }
62   }
63   setupForm();
64   </script>
65
66   </body>
67   </html>
```

5-25

JavaScript output

JavaScript commands can access and edit HTML elements outside of the <script> tags, and write directly to the web page document using the command document.write("Hello World"); for example. The attribute .innerHTML of an HTML element can be edited directly. (See line 28 above.)

Q3: What is the effect of line 57 of the JavaScript code?

Another method is to cause the browser to display a pop-up alert box with a custom message requiring the user's attention. Line 54 displays an alert box once the user has submitted valid details.

JavaScript Alert box

Functions and variables

JavaScript functions are declared within curly brackets {} and called using the function name e.g. `setupForm();`. Function parameters may be included inside the round brackets, but if there are none, empty brackets must be used.

Q4: What are the identifiers of **two** variables used in the JavaScript code?

Q5: The function setupForm is called and executed using the command `setupForm();` on line 63.

(a)   What is the purpose of the function?

(b)   Looking at the HTML form script, when else is this function used?

Validation

Validation routines are commonly built in to webpages using JavaScript since the script is executed locally on the client's machine. The function `validateForm()` checks the user input and either changes form labels and styling in response to an invalid entry, or displays the alert box above.

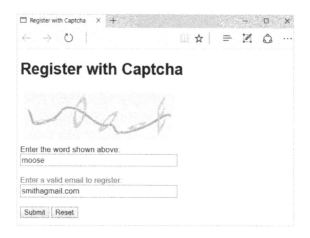

Arrays in JavaScript

JavaScript arrays can hold any type of data. In this example there are two arrays – one to hold a set of three captcha images and the other to hold the answers to each of them.

```
var captcha=["captcha1.jpg","captcha2.jpg","captcha3.jpg"];
var captchaAnswer=["weasel","moose","polecat"];
```

On line 35, a math function generates an average number between 1 and the length of the array (i.e. 3 in this case), and assigns it to variable j. JavaScript array indexes begin at 0, so 1 is subtracted from j using the simplified command $j--$ to decrement j by 1 in order to reference array indices 0-2.

Exercises

1. A website contains Javascript code.

   (a) Describe what is meant by the term *JavaScript*. [2]

   (b) Explain why JavaScript is usually interpreted rather than compiled. [2]

2. The website www.postrates.com offers a rate check service for sending letters and parcels.
   The homepage contains a button hyperlinked to the following webpage:

```
1    <!doctype html>
2    <html>
3    <head>
4        <title>Shipping rates</title>
5    </head>
6
7    <body>
8    Calculate shipping rates
9    <script Language = "JavaScript">
10   var weight = prompt("Enter the parcel weight in kg", "");
11   var length = prompt("Enter the largest dimension in cm", "");
12
13   if (weight < 1 && length <= 20)
14   {
15       alert("Letter rate: £0.65");
16   }
17
18   if (weight < 1 && length > 20)
19   {
20       alert("Small parcel rate: £1.85");
21   }
22
23   if (weight >= 1)
24   {
25       alert("Large parcel rate: £3.50");
26   }
27   </script>
28
29   </body>
30   </html>
```

5-25

   (a) Which lines of code contain JavaScript code? [1]

   (b) Give the identifiers of **two** variables used in the code. [2]

   (c) Looking at the webpage code, what is the purpose of the JavaScript function called `prompt` on line 10? [2]

   (d) When the webpage is requested, what would happen if a parcel weight of 1kg and a maximum length of 10cm is entered? [2]

Chapter 26 – Search engine indexing

Objectives

(A) • Understand how web pages are indexed by search engines

(A) • Understand the PageRank algorithm

(A) • Be able to interpret and apply the PageRank algorithm to a given scenario

Search engines

Search engines such as Google are systems that locate resources on the Internet. These resources could be web pages, documents, images or other files.

Search engine indexing

Search engines rely on a database or index of web pages to find the pages you are looking for. To build this index, a software program called a web crawler or spider is used. This constantly goes out to all the pages currently on the index, and then on to fetch all those sites linked to by those sites and so on until they have linked to all or nearly all web pages and resources on the Internet. Different search engines use their own crawler programs so a search in one engine might return different results from another.

> **Q1:** What resources and file types might be accessed via your school website?

> **Q2:** If you create a new website, why might it not appear in search results immediately?

Key words, meta tags, and descriptions

Search engines look for key words and phrases within web pages or resource content that match your search terms. These are visible to the user and part of the main web page content.

> Tolpuddle Martyrs: Welcome
> www.**tolpuddlemartyrs**.org.uk/ ▾
> Tells the tale of six labourers' arrest, trial and deportation for unionising, leading to the foundation of modern trade unionism.

Meta tags and descriptions are a list of keywords or concise phrases specified by the website owner that are built into each webpage. Descriptions are displayed with the page title in search results as shown above. These can be defined in the HTML documents within the <head> section to help searches.

```
 1  <!doctype html>
 2  <html>
 3  <head>
 4  <meta http-equiv="Content-Type" content="text/html; charset=utf-8">
 5  <TITLE>Tolpuddle Martyrs</TITLE>
 6  <META NAME="Keywords" CONTENT="martyr, tolpuddle, farm, worker,
    labourer, dorset, loveless, 1834, union, liberty, australia">
 7  <META NAME="Description" CONTENT="In the 1830s life in rural
    villages like Tolpuddle was hard and getting worse. Farm workers
    could not bear yet more cuts to their pay. Some fought back against
    land owners and formed the first trade unions.">
 8  <head>
 9  <body>
10  </body>
11  </html>
```

5-26

Search results

There are believed to be over 200 factors affecting search results that may help position your own website nearer the top of the results list. Other than metatags and descriptions, these include:

- using keywords in the `<title>` tag
- the age of your website and date of last update (or frequency of updates)
- the number and relevancy of keywords appearing in `<h1>` tags and
- the relevancy of the domain name to the content

Google's PageRank algorithm

In the 1990s two postgraduate Computer Science students called Larry Page and Sergey Brin met at Stanford University. Brin was working on data mining systems and Page was working on a system to rank the importance of a research paper according to how often it was cited in other papers.

The pair realised that this concept could be used to build a far superior search engine to the existing ones, and they started to work on a new Search Engine for the Web. The problem they set themselves was how to rank the thousands or even millions of web pages that had a reference to the search term typed in by a user. To make a search engine useful, the most reliable and relevant pages need to appear first in the list of links.

Until that point, pages had generally been ranked simply by the number of times the search term or its synonyms appeared on the page. Page's and Brin's insight was to realise that the usefulness and therefore the **rank** of a given page, say Page X, can be determined by how many visits to Page X result from other web pages containing links to the page. Taking this further, links from a Page Y that itself has a high rank are more significant than those from pages which have themselves only had a few visits. The importance or authority of a page is also taken into account so that a link from a .gov page or a page belonging to the BBC site, for example, may be given a higher PageRank rating.

An initial version of Google was launched in August 1996 from Stanford University's website. By mid-1998 they had 10,000 searches a day, and realised the potential of their invention.

They represented the Web as a **directed graph** of pages, using an algorithm to calculate the PageRank (named after Larry Page) of each page. Every web page is a node and any hyperlinks on the page are edges, with the edge weightings dependent on the PageRank algorithm.

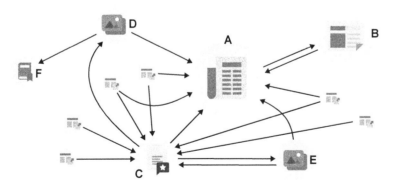

*Using PageRank, **B** has a higher page rank than **C** because it is a more authoritative source.*

By 2015, Google was processing 40,000 search queries every second, worldwide. David Vise, the author of The Google Story noted that "Not since Gutenberg* … has any new invention empowered individuals, and transformed access to information, as profoundly as Google."

(* Gutenberg invented the printing press in the fifteenth century)

A-Level only

> **Q3:** Page X has outbound links to ten well-regarded and high-ranking websites. Page Y has 10 inbound links from the same ten websites. Which is more likely to have a higher page rank and why?

Calculating PageRank

PageRank is effectively a popularity contest between websites defined by the number of votes or inbound links they receive, with a weighting to give more importance to some votes than others. This weighting is swayed by either the number of outbound links a site has or the importance (or PageRank) of a site. A website with a good reputation and high PageRank will have a higher weighting assigned to its 'votes' but its total vote is shared or diluted amongst all of the sites it links to.

The PageRank algorithm itself is defined as:

$$\texttt{PR(A) = (1-d) + d (PR(T1)/C(T1) + ... + PR(Tn)/C(Tn))}$$

where:

- **`PR(A)`** is the PageRank of page A

- **`C(Tn)`** is the total count of outbound links from web page n including the inbound link to page A. All webpages have a notional vote of 1. This is shared between all those it links to.

- **`PR(Tn)/C(Tn)`** is the share of the vote that page A gets from pages T1 ... Tn. Each of these vote fractions is added together and multiplied by d.

- **`d`** is the damping factor set to prevent `PR(Tn)/C(Tn)` from having too much influence. It is notionally set to 0.85, which in probability terms says that after roughly six click-through links, the average user will either stop their session or enter a new web address in their browser directly rather than following another link.

The PageRank of a page is constantly being recalculated and updated.

> **Q4:** Google's PageRank algorithm uses a damping factor. What is the purpose of the damping factor?

Applying the algorithm

The PageRank of one web page is determined in part by the PageRank of other pages that link to it. However, the PageRank algorithm works without the need to know any of the other PageRanks of back-linked pages. (A *back-link* can be defined as an inbound link from another site.) Instead, a guess can be made in the first instance and after several iterations of the algorithm, the PageRank begins to home in on the correct figure. It can take dozens, if not hundreds or even millions of iterations before this number finally stops moving. Once settled, the average PageRank of all pages will be 1.

Example 1

In this simplest of examples with a hypothetical world wide web consisting of just two web pages, pages A and B would have equal ranking if there is one inbound and one outbound link between them.

This can be calculated using the PageRank algorithm to give an equal ranking of 1:

d = 0.85

PR(A) = (1 − d) + d(PR(B)/1) PR(A) = 0.15 + 0.85 * 1 = **1**

PR(B) = (1 − d) + d(PR(A)/1) PR(B) = 0.15 + 0.85 * 1 = **1**

5-26

A-Level only

Example 2 shows the iterative process used to calculate and recalculate the PageRank (PR) of a group of webpages where the starting point is unknown.

Example 2

As the number of web pages grows, more complex link structures are created. After the addition of one extra web page, the PageRank is recalculated and adjusted to reflect the new pages and links.

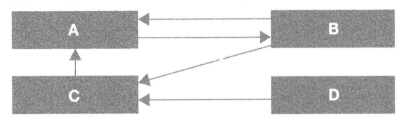

First iteration: (Assumes a PR of 1 for each page where not known.)

    d = 0.85

PR(A) = (1 – d) + d(PR(B)/2 + PR(C)/1)   PR(A) = 0.15 + 0.85 * (0.5 + 1) = **1.425**

PR(B) = (1 – d) + d(PR(A)/1)   PR(B) = 0.15 + 0.85 * 1.425 = **1.361**

PR(C) = (1 – d) + d(PR(B)/2 + PR(D)/1)   PR(C) = 0.15 + 0.85 * (0.681 + 1) = **1.578**

PR(D) = (1 – d) + d(0)   PR(D) = **0.15**

Second iteration: (Uses new PR figures from first iteration.)

    d = 0.85

PR(A) = (1 – d) + d(PR(B)/2 + PR(C)/1)   PR(A) = 0.15 + 0.85 * (0.681 + 1.578) = **2.07**

PR(B) = (1 – d) + d(PR(A)/1)   PR(B) = 0.15 + 0.85 * 2.07 = **1.909**

PR(C) = (1 – d) + d(PR(B)/2 + PR(D)/1)   PR(C) = 0.15 + 0.85 * (0.955 + 0.15) = **1.089**

PR(D) = (1 – d) + d(0)   PR(D) = **0.15**

Third iteration:

    d = 0.85

PR(A) = (1 – d) + d(PR(B)/2 + PR(C)/1)   PR(A) = 0.15 + 0.85 * (0.955 + 1.089) = **1.887**

PR(B) = (1 – d) + d(PR(A)/1)   PR(B) = 0.15 + 0.85 * 1.887 = **1.754**

PR(C) = (1 – d) + d(PR(B)/2 + PR(D)/1)   PR(C) = 0.15 + 0.85 * (0.877 + 0.15) = **1.023**

PR(D) = (1 – d) + d(0)   PR(D) = **0.15**

After three iterations, the PageRank of each page begins to settle. In reality many more iterations would be necessary before the figures stop moving, but three iterations get us close enough to understand the process and begin to see some results.

Page A now has a slightly higher ranking than B since it has another vote from page C. Page B has a higher rank than pages C and D because it has 100% of the votes from A, a high ranking page in itself. Page C has a comparatively moderate ranking since it has two inbound links from other pages that also have inbound links. C's vote from page D however is not given significant importance since page D has no inbound links and therefore has a low PageRank.

Q5: What factors may result in a web page A's rank rising or falling over time as it is revised?

5-26

A-Level only

Exercises

1. The owner of website www.inflatablecastle.com is trying to improve the positioning of his homepage inflatablecastle.com/index.html in search engine listings.

   (a) Other than PageRank, give **three** design factors that may affect the company homepage's positioning in search results. [3]

   Google's PageRank algorithm $PR(A) = (1-d) + d\ (PR(T1)/C(T1) + \ldots + PR(Tn)/C(Tn))$ calculates a ranking for each web page that has a significant bearing on search results.

   (b) With reference to the diagram below, explain which page is likely to have the highest PageRank. You are not expected to perform any calculations. [2]

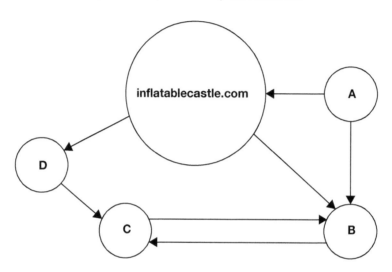

   (c) Looking at the algorithm, what factors directly influence the PageRank of the homepage index.html at inflatablecastles.com? [2]

   (d) PageRank uses a damping factor d in its algorithm. Explain the purpose of *d*. [2]

2. Search engines provide a listing of all web pages with content relevant to a set of search terms.

   (a) Explain how search engines produce this list. [2]

   (b) With reference to the screenshot below, state which line of code contains metatags. [1]

   (c) Briefly explain the purpose of the meta description. [2]

```
1  <html>
2  <head>
3  <meta http-equiv="Content-Type" content="text/html; charset=utf-8">
4  <TITLE>Fossils</TITLE>
5  <META NAME="Keywords" CONTENT="dinosaur, lyme, regis, limestone,
   ammonite, bone, jurassic, strata, rock, geology, paleontology">
6  <META NAME="Description" CONTENT="Fossils are the preserved remains
   of animals or plants, commonly found embedded in sedimentary
   layers of rock.">
7  <head>
8  <body>
9  </body>
10 </html>
```

5-26

Ⓐ

Chapter 27 – Client server and peer-to-peer

Objectives

- Understand the client-server and peer-to-peer models

- Describe situations where each model may be used

A • Explain the difference between client- and server-side processing and the advantages of each

A • Identify the different uses of client- and server-side processing and describe situations when one or the other may be more practical

A • Identify the advantages and disadvantages of client- and server-side processing

Client-server networking

In a client-server network, one or more computers known as **clients** are connected to a powerful central computer known as the **server**. Each client may hold some of its own files and resources such as software, and can also access resources held by the server. In a large network, there may be several servers, each performing a different task.

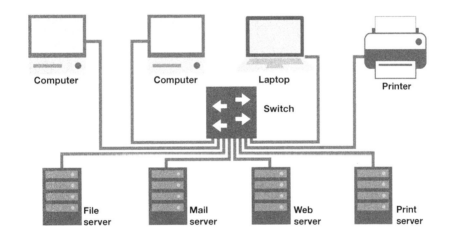

- File server holds and manages data for all the clients
- Print server manages print requests
- Web server manages requests to access the Web
- Mail server manages the email system
- Database server manages database applications

In a client-server network, the client makes a request to the server which then processes the request.

Advantages of a client-server network

- Security is better, since all files are stored in a central location and access rights are managed by the server

- Backups are done centrally so there is no need for individual users to back up their data. If there is a breakdown and some data is lost, recovery procedures will enable it to be restored

- Data and other resources can be shared

Disadvantages of a client-server network

- It is expensive to install and manage

- Professional IT staff are needed to maintain the servers and run the network

Cloud computing

Cloud computing refers to a growing service-based industry providing access to software or files via the Internet using the client-server model. File storage companies such as DropBox, OneDrive or Google Drive offer file storage facilities where users' files are kept on remote servers. Other companies offer software via the cloud, a provision known as Software as a Service (**SaaS**). Microsoft, for example offers cloud-based Office applications. Accounting packages are also available through website logins where all the company data and application are stored offsite.

> **Q1:** Cloud-based storage facilities such as DropBox and Google Drive store files for users. What are the advantages of using cloud-based services? What happens when a user requests a file?

Peer-to-peer networks

In a **peer-to-peer** network, there is no central server. Individual computers are connected to each other, either locally or over a wide area network so that they can share files. In a small local area network, such as in a home or small office, a peer-to-peer network is a good choice because:

- it is cheap to set up

- it enables users to share resources such as a printer or router

- it is not difficult to maintain

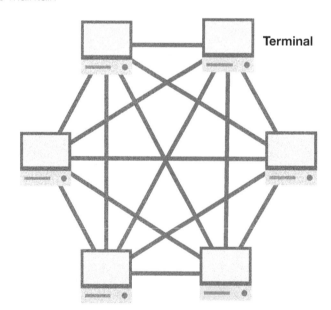

Peer-to-peer networks are also used by companies providing, for example, video on demand. A problem arises when thousands of people simultaneously want to download the latest episode of a particular TV show. Using a peer-to-peer network, hundreds of computers can be used to hold parts of the video and so share the load. This is the main principle behind dozens of **torrent** websites that enable the sharing of files, often containing copyright material.

5-27

The downside of peer-to-peer networking

Peer-to-peer networking has been widely used for online piracy, since it is impossible to trace the files which are being illegally downloaded. In 2011, the US Chamber of Commerce estimated that piracy sites attracted 53 billion visits each year. The analyst firm *NetNames* estimated that in January 2013 alone, 432 million unique Web users actively searched for content that infringes copyright.

Case study: Piracy sites

In January 1999, 19-year-old Shawn Fanning and Sean Parker created the Napster software, which enabled the peer-to-peer "sharing" of music – in actual fact, the theft of copyright music. Instead of storing the MP3 files on a central computer, the songs are stored on users' machines. When you want to download a song using Napster, you are downloading it from another person's machine, which may be next door or on the other side of the world.

All you need is a copy of the Napster utility and an Internet connection. Napster was sued for copyright infringement in 2000 but argued that they were not responsible for copyright infringement on other people's machines. However, they lost the case and were pushed into bankruptcy, but the service has since reinvented itself on a legitimate, subscription basis.

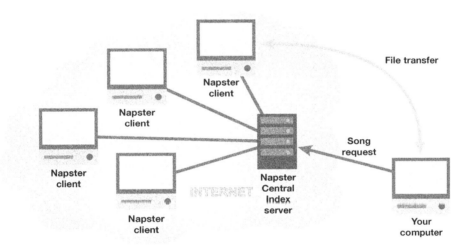

The consequences of piracy

In 2014, Popcorn Time was launched, allowing a decentralised peer-to-peer service for illegal streaming of movies. Popcorn Time has already been translated into 32 languages and has been described as a "nightmare scenario" for the movie industry. The more movies that are stolen and illegally downloaded online, the fewer resources moviemakers have to invest in new films. In 2013 there was a 21% drop in the 18-24 age group buying tickets to watch movies, and numbers may plummet further in the next few years.

A 2011 report by the London-based International Federation of the Phonographic Industry (IFPI) estimated that 1.2 million European jobs would be destroyed by 2015 in the music, movie, publishing and photography industries because of online piracy.

Q2: Look up the Copyright, Designs and Patents Act 1988. What types of work are protected by this Act? For what period of time is a work protected by copyright?

A-Level only

Client- and server-side processing

In the **client-server** model, data may be processed on either side; by either client, server or both.

Web servers

A client will send a request message to a server which should respond with the data requested or a suitable message otherwise.

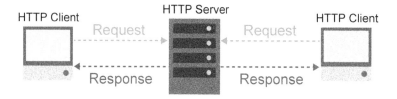

This is commonly seen when a client browser sends an HTTP request to a web server for dynamic web page data or a web resource, or when using a web page with an online search facility such as checking availability via a booking form.

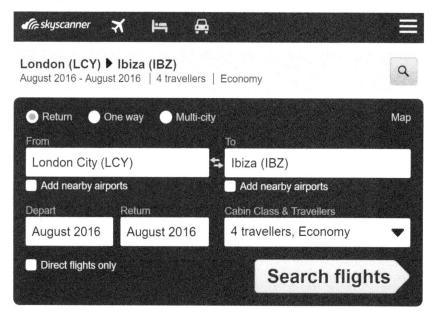

The page data is sent back from the HTTP server by way of response and the browser renders the web page on the client's computer.

Client-side processing

Client-side processing describes situations where data is processed on the client computer, rather than on the server. This may happen because the client computer has specific software that can process the information, or to lighten the load on the server's processor. Processing data on the client-side can also improve security as it can avoid unnecessary data transfer. JavaScript is a client-side language and is frequently used to provide interactivity on a web page. Client-side processing can also adjust styles for different platforms or screen sizes.

JavaScript validation

JavaScript is commonly used for processing data on the client side to validate data entry before it is sent to the server.

```
<script>
function validate() {
   var airport = document.forms["departure"]["arrival"];
   if (airport.value == "") {
       airport.style.borderColor = "red";
         alert("Departure and arrival airports cannot be left blank.");
         return false;
   }
}
</script>
```

Q3: What are the advantages of validating data on the client side before it is sent to the server?

Server-side processing

Servers often process an enormous volume of data on behalf of multiple clients. They can also process the data much faster than a client computer. There are specific languages that are used for server-side processing such as **SQL** or **PHP**. Search requests (e.g. for a search engine or a company database) may be sent to the server where they may be applied to a database using SQL. Database search results are then sent back to the client browser. Validation may also be carried out on the server where an invalid entry must be compared with data already on a server database. Examples may include checking user credentials, or looking up valid airport locations. JavaScript may also be circumvented malicously so server-side validation is important for the integrity of server data.

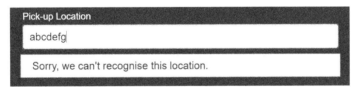

Server-side validation

Client-side Processing	Server-side Processing
1. Initial data validation	1. Provides further validation
2. Provides web page interactivity	2. Used to query a Database
3. Manipulates user interface elements	3. Updates server databases
4. Applies styles (CSS)	4. Performs complex calculations
5. Reduces the load on the server	5. Encodes data to readable HTML
6. Reduces the amount of web traffic	6. Keeps organisational data secure

5-27

A-Level only

API (Application Programming Interface)

An **API** is a set of protocols (rules) that governs how two applications should interact with one another. An API sets out the format of requests and responses between a client and a server and enables one application to make use of the services of another. An organisation may use the Twitter API to enable relevant tweets to be regularly fed through to a display window within their own website. Price comparison websites may also use an API to gather data from individual company websites in order to display a list of each of them for the consumer.

Thin- versus thick-client computing

The 'thickness' of a client computer refers to the level of processing and storage that it does compared with the server it is connected to. The more processing and storage that a server does, the 'thinner' the client becomes. If all the processing and storage is done by the server, then all that is required for the thinnest-client computer is a very basic machine with very little processor power and no storage. This is often known as a dumb terminal. The decision to go 'thick' or 'thin' rather depends on your specific requirements and each option comes with its own advantages and disadvantages.

Q4: How might you design a mobile GPS navigation app in order to optimise its use, given the advantages and disadvantages of thin- and thick-client systems?

	Advantages	Disadvantages
Thin-client	Easy to set up, maintain and add terminals to a network with little installation required locally. Software and updates can be installed on the server and automatically distributed to each client terminal. More secure since data is all kept centrally in one place.	Reliant on the server, so if the server goes down, the terminals lose functionality. Requires a very powerful, and reliable server which is expensive. Server demand and bandwidth increased. Maintaining network connections for portable devices consumes more battery power than local data processing.
Thick-client	Robust and reliable, providing greater up-time. Can operate without a continuous connection to the server. Generally better for running more powerful software applications.	More expensive, higher specification client computers required. Installation of software required on each terminal separately and network administration time is increased. Integrity issues with distributed data.

5-27

Exercises

1. Explain the difference between client-server and peer-to-peer networking, and give an example of where each might be used. [6]

2. A travel agency is planning to install a new computer system based on the client-server model, for its agents to use for flight and hotel bookings and enquiries at multiple workstations.

   (a) What is meant by the client-server model? [2]

   After some consideration, the company has decided to use a thin-client network.

   (b) Explain how a thin-client network operates. [3]

   (c) How would the decision to use a thin- rather than thick-client network affect the choice of hardware? [2]

   A-Level only

3. A company is designing a website which will allow its customers to place orders online. The individual web pages that describe each product will be generated dynamically using server-side scripting.

   Explain what a server-side script is. [2]

4. A website is set up to enable users to access on-demand television programs. Users can sign up to the website and download a recent series episode or film. Programs are downloaded and stored on the user's device. When others choose to download the same program, parts of the program data may come from multiple devices belonging to other users.

   (a) State what this model of network is called. [1]

   (b) (i) Give **one** advantage to the company of this model. [1]

   (ii) Give **one** advantage to the user of this model. [1]

   (c) JavaScript is used to validate that the user's email address is in a valid format when a booking is made.

   (i) Give **two** advantages of client-side validation. [2]

   (ii) Client- and server-side validation should happen in partnership. Explain why it is important to validate the email address again once it reaches the server. [1]

5-27

Ⓐ

Section 6

Data types

In this section:

6

Chapter 28

Primitive data types, binary and hexadecimal

Objectives

- List and define primitive data types
- Represent positive integers in binary and hexadecimal
- Convert between binary, hexadecimal and denary

Primitive data types

A **primitive data type** is one which is provided by a programming language. They include:

- integer   a whole number such as -25, 0, 3, 28679
- real/float   a number with a fractional part such as -13.5, 0.0, 3.142, 100.0001
- Boolean   a Boolean variable can only take the value TRUE or FALSE
- character   a letter, number or special character typically represented in ASCII, such as a, A, 4, ? or %. Note that the character "4" is represented differently in the computer from the integer 4 or the real number 4.0
- string   anything enclosed in quote marks is a string, for example "Peter", "123", or "This is a string". Either single or double quotes are acceptable.

All data types are held in the computer in binary, and this chapter describes how integers are represented.

6-28

Number bases

Our familiar **decimal** (or **denary**) number system uses the numbers 0 through 9 and therefore has a base of 10. **Binary** uses only the numbers 0 and 1 and has a base of 2. **Hexadecimal** uses a base of 16 with numbers 0-9 and letters A to F. A number's base can be written as a subscript to denote its value in the correct number system. For example 11_{10} denotes the number eleven in denary. 11_2 would denote a binary value, (with a denary equivalent of three) and 11_{16} would denote a hexadecimal value. (17 in denary.)

The binary number system

In order to better understand the simplicity of the binary number system, it is a good idea to examine how our familiar denary number system works. Columns, right-to-left, represent units, tens and hundreds etc. We mentally multiply the values with their column value and add the totals together.

1000s	100s	10s	1s	
5	**0**	**7**	**4**	
5000		+ 70	+ 4	**= 5074**

The principle is exactly the same in the binary number system. As we move from left to right, each digit is worth twice as much as the previous one, instead of ten times as much.

128	64	32	16	8	4	2	1	
1	**1**	0	0	1	0	1	1	
128 +	64			+ 8		+ 2 +	1	= **203**

The minimum and maximum values that can be represented in n bits using unsigned binary are 0 and $2^n - 1$ respectively.

Q1: Convert the binary numbers 0011 1001 and 1111 1111 into denary.

Converting from denary to binary

To convert a denary number to binary, first write headings of 1, 2, 4, 8 ... 128 from right to left. (If the number is greater than 255, continue writing headings.)

To convert a denary number, for example 73, into binary, write a 1 under the largest heading less than 73 (i.e. 64). You now have 73 – 64 = 9 remaining, to be converted to binary. 9 = 8 + 1 so put 1 under 8 and under 1. Fill the spaces with zeros. The binary number representing 73 is 01001001.

128	64	32	16	8	4	2	1	
0	**1**	0	0	1	0	0	1	= **1001**

6-28

Q2: Convert the denary numbers 37 and 100 into binary.

The hexadecimal number system

The hexadecimal system, often referred to as simply '*hex*', uses a base of 16 as follows:

Denary	Hexadecimal	Binary
0	0	0
1	1	1
2	2	10
3	3	11
4	4	100
5	5	101
6	6	110
7	7	111
8	8	1000
9	9	1001
10	A	1010
11	B	1011
12	C	1100
13	D	1101
14	E	1110
15	F	1111
16	10	10000

Converting from binary to hexadecimal and vice versa

To convert a binary number to hexadecimal, split the binary number into groups of 4 binary digits.

Binary	0011	1010	1111	1010
Hex	3	A	F	9

The hex representation of 0011 1010 1111 1010 is therefore 3AF9.

To convert from hex to binary, perform this operation in reverse by grouping the bits in groups of 4 and translating each group into binary. For example, to convert the number 23_{16} to binary:

Hex	2	3	
Binary	0010	0011	– 00100011

Q3: Convert the hexadecimal number A7 into binary.

Q4: What is 1111 1111 in hexadecimal?

Converting from hexadecimal to denary and vice versa

To convert from hexadecimal to denary, remember that the left column now represents 16s and not tens. For example, to convert 27_{16} to denary:

	16s	1s
Hex	2	7= 2 x 16 + 7 = 39

To convert a denary number to hex, the easiest way is to first convert the denary number to binary and then translate from binary to hex. For example, to convert 75_{10} to hex:

	128	64	32	16	8	4	2	1
Binary	0	1	0	0	1	0	1	1
Hex			4		B			

Therefore $75_{10} = 4B_{16}$ (75/16 = 4 remainder 11, or 4B, since 11 is B in hexadecimal.)

Q5: Convert the denary numbers 37 and 100 into hexadecimal.

Q6: Convert the hexadecimal numbers 3B and 14 into binary.

Why the hexadecimal number system is used

The hexadecimal system is used as a shorthand for binary since it is simple to represent a byte in just two digits, and fewer mistakes are likely to be made in writing a hex number than a string of binary digits. It is easier for technicians and computer users to write or remember a hex number than a binary number. Colour codes in images often use hexadecimal to represent the RGB values, as they are much easier to remember than a 24-bit binary string. In the example overleaf #364DB2 represents 36_{16} for Red, $4D_{16}$ for Green and $B2_{16}$ for Blue values, which can be displayed or printed in the Colour Picker window more compactly than in binary.

6-28

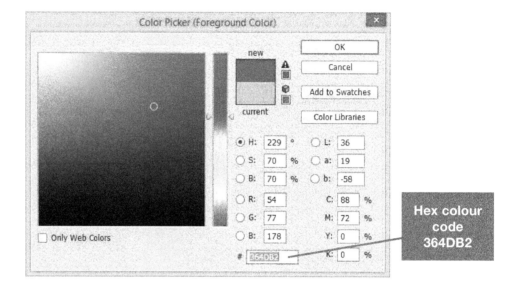

Exercises

1. A school keeps data about each of its pupils. State the most suitable data type for each of the following data items:

    Pupil's surname

    A single letter indicating whether they are male or female

    The amount owed for school trips

    The number of school trips they have participated in

    Whether or not the pupil is entitled to free school meals   [5]

2. Represent the denary number 123 in binary using 8 bits.   [1]

3. How many different denary numbers can be represented using 8-bit binary?   [1]

4. What is the hexadecimal equivalent of the denary number 123?   [1]

5. Why are bit patterns often displayed using hexadecimal instead of binary?   [2]

6. Figure 1 shows the contents of a memory location.

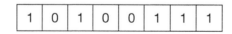

Figure 1

    What is the denary equivalent of the contents of this memory location if it represents an unsigned binary integer?   [1]

7. What is the hexadecimal equivalent of the binary pattern shown in Figure 1?   [1]

8. Convert the hexadecimal number DA to denary.   [1]

6-28

Chapter 29 ASCII and Unicode

Objectives

- Define a bit as a 1 or a 0, and a byte as a group of eight bits
- Know that 2^n different values can be represented with n bits
- Use names, symbols and corresponding powers of 2 for binary prefixes e.g. Ki, Mi
- Differentiate between the character code of a denary digit and its pure binary representation
- Describe how character sets (ASCII and Unicode) are used to represent text

Bits and bytes

A **bit** is the fundamental unit of information in the form of either a single 1 or 0. 1 and 0 are used to represent the two electronic states: on and off, or more accurately a switch that is closed (to complete a circuit) or open (to break it). A **byte** is a set of eight bits, for example 0110 1101. One byte holds one character of text.

Q1: Why is the on / off symbol designed like this:

The number of values that can be represented with n bits is 2^n. Two bits can represent 4 different values: 00, 01, 10 and 11. Three bits can represent 8 values and four bits can represent 16 different values, since $2 \times 2 \times 2 \times 2 = 16$.

6-29

Unit nomenclature

Although we frequently refer to 1024 bytes as a kilobyte, it is in fact a **kibibyte**. To avoid any confusion between references to 1024 bytes rather than 1000 bytes, an international collaboration between standards organisations decided in 1996 that kibi would represent 1024, and kilo would represent 1000. Kibi is a combination of the words kilo and binary. The same is true of the other familiar names Mega, Giga and Tera being replaced by mebi, gibi and tebi. The table below outlines the nomenclature for increasing quantities of bytes, in which a **KiB** is a **kibibyte** and a **MiB**, a **mebibyte**.

Name	Symbol	Power	Value
kibi	Ki	2^{10}	1024
mebi	Mi	2^{20}	1,048,576
gibi	Gi	2^{30}	1,073,741,824
tebi	Ti	2^{40}	1,099,511,627,776
pebi	Pi	2^{50}	1,125,899,906,842,624
exbi	Ei	2^{60}	1,152,921,504,606,846,976
zebi	Zi	2^{70}	1,180,591,620,717,411,303,424
yobi	Yi	2^{80}	1,208,925,819,614,629,174,706,176

Name	Symbol	Power
Kilo	K or k	10^3
Mega	M	10^6
Giga	G	10^9
Tera	T	10^{12}
Peta	P	10^{15}
Exa	E	10^{18}
Zetta	Z	10^{21}
Yotta	Y	10^{24}

The ASCII code

Historically, the standard code for representing the characters on the keyboard was ASCII (American Standard Code for Information Interchange). This uses seven bits which form 128 different bit combinations, more than enough to cover all of the characters on a standard English-language keyboard. The first 32 codes represent non-printing characters used for control such as **backspace** (code 8), the **Enter** or **Carriage Return** key (code 13) and the **Escape** key (code 27). The **Space** character is also included as code 32 and **Delete** as code 127.

ASCII	DEC	Binary	ASCII	DEC	Binary	ASCII	DEC	Binary	ASCII	DEC	Binary
NULL	000	000 0000	space	032	010 0000	@	064	100 0000	`	096	110 0000
SOH	001	000 0001	!	033	010 0001	A	065	100 0001	a	097	110 0001
STX	002	000 0010	"	034	010 0010	B	066	100 0010	b	098	110 0010
ETX	003	000 0011	#	035	010 0011	C	067	100 0011	c	099	110 0011
EOT	004	000 0100	$	036	010 0100	D	068	100 0100	d	100	110 0100
ENQ	005	000 0101	%	037	010 0101	E	069	100 0101	e	101	110 0101
ACK	006	000 0110	&	038	010 0110	F	070	100 0110	f	102	110 0110
BEL	007	000 0111	'	039	010 0111	G	071	100 0111	g	103	110 0111
BS	008	000 1000	(	040	010 1000	H	072	100 1000	h	104	110 1000
HT	009	000 1001	)	041	010 1001	I	073	100 1001	i	105	110 1001
LF	010	000 1010	*	042	010 1010	J	074	100 1010	j	106	110 1010
VT	011	000 1011	+	043	010 1011	K	075	100 1011	k	107	110 1011
FF	012	000 1100	,	044	010 1100	L	076	100 1100	l	108	110 1100
CR	013	000 1101	-	045	010 1101	M	077	100 1101	m	109	110 1101
SO	014	000 1110	.	046	010 1110	N	078	100 1110	n	110	110 1110
SI	015	000 1111	/	047	010 1111	O	079	100 1111	o	111	110 1111
DLE	016	001 0000	0	048	011 0000	P	080	101 0000	p	112	111 0000
DC1	017	001 0001	1	049	011 0001	Q	081	101 0001	q	113	111 0001
DC2	018	001 0010	2	050	011 0010	R	082	101 0010	r	114	111 0010
DC3	019	001 0011	3	051	011 0011	S	083	101 0011	s	115	111 0011
DC4	020	001 0100	4	052	011 0100	T	084	101 0100	t	116	111 0100
NAK	021	001 0101	5	053	011 0101	U	085	101 0101	u	117	111 0101
SYN	022	001 0110	6	054	011 0110	V	086	101 0110	v	118	111 0110
ETB	023	001 0111	7	055	011 0111	W	087	101 0111	w	119	111 0111
CAN	024	001 1000	8	056	011 1000	X	088	101 1000	x	120	111 1000
EM	025	001 1001	9	057	011 1001	Y	089	101 1001	y	121	111 1001
SUB	026	001 1010	:	058	011 1010	Z	090	101 1010	z	122	111 1010
ESC	027	001 1011	;	059	011 1011	[	091	101 1011	{	123	111 1011
FS	028	001 1100	<	060	011 1100	\	092	101 1100			124	111 1100
GS	029	001 1101	=	061	011 1101	]	093	101 1101	}	125	111 1101
RS	030	001 1110	>	062	011 1110	^	094	101 1110	~	126	111 1110
US	031	001 1111	?	063	011 1111	_	095	101 1111	DEL	127	111 1111

6-29

Q2: How would the word 'Cat' be stored?

Character form of a denary digit

Although numbers are represented within the code, the number character is not the same as the actual number value. The ASCII value 0110111 will print the character '7', even though the same binary value equates to the denary number 55. Therefore ASCII cannot be used for arithmetic and would use unnecessary space to store numbers. Numbers for arithmetic are stored as pure binary numbers.

'7' + '7' (i.e. 0110111 + 0110111 in ASCII) would be 77, not 14 or 110.

The development of ASCII

ASCII originally used only 7 bits, but an 8-bit version was developed to include an additional 128 combinations to represent symbols such as æ, © and ƒ. You can try holding down the ALT key and typing in the code number using the number pad to type one of these symbols. For example, ALT+130 will produce é, as used in *café*. The 7-bit ASCII code is compatible with the 8-bit code and simply adds a leading 0 to all binary codes.

Unicode

By the 1980s, several coding systems had been introduced all over the world that were all incompatible with one another. This created difficulty as multilingual data was being increasingly used and a new, unified format was sought. As a result, a new 16-bit code called **Unicode (UTF-16)** was introduced. This allowed for 65,536 different combinations and could therefore represent alphabets from dozens of languages including Latin, Greek, Arabic and Cyrillic alphabets. The first 128 codes were the same as ASCII so compatibility was retained. A further version of Unicode called **UTF-32** was also developed to include just over a million characters, and this was more than enough to handle most of the characters from all languages, including Chinese and Japanese.

This meant that whilst there is now just one globally recognised system to maintain, one character in this scheme uses four bytes instead of two, significantly increasing file sizes and data transmission times.

6-29

Q3: Using the Unicode UTF-16 system, how much memory would be used for the word 'Mouse'?

Exercises

1. The ASCII system uses 7 bits to represent a character. The ASCII code in denary for the numeric character '0' is 48; other numeric characters follow on from this in sequence.
   (a) Using 7 bits, what is the ASCII code for the character '2' in binary?   [1]
   (b) How many different characters can be represented using ASCII?   [1]

2. One character encoding scheme is Unicode. An alternative character encoding scheme is ASCII.
   (a) State **one** difference between Unicode and ASCII.   [1]
   (b) State one advantage and one disadvantage of using ASCII rather than Unicode for representing characters.   [2]

3. How many times greater is the storage capacity of a 1 terabyte hard disk drive than that of a 256 megabyte hard disk drive?

   Show each stage of your working.   [2]

Chapter 30 Binary arithmetic

Objectives

- Use sign and magnitude to represent negative numbers in binary
- Use two's complement to represent negative numbers in binary
- Add and subtract binary integers
- Represent fractions in fixed point binary

Binary addition

Binary addition works in a similar way to denary addition. If two numbers added together are equal to or greater than the base value, (in the case of denary, 10) then the 'tens' are carried. In binary, an addition that equals 2 or more results in a carry over to the next column.

In binary, the rules for addition are as follows:

1. 0 + 0 = 0
2. 0 + 1 = 1
3. 1 + 0 = 1
4. 1 + 1 = 0 Carry 1 (This is 2 in denary or 10 in binary.)
5. 1 + 1 + 1 = 1 Carry 1 (This is 3 in denary or 11 in binary.)

6-30

Use the following worked example as a guide to where and how each of the rules is implemented.

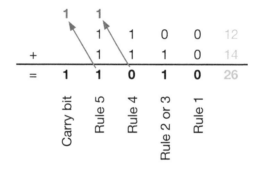

Q1: Calculate 00100111 + 00011001.

Overflow

In the following example, 8 bits are used to store the result of an addition. The result of the addition is greater than 255, and an overflow error occurs where a carry from the most significant bit requires a ninth bit.

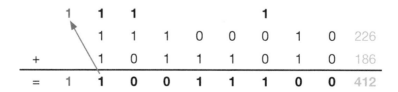

Representing negative numbers using sign and magnitude

One way to represent negative numbers is to make the leftmost bit, called the **most significant bit**, a sign bit.

- If the most significant bit is zero, the number is positive

- if the most significant bit is one, the number is negative.

In essence we are coding a plus sign as 0 and a minus sign as 1. This is known as the **sign and magnitude** representation of binary numbers. For example, using one-byte numbers,

00000011 = 3

10000011 = -3

> **Q2:** Add together these two numbers. What is the result?

Binary arithmetic using the sign and magnitude representation does not work as you would expect. A much better way of representing numbers in binary is called **two's complement**.

Representing negative numbers using two's complement

Two's complement binary works in a similar way to numbers on an analogue counter. Moving the wheel forwards one, will create a reading of 0001; turn back one, and the reading will become 9999. 9999 is interpreted as -1.

6-30

In binary:

11111101	=	-3
11111110	=	-2
11111111	=	-1
00000000	=	0
00000001	=	1
00000010	=	2
00000011	=	3

> **Q3:** Add together the two's complement numbers 3 and -3. What is the result?

Calculating the range

The range that can be represented with two's complement using n bits is given by the formula:

$$-(2^{(n-1)}) \dots 2^{(n-1)} - 1$$

With eight bits, the maximum denary range that can be represented is -128 to 127 because the leftmost bit is used as a sign bit to indicate whether a number is negative. If the leftmost number is a 1, it is a negative number. Thus 10000000 represents -128.

Q4: What is the range that can be represented using 16 bits?

Converting a negative denary number to binary

Start by working out the positive equivalent of the number, flip all of the bits and add 1. For example, to convert the denary number -9 to binary:

		-9
Positive binary	:	00001001
Flip the bits	:	11110110
Add one	:	1
		11110111

Q5: Convert the number -65 to binary

Converting a negative two's complement binary number to denary

The same method works the other way. Flip all of the bits and add 1. Then work out the result in denary using the normal method. For example, to convert the binary number 11100101 to denary:

		11100101
Flip the bits	:	00011010
Add one	:	1
Convert	:	- 00011011
		-27

Q6: Convert the binary number 11110111 to denary.

Binary subtraction using two's complement

Binary subtraction is best done by using the negative two's complement number and then adding the second number. For example denary 17-14 would be:

14	=	00001110
-14	=	11110010
17	=	00010001
17 + (-14) =	(1)	00000011

The carry on the addition is ignored, and the correct answer is given.

Q7: Convert the following pairs of denary numbers to binary, and subtract the second number from the first

(i) 14 and 27 (ii) 14 and 8

Fixed point binary numbers

Fixed point binary numbers can be a useful way to represent fractions in binary. A binary point is used to separate the whole place values from the fractional part on the number line:

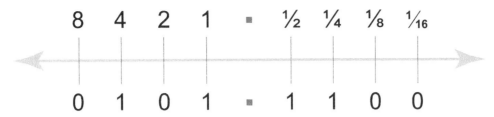

In the binary example above, the left hand section before the point is equal to 5 (4+1) and the right hand section is equal to ½ + ¼ (¾), or 0.5 + 0.25 = 0.75. So, using four bits after the point, 0101 1100 is 5.75 in denary. A useful table with some denary fractions and their equivalents is given below:

Q8: How is 19.25 represented using a single byte with 3 bits after the point?

Binary fraction	Fraction	Denary fraction
0.1	1/2	0.5
0.01	1/4	0.25
0.001	1/8	0.125
0.0001	1/16	0.0625
0.00001	1/32	0.03125
0.000001	1/64	0.015625
0.0000001	1/128	0.0078125
0.00000001	1/256	0.00390625

Converting a denary fraction to fixed point binary

To convert the fractional part of a denary number to binary, you can employ the same technique as you would when converting any denary number to binary. Take the value and subtract each point value from the amount until you are left with 0. Take the example 3.5625 using 4 bits to the right of the binary point:

Subtract 0.5:	0.5625 – 0.5 = 0.0625	**1**
Subtract 0.25 from 0.0625:	Won't go	**0**
Subtract 0.125 from 0.0625:	Won't go	**0**
Subtract 0.0625 from 0.0625:	0.0625 – 0.0625 = 0	**1**

3 = 0011 in binary. 0.5625 = 1001. So 3.5625 = 0011 1001

It is worth noticing that this system is not only less accurate than the denary system, but some fractions cannot be represented at all. 0.2, 0.3 and 0.4, for example, will require an infinite number of bits to the right of the point. The number of fractional places would therefore be truncated and the number will not be accurately stored, causing rounding errors. In our denary system, two denary places can hold all values between .00 and .99. With the fixed point binary system, 2 digits after the point can only represent 0, ¼, ½, or ¾ and nothing in between.

32	16	8	4	2	1	▪	½	¼

16	8	4	2	1	▪	½	¼	⅛

The **range** of a fixed point binary number is also limited by the fractional part. For example, if you have only 8 bits to store a number to 2 binary places, you would need 2 digits after the point, leaving only 6 bits before it. 6 bits only gives a range of 0-63. Moving the point one to the left to improve accuracy within the fractional part only serves to half the range to just 0-31. Even with 32 bits used for each number, including 8 bits for the fractional part after the point, the maximum value that can be stored is only about 8 million. Another format called **floating point binary** can hold much larger numbers, with greater accuracy.

Floating point form is covered in the next chapter.

Exercises

1. Represent the denary value -19 as an 8-bit two's complement binary integer. [2]

2. What is the largest positive denary value that can be represented using 8-bit two's complement binary? [1]

3. Describe how 8-bit two's complement binary can be used to subtract one number from another number. In your answer show how the calculation 25 – 49 would be completed using the method that you have described. [2]

4. A computer stores the current temperature of a supermarket delivery van. The temperature in °C is stored as a two's complement integer using a single byte.

    (a) Convert the freezer temperature value of -19 into binary. [2]

    (b) State the range of temperature values that can be stored using 8 bits. [1]

5. A memory location contains the value 10101011. What is its denary equivalent if it represents a two's complement binary integer? [2]

Chapter 31 – Floating point arithmetic

A-Level only

Objectives

Ⓐ • Represent positive and negative numbers with a fractional part in floating point form

Ⓐ • Normalise un-normalised floating point numbers with positive or negative mantissas

Ⓐ • Add and subtract floating point numbers

Ⓐ • Explain underflow and overflow and describe the circumstances in which they occur

Fixed point binary numbers

In the last chapter we looked briefly at how numbers with a fractional part can be held in fixed point format, which assumes a predetermined number of bits before and after the point. This makes fixed point numbers simpler to process but there is a compromise in the **range** and **precision** of values that can be represented in a given number of bits. Moving the point to the right increases the range but reduces the precision, or accuracy, of the fractional part and vice versa.

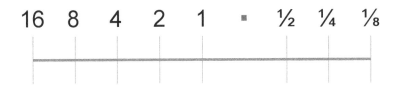

In the example above, only numbers which are multiples of 1/8 can be represented. The value 4.9, for example would be 'rounded' to 4.875 or 00100111 with three fractional bits to the right of the point.

Q1: Using 1 byte to hold each number with the three least significant bits to the right of the point, convert the following binary numbers to denary:

(a) 01010100   (b) 01011101   (c) 00111011   (d) 01010111

Q2: Convert the following numbers to 8-bit binary assuming four bits after the point:

(a) 2.75   (b) 10.875   (c) 7.5625   (d) 3.4375

Q3: What are the largest and smallest unsigned numbers that can be held in two bytes with four bits after the point? See Figure 31.1

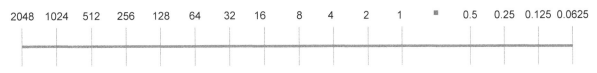

Figure 31.1

Floating point binary numbers

Using 32 bits (4 bytes), the largest fixed point number that can be represented with just one bit after the point is only just over two billion. Floating point binary allows very large numbers to be represented.

When ordinary denary numbers become very large, they are written in a more convenient scientific notation $m \times 10^n$ where m is known as the **mantissa** or coefficient, and n is the **exponent** or order of magnitude. 5000 can therefore written as 0.5×10^4, and 42,750.254 can be written as 0.42750254×10^5, moving the decimal point five places to the left.

This technique can easily be applied to binary numbers too, where the mantissa and exponent are represented for example using 12 bits, with 8 bits for the mantissa and 4 bits for the exponent. The leftmost bit of both the mantissa and the exponent is a sign bit, with 0 indicating a positive number, and 1 a negative number. In a computer, of course, many more bits than this will be used to represent a floating point number, with 32-, 64- and 128-bit floating point numbers all being common.

In all the examples below, eight bits are used for the mantissa and four bits for the exponent. The implied binary point is to the right of the sign bit.

Sign bit	Mantissa	Exponent
0 •	1 0 1 1 0 1 0	0 0 1 1

$0 • 1011010\ 0011 = 0.101101 \times 2^3 = 0101.101 = 4+1+0.5+0.125 = 5.625$

To convert the floating point binary number above to denary:

- Write down the mantissa, 0.1011010

- Translate the exponent from binary to denary 0011 = 3. This means that you have to move the point 3 places to the right, as the mantissa has to be multiplied by 2^3.

- The binary number is therefore 101.1010

- Translate this to binary using the table in Figure 31.1. The number is 5.625.

Q4: Convert the following floating point numbers to denary: You can use *Figure 1* to help you.
(a) 0 • 1101010 0100   (b) 0 • 1001100 0011

Negative exponents

If the exponent is negative, the decimal point must be moved left instead of right.

$0 • 1000000\ 1110 = 0.1 \times 2^{-2} = 0.001 = 0.125$

The example above has a positive mantissa of 0.1000000 and a negative exponent of -2.

- Find the two's complement of the exponent. (Remember that to convert a positive to negative binary number using two's complement you must flip the bits and add 1.) Exponent = -2

- Move the binary point of the mantissa two places to the left, to make it smaller. The mantissa is therefore 0.001 (You can ignore the trailing zeros)

- Translate this to denary with the help of Figure 31.1. The answer is 0.125.

6-31

Q5: Convert the following floating point number to denary: 0 • 1100000 1110

Handling negative mantissas

A negative floating point number will have a 1 as the sign bit or MSB (Most Significant Bit) of the mantissa indicating a negative place value.

$$1 \bullet 0101101 \; 0101 = -0.1010011 \times 2^5 = -10100.11 = -20.75$$

The example above has a negative mantissa of 1.0101101 and a positive exponent of 0101.

- Find the twos complement of the mantissa. It is 0.1010011, so the bits represent -0.1010011
- Translate the exponent to denary, 0101 = 5
- Move the binary point 5 places to the right to make it larger. The mantissa is -10100.11
- Translate this to binary with the help of Figure 31.1. The answer is -20.75.

Q6: Convert the following binary numbers to denary:
    (a) 0 • 1000000 1110   (b) 1 • 0011000 0100

Normalisation

Normalisation is the process of moving the binary point of a floating point number to provide the maximum level of precision for a given number of bits. This is achieved by ensuring that the first digit after the binary point is a significant digit. To understand this, first consider an example in denary.

In the denary system, a number such as $5,842,130_{10}$ can be represented with a 7-digit mantissa in many different ways

       $0.584213 \times 10^7 = 5,842,130$

       $0.058421 \times 10^8 = 5,842,100$

       $0.005842 \times 10^9 = 5,842,000$

The first representation, with a significant (non-zero) digit after the decimal point, has the maximum precision.

A number such as 0.00000584213 can be represented as 0.584213×10^{-5}.

Normalising a positive binary number

In binary arithmetic, the leading bit of both mantissa and exponent represent the sign bit.

In normalised floating point form:

      A positive number has a sign bit of 0 and the next digit is always 1.

This means that the mantissa of a positive number in normalised form always lies between ½ and 1.

A-Level only

Example 1

Normalise the binary number 0.0001011 0101, held in an 8-bit mantissa and a 4-bit exponent.

- The binary point needs to move 3 places to the right so that there is a 1 following the binary point.
- Making the mantissa larger means we must compensate by making the exponent smaller, so subtract 3 from the exponent, resulting in an exponent of 0010.
- The normalised number is 0.1011000 0010

Normalising a negative binary number

An unnormalised number will have a sign bit of 1 and one or more 1s after the binary point.

Example 2

Normalise the binary number 1.1110111 0001, held in an 8-bit mantissa and a 4-bit exponent.

- Move the binary point right 3 places, so that it is just before the first 0 digit. The mantissa is now 1.0111000

- Moving the binary point to the right makes the number larger, so we must make the exponent smaller to compensate. Subtract 3 from the exponent. The exponent is now $1 - 3 = -2 = 1110$

- The normalised number is 1.0111000 1110

A normalised negative number has a sign bit of 1 and the next bit is always 0.

The mantissa of a negative number in normalised form always lies between -½ and -1.

Example 3

What does the following binary number (with a 5-bit mantissa and a 3-bit exponent) represent in denary?

-1	1/2	1/4	1/8	1/16	-4	2	1
0	1	1	1	1	0	1	1

This is the largest positive number that can be held using a 5-bit mantissa and a 3-bit exponent, and represents $0.1111 \times 2^3 = 7.5$

Example 4

The most negative number that can be held in a 5-bit mantissa and 3-bit exponent is:

-1	1/2	1/4	1/8	1/16	-4	2	1
1	0	0	0	0	0	1	1

This represents $-1.0000 \times 2^3 = -1000.0 = -8$

Note that the size of the mantissa will determine the **precision** of the number, and the size of the exponent will determine the **range** of numbers that can be held.

Q7: Normalise the following numbers, using an 8-bit mantissa and a 4-bit exponent

(a)   0.0000110 0001

(b)   1.1110011 0011

Converting from denary to normalised binary floating point

To convert a denary number to normalised binary floating point, first convert the number to fixed point binary.

Example 5

Convert the number 14.25 to normalised floating point binary, using an 8-bit mantissa and a 4-bit exponent.

- In fixed point binary, 14.25 = 01110.010

- Remember that the first digit after the sign bit must be 1 in normalised form, so move the binary point 4 places left and increase the exponent from 0 to 4. The number is equivalent to 0.1110010×2^4

- Using a 4-bit exponent, 14.25 = 0 1110010 0100

Example 6

If the denary number is negative, calculate the two's complement of the fixed point binary:

e.g. Calculate the binary equivalent of -14.25

14.25 = 01110.010

-14.25 = 10001.110 (two's complement)

In normalised form, the first digit after the point must be 0, so the point needs to be moved four places left.

$10001.110 = 1.0001110 \times 2^4 = 10001110\ 0100$

Q8: Convert the following numbers to normalised binary floating point numbers, using an 8-bit mantissa and 4-bit exponent:

    (a) 16.75   (b) -4.5

Floating point addition and subtraction

Before looking at these operations in binary, we can gain an understanding of the principles involved in floating point arithmetic by looking at equivalent calculations in denary.

In denary, when adding two numbers involving decimal points, we first have to line up the points.

For example: 132.156

+   1.0318

133.1878

In their "normalised form", the two numbers above would be represented as

.132156 $\times 10^3$ and

.103180 $\times 10^1$

Clearly we do not simply add the mantissas, and the same principle holds true in binary. The rules for addition and subtraction can be stated as:

- line up the points by making the exponents equal

- add or subtract the mantissas

- normalise the result

A-Level only

Q9: Using the above rules, add together the denary numbers 1.562 x 10^4 and 3.128 x 10^2.

Example 7

Convert the denary numbers 0.25 and 10.5 to normalised floating point binary form using an 8-bit mantissa and a 4-bit exponent. Add together the two normalised binary numbers, giving the result in normalised floating point binary form.

Step 1: The numbers in normalised form are:

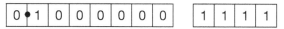

| 0●1 | 0 | 0 | 0 | 0 | 0 | 0 | | 1 | 1 | 1 | 1 |

| 0●1 | 0 | 1 | 0 | 1 | 0 | 0 | | 0 | 1 | 0 | 0 |

Step 2: Write the mantissas with a binary point, and convert the exponents to denary, giving

0.1000000   exponent -1 and

0.1010100   exponent 4

Step 3: Make both exponents 4 and shift the binary points accordingly

0.0000010   (make the number *smaller* as you *increase* the exponent)

0.1010100

Step 4: Add the numbers, giving 0.1010110 exponent 4 (In this case it's already normalised)

Result is

| 0●1 | 0 | 1 | 0 | 1 | 1 | 0 | | 0 | 1 | 0 | 0 |

Q10: Add together the two binary numbers given below, leaving the result in normalised floating point binary form.

| 0●1 | 1 | 0 | 0 | 0 | 0 | 0 | | 1 | 1 | 1 | 1 |

| 0●1 | 1 | 0 | 1 | 0 | 0 | 0 | | 0 | 0 | 1 | 0 |

Example 8

Subtract the second of the two numbers given below from the first, giving the result in normalised floating point binary form.

| 0●1 | 0 | 0 | 0 | 1 | 0 | 0 | | 0 | 1 | 1 | 0 |

| 0●1 | 0 | 0 | 0 | 0 | 1 | 0 | | 0 | 1 | 0 | 1 |

Step 1: Convert the exponents to denary, giving

0.1000100   exponent 6 and

0.1000010   exponent 5

Step 2: Make both exponents 6 and shift the binary point of the second number accordingly

0.1000100 exp 6

0.0100001 exp 6 (make the number *smaller* as you *increase* the exponent)

Step 3: Find the twos complement of the second number

1.1011110 +1 = 1.1011111

6-31

A-Level only

Step 4:   Add the numbers

0.1000100

1.1011111

(1)0.0100011   exp 6 (ignore the carry)

Now normalise the number by moving the binary point right 1 place, which increases the number, and decrease the exponent by 1

Result is

Q11:   Subtract the number 01001000 0011 from 01011000 0000

Underflow and overflow

Underflow occurs when a number is too small to be represented in the allotted number of bits. If, for example, a very small number is divided by another number greater than 1, underflow may occur and the result will be represented by 0.

Overflow occurs when the result of a calculation is too large to be held in the number of bits allocated.

Exercises

1. A normalised floating point representation uses an 8-bit mantissa and a 4-bit exponent, both stored using **two's complement format**.

    (a) This is a floating point representation of a number:

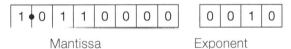

Mantissa   Exponent

Calculate the denary number. Show your working.   [2]

    (b) Write the normalised representation of the denary value 12.75 in the boxes below:

Mantissa   Exponent   [2]

    (c) Floating point numbers are usually stored in normalised form.

         State **two** advantages of using a normalised representation.   [2]

2. Convert the following denary numbers to normalised floating point binary form, using an 8-bit mantissa and a 4-bit exponent.

    (a) -18.75   [2]

    (b) 0.0625   [2]

6-31

`A-Level only`

Chapter 32 Bitwise manipulation and masks

Objectives

Ⓐ • Perform logical, arithmetic and circular shifts on binary data

Ⓐ • Perform bitwise operations AND, OR and XOR

Ⓐ • Use masks to manipulate bits

Logical shift instructions

All the bits move right or left. A logical shift right causes the least significant bit (lsb) to be shifted into the carry bit, and a zero moves into the most significant bit (msb) to occupy the vacated space.

Example 1

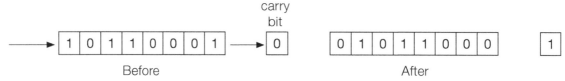

It is useful for examining the least significant bit of a number. After the operation, the carry bit can be tested and a conditional branch executed.

Example 2

A logical shift left works in the same way, but the bits move left. The most significant bit (msb) moves into the carry bit and a zero moves into the lsb. You can visualise the carry bit as being on the left of the byte.

Q1: Shift the binary pattern 0100 0111 right twice and then left once. What are the contents of the byte and the carry bit after these shifts?

Arithmetic shift instructions

An arithmetic shift is similar, but it takes into account the sign bit, which always remains the same.

Example 3

Shifting right has the effect of dividing by 2. If the sign bit is 1, 1 is moved in from the left instead of 0.

Q2: Convert the number -16 to binary, and divide by 8 using arithmetic shifts.

Example 4

Shifting left multiplies by 2. The shift bypasses the sign bit, leaving the msb the same whatever the value of the other bits. However, this may result in arithmetic overflow, as shown below.

Before   After

Q3: Convert the number 14 to binary and then multiply it by 4 using arithmetic shifts. Convert the result back to denary.

Multiplying two numbers using arithmetic shifts

Using a combination of shifts and addition, two binary numbers may be multiplied together.

Example 5

Multiply 9 by 5 using shifts and addition:

Multiply 9 x 1	0000 1001
Multiply 9 by 4 with 2 left shifts:	0010 0100
Add together:	0010 1101 = 45

Q4: Multiply 12 by 6 using shifts and addition.

6-32

Circular shift instructions

A rotate or circular shift is useful for performing shifts in multiple bytes. In a circular shift right, the value in the least significant bit (lsb) is moved into the carry bit, and the carry bit is moved into the most significant bit (msb).

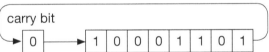

A circular shift right of the bit pattern shown above will result in the following:

Example 6

Assume that R0 and R1, shown below, are two 8-bit registers being used as a double register to hold a 16-bit binary integer, with R0 holding the high half of the number. Show how a combination of shift instructions may be used to divide the 16-bit integer by 2.

R0   carry bit   R1

Answer: First perform an arithmetic shift right on R0. 1 is shifted into the carry bit.

R0   carry bit   R1

Then perform a circular shift on R1. This places the carry bit into the msb of R1, and the carry bit is replaced with the lsb of R1.

| 0 | 0 | 1 | 0 | 1 | 1 | 0 | 0 |

R0   carry bit 0   R1 1 1 1 0 1 1 0 0

Q5: A 16-bit integer is held in R0 and R1 which are being used as a double register. Show the effect on the registers of doing an arithmetic shift right of 1 place in R0, followed by a circular shift right of 1 place in R1.

| 1 | 0 | 0 | 1 | 1 | 0 | 1 | 1 | carry bit | 0 | 1 | 0 | 1 | 1 | 1 | 0 | 1 |

R0   carry bit   R1

Logical instructions

Boolean algebra is covered in Section 8, Chapters 40 and 41.

The instructions NOT, AND, OR and XOR (exclusive OR) have the following effects:

		NOT	AND	OR	XOR
Input	A	1010	1010	1010	1010
Input	B		1100	1100	1100
Result		0101	1000	1110	0110

Explanation: In Boolean logic, 1 represents True and 0 represents False. A NOT instruction has only one input. If the input is True (i.e. 1), the output is False (i.e. 0). With the AND gate, if both inputs are True, (i.e.1) the output is True. Otherwise, the output is False. With the OR gate, if either of the inputs is True (i.e. 1) the output is True. Otherwise, the output is False. With the XOR gate, if either, but not both, of the inputs is True, the output is True. Otherwise, the output is False.

Q6: What will be the output from the following operations?
(a) 0010 1101 OR 1111 0000   (b) 0010 1101 AND 1111 0000

Masks

The OR function may be used to set selected bits to 1 without affecting the other bits.

Example 7

A system has 8 lights that can be turned ON (output 1) of OFF (output 0), controlled by an 8-bit binary code. At present, lights 1 to 4 are ON, lights 5 to 8 are OFF. Lights 5 and 6 are to be turned ON.

Light number	1 2 3 4 5 6 7 8
Present state	1 1 1 1 0 0 0 0
OR with	0 0 0 0 1 1 0 0
Result	1 1 1 1 1 1 0 0

The AND function may be used to mask particular bits, by setting them to zero.

A-Level only

Example 8

The ASCII bit pattern for the number "5" is 0011 0101. Convert this to a pure binary number using a mask.

We need to mask out the first four bits. This can be done with an AND operation.

ASCII "5"	0 0 1 1 0 1 0 1
AND with	0 0 0 0 1 1 1 1
Result	0 0 0 0 0 1 0 1 = 5 in binary

The XOR function may be used to invert chosen bits.

Example 9

Convert an uppercase letter represented in ASCII to its lowercase equivalent.

The letter "C", for example, is 0100 0011 in ASCII. The lowercase letter "c" is 0110 0011. We want to change the third bit (counting from the left) from 0 to 1.

ASCII "C"	0 1 0 0 0 0 1 1
XOR with	0 0 1 0 0 0 0 0
Result	0 1 1 0 0 0 1 1 = "c"

Exercises

1. An 8-bit word holds the binary pattern 10110010. Start with this bit pattern in each of parts (a), (b) and (c). There is no need to show the contents of the carry bit.

   (a) State the contents of the word after a logical left shift of 2 bits. [1]

   (h) Interpreting the word as a number in two's complement form, state the contents of the word after an arithmetic right shift of 2 bits. [1]

   (c) State the contents of the word after a circular shift left of 3 bits. [1]

2. In a particular computer, characters are represented in 8 bits using the ASCII code.

   The codes for uppercase letters are from 0100 0001 for A to 0101 1010 for Z.

   The codes for lowercase letters are from 0110 0001 for a to 0111 1010 for z.

   Give an 8-bit mask and the appropriate logical operation which will:

   (a) change any uppercase letter into its lowercase equivalent [2]

   (b) change any lowercase letter into its uppercase equivalent. [2]

3. A 32-bit register holds a four byte value. The bytes are numbered so that the first byte is leftmost. What mask and logical operator is required to achieve each of the following results:

   (a) complement the second byte [2]

   (b) set the third byte to zero? [2]

6-32

A

Section 7

Data structures

In this section:

7

Chapter 33 – Arrays, tuples and records

Objectives

- Be familiar with the concept of a data structure
- Be familiar with arrays of up to 3 dimensions, tuples and records

Data structures

Computer languages such as Python, Pascal and VB have built-in **elementary data types** such as **integer**, **real**, **Boolean** and **char**. They also have some built-in structured data types such as **string**, **array** and **record**. These are made up of a number of elements of a specified type such as char, integer, real or string.

1-dimensional arrays

An array is defined as a finite, ordered set of elements of the same type, such as integer, real or char. **Finite** means that there is a specific number of elements in the array. **Ordered** implies that there is a first, second, third etc. element of the array.

For example, (assuming the first element of the array is `myArray[0]`:

```
myArray = [51, 72, 35, 37, 0, 3]
x = myArray[2]      #assigns 35 to x
```

Example 1

7-33

Every year the RSPB organises a Big Garden Birdwatch to involve the public in counting the number of birds of different types that they see in their gardens on a particular weekend. During 30-31 January 2016, more than 8 million birds were counted and reported.

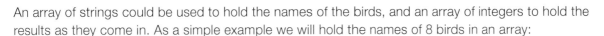

The scientists add all the sightings together, and once the data has been analysed, they can discover trends and understand how different birds and other wildlife are faring.

An array of strings could be used to hold the names of the birds, and an array of integers to hold the results as they come in. As a simple example we will hold the names of 8 birds in an array:

```
birdName = ["robin", "blackbird", "pigeon", "magpie", "bluetit",
"thrush", "wren", "starling"]
```

We can reference each element of the array using an **index**. For example:

```
birdName[2] = "pigeon"   #the index here is 2
```

Most languages have a function which will return the length of an array, so that

```
numSpecies = len[birdName]
```

will assign 8 to `numSpecies`.

To find at which position of the array a particular bird is, we could use the following pseudocode algorithm:

```
bird = input("Enter bird name: ")
birdFound = False
numSpecies = len(birdName)
for count = 0 to numSpecies - 1
   if bird == birdName[count] then
      birdIndex = count
      birdFound = True
   endif
next count
if birdFound == False then
   print("Bird species not in array")
else
   print("Bird found at",birdIndex)
endif
```

We need a second array of integers to accumulate the totals of each bird species observed. We can initialise each element to zero.

```
birdCount = [0,0,0,0,0,0,0,0]
```

To add 5 to the blackbird count (the second element in the list) we can write a statement

```
birdCount[1] = birdCount[1] + 5
```

The following algorithm enables a member of the Birdwatch team to enter results as they come in from members of the public.

```
birdName = ["robin", "blackbird", "pigeon", "magpie", "bluetit",
                          "thrush", "wren", "starling"]
birdCount = [0,0,0,0,0,0,0,0]
bird = input("Please input name of bird (x to end): ")
while bird != "x"
   birdFound = False
   for count = 0 to 7
      if bird == birdName[count] then
         birdFound = True
         birdsObserved = input("number observed: ")
         birdCount[count] = birdCount[count] + birdsObserved
      endif
   next count
   if birdFound == False then
      print("Bird species not in array")
   endif
   bird = input("Please input name of bird (x to end): ")
endwhile
#now print out the totals for each bird
for count = 0 to 7
   print(birdName[count], birdCount[count])
next count
```

7-33

2-dimensional arrays

An array can have two or more dimensions. A two-dimensional array can be visualised as a table, rather like a spreadsheet.

Imagine a 2-dimensional array called `numbers`, with 3 rows and 4 columns. Elements in the array can be referred to by their row and column number, so that `numbers[1,3]` = 8 in the example below.

	Column 0	Column 1	Column 2	Column 3
Row 0	1	2	3	4
Row 1	5	6	7	8
Row 2	9	10	11	12

Q1: What is the value of `numbers[2,1]`?

Example 2

Write a pseudocode algorithm for a module which prints out the quarterly sales figures (given in integers) for each of 3 sales staff named Anna, Bob and Carol, together with their total annual sales. Assume that the sales figures are already in the 2-dimensional array `quarterSales`. The staff names are held in a 1-dimensional array `staff`.

```
staff = ["Anna","Bob","Carol"]
quarterSales = [[100,110,120,110],
                [350,355,360,360],
                [200,210,220,220]]
for s = 0 to 2
   annualSales = 0
   #output staff name
   (insert statement here)

   for q = 0 to 3
      print("Quarter ", q, quarterSales[s,q])
      annualSales = annualSales + quarterSales[s,q]
   next q
   print("Annual sales: ", annualSales)
next s
```

Q2: What statement needs to be inserted after the comment `#output staff name` in order to output the staff name?

Arrays of three dimensions

Arrays may have more than two dimensions. An n-dimensional array is a set of elements of the same type, indexed by n integers. In a 3-dimensional array `x`, a particular element may be referred to as `x[4,5,2]`, for example. The first element would be referred to as `x[0,0,0]`.

7-33

Tuples

A **tuple** is an ordered set of values, which could be elements of any type such as strings, integers or real numbers, or even graphic images, sound files or arrays. Unlike arrays, the elements do not all have to be of the same type. However, a tuple, like a string, is **immutable**, which means that its elements cannot be changed, and you cannot dynamically add elements to or delete elements from a tuple.

In Python a tuple is written in parentheses, for example:

```
pupil = ("John", 78, "a")
```

You can refer to individual elements of a tuple, for example:

```
name = pupil[0]
```

but the following statement is invalid:

```
pupil[0] = "Mary"
```

Records

If you want to store data permanently so that you can read or update it at a future date, the data needs to be stored in a file on disk. The most common way of storing large amounts of data conveniently is to use a database, but sometimes you need to create and interrogate your own files.

Generally, a **file** consists of a number of **records**. A record contains a number of **fields**, each holding one item of data. For example, in a file holding data about students, you might have the following record structure:

ID	Firstname	Surname	DateOfBirth	Class
1453	Gemma	Baines	01/05/2004	2G
1768	Paul	Gerrard	17/11/2003	2G
2016	Brian	Davidson	03/08/2002	3H

The table shows a file containing three records, each record having 5 fields. In some languages, a record type will be declared in the following manner:

```
studentType = record
    integer ID
    string firstname
    string surname
    date dateOfBirth
    string class
end record
```

This is an example of a user-defined data type named `studentType`.

A variable `student` of type `studentType` may then be declared as

```
student : studentType
```

Every field in a record can be identified by `<recordName>.<fieldName>`.

The surname of the student, for example, would be referred to as `student.surname`.

Exercises

1. Referring to the BirdWatch program given earlier in this chapter:

   (a) Explain why the `for… next` loop repeated below is not the most efficient type of loop in this situation. [1]

   ```
   for count = 0 to 7
      if bird == birdName[count] then
         birdFound = True
         birdsObserved = input("Enter number of birds observed: ")
         birdCount[count] = birdCount[count] + birdsObserved
      endif
   next count
   ```

   (b) Rewrite the algorithm using a different type of loop. [3]

2. The birth weights in grams of 100 babies, which vary between 1500 to 4000 grams, are held in an array `weight`.

   Write pseudocode for an algorithm which calculates the average birth weight, and then prints out the number of babies who are more than 500 grams below the average weight, together with the average weight of these. [5]

3. The marks for 3 assignments, each marked out of 10, for a class of 5 students are to be input into a two-dimensional array `mark` so that `mark[3,1]`, for example, holds the second mark achieved by the 4th student. Any missing assignments are given a mark of zero.

   Draw a table representing this array, and fill it with test data. [2]

   Write a pseudocode algorithm which allows the user to enter the marks for the class. Calculate the average mark for each student, and the class average. [4]

4. In a certain game, treasure is hidden in a 10x10 grid. The grid coordinates are given by `grid[row,col]` where `grid[0,0]` represents the top left hand corner and `grid[9,9]` the bottom right corner. The grid coordinates of the treasure are signified by a 1 at `grid[row,col]`. All other grid elements are filled with zeros.

   What is the purpose of the following pseudocode algorithm? [2]

   ```
   for row = 0 to 9
      for col = 0 to 9
         if grid[row, col] == 1 then
            print("row ", row, " column ", col)
         endif
      next col
   next row
   ```

   Write pseudocode statements to initialise the grid and "hide the treasure" at a random location inside the grid. [5]

7-33

Chapter 34 – Queues

Objectives

- Understand the concept of an abstract data type

- Be familiar with the concept and uses of a queue

(A) • Describe the creation and maintenance of data within a queue (linear, circular, priority)

(A) • Describe and apply the following to a linear, circular and priority queue

  o   add an item

  o   remove an item

  o   test for an empty queue

  o   test for a full queue

Abstract data types

An **abstract data type** is one that is created by the programmer, rather than defined within the programming language. They include structures such as queues, stacks, trees and graphs. These can easily be shown in graphical form, and it is not hard to understand how to perform operations such as adding, deleting or counting elements in each structure. However, programming languages require data types to represent them. An abstract data type (**ADT**) is a logical description of how the data is viewed and the operations that can be performed on it, but how this is to be done is not necessarily known to the user. It is up to the programmer who creates the data structure to decide how to implement it, and it may be built in to the programming language. This is a good example of **data abstraction**, and by providing this level of abstraction we are creating an **encapsulation** around the data, hiding the details of implementation from the user.

As a programmer, you will be quite familiar with this concept. When you call a built-in function such as `random` to generate a random number, or `sqrt` to find the square root of a number, you are not at all concerned with how these functions are implemented.

Queues

A queue is a **First In First Out (FIFO)** data structure. New elements may only be added to the end of a queue, and elements may only be retrieved from the front of a queue. The sequence of data items in a queue is determined, therefore, by the order in which they are inserted. The size of the queue depends on the number of items in it, just like a queue at traffic lights or at a supermarket checkout.

Queues are used in a variety of applications:

- Output waiting to be printed is commonly stored in a queue on disk. In a room full of networked computers, several people may send work to be printed at more or less the same time. By putting the output into a queue on disk, the output is printed on a first come, first served basis as soon as the printer is free.

- Characters typed at a keyboard are held in a queue in a keyboard buffer.

- Queues are useful in simulation problems. A simulation program is one which attempts to model a real-life situation so as to learn something about it. An example is a program that simulates customers arriving at random times at the check-outs in a supermarket store, and taking random times to pass through the checkout. With the aid of a simulation program, the optimum number of check-out counters can be established.

Operations on a queue

The abstract data type **queue** is defined by its logical structure and the operations which can be performed on it. It is described as an ordered collection of items which are added at the rear of the queue, and removed from the front.

When Eli leaves the queue, the front pointer is made to point to Jason; the elements themselves do not move. When Adam joins the queue, the rear pointer points to Adam. Think of a queue in a doctor's surgery – people leave and join the queue, but no one moves chairs.

The following queue operations are needed:

- enQueue(item)   Add a new item to the rear of the queue
- deQueue()   Remove the front item from the queue and return it
- isEmpty()   Test to see whether the queue is empty
- isFull()   Test to see whether queue is full

7-34

Q1: Complete the following table to show the queue contents and the value returned by the function or **method**. The queue is named **q** and is of length 6.

Queue operation	Queue contents	Return value
q.isEmpty()	[]	True
q.enQueue("Blue")	["Blue"]	(none)
q.enQueue("Red")	["Blue", "Red"]	(none)
q.enQueue("Green")		
q.isFull()		
q.isEmpty()	["Blue", "Red", "Green"]	
q.deQueue()		
q.enQueue("Yellow")		

Dynamic vs static data structures

An abstract data type may be implemented using either a dynamic or a static data structure.

A **dynamic data structure** refers to a collection of data in memory that has the ability to grow or shrink in size. It does this with the aid of the **heap**, which is a portion of memory from which space is automatically allocated or de-allocated as required.

Languages such as Python, Java and C support dynamic data structures, such as the built-in `list` data type in Python. A potential drawback of using a dynamic data structure is that the data structure may cause **overflow** if it exceeds the maximum memory limit, and the program will crash.

Dynamic data structures are very useful for implementing data structures such as queues when the maximum size of the data structure is not known in advance. The queue can be given some arbitrary maximum to avoid causing memory overflow, but it is not necessary to allocate space in advance. A further advantage of using a built-in dynamic data structure such as a `list` is that many methods or functions such as `append`, `remove`, `length`, `insert`, `search` and `pop` may already be written and can be used in the implementation of other data structures such as a queue or stack.

A **static data structure** such as an `array` is fixed in size, and cannot increase in size or free up memory while the program is running. An array is suitable for storing a fixed number of items such as the months of the year, monthly sales or average monthly temperatures. The disadvantage of using an array to implement a dynamic data structure such as a queue is that the size of the array has to be decided in advance by the programmer, and if the number of items added fills up the array, then no more can be added, regardless of how much free space there is in memory. Python does not have a built-in `array` data structure.

7-34

A-Level only

Implementing a linear queue

There are basically two ways to implement a linear queue in an array or list:

1. As items leave the queue, all of the other items move up one position in allocated memory so that the front of the queue is always the first element of the structure, e.g. q[0]. With a long queue, this may require significant processing time.

2. A linear queue can be implemented as an array with pointers to the front and rear of the queue. An integer holding the size of the array (the maximum size of the queue) is needed, as well as a variable giving the number of items currently in the queue. However, clearly a problem will arise as many items are added to and deleted from the queue, as space is created at the front of the queue which cannot be filled, and items are added until the rear pointer points to the last element of the data structure.

> **Q2:** The queue of names pictured above containing Jason, Milly, Bob and Adam has space for six names. What will be the situation when Jason and Milly leave the queue, and Jack joins it? How many names are now in the queue? How many free spaces are left?

A circular queue

One way of overcoming the limitation of a static data structure such as an array is to implement the queue as a **circular queue**, so that when the array fills up and the rear pointer points to the last element of the array, say q[5], it will be made to point to the first element, q[0], when the next person joins the queue, assuming this element is empty. This solution requires some extra effort on the part of the programmer, and is less flexible than a dynamic data structure if the maximum number of items is not known in advance.

Q3: A circular queue is implemented in a fixed size array of six elements, indexed from 0. Show the contents of the queue and the front and rear pointers for a circular queue of 6 items when

(a) it is empty

(b) Ali, Ben, Charlie, Davina, Enid, Fred join the queue. Ali, Ben and Charlie leave, and Greg joins the queue.

Pseudocode for implementing a circular queue

To initialise the queue:

```
procedure initialise
    front = 0
    rear = -1
    size = 0
    maxSize = size of array
endprocedure
```

To test for an empty queue:

```
function isEmpty
    if size == 0 then
        return True
    else
        return False
    endif
endfunction
```

To test for a full queue:

```
function isFull
    if size == maxSize then
        return True
    else
        return False
    endif
endfunction
```

To add an element to the queue:

```
procedure enqueue(newItem)
    if isFull then
        print("Queue full")
    else
        rear = (rear + 1) MOD maxSize
        q[rear] = newItem
        size = size + 1
    endif
endprocedure
```

To remove an item from the queue:

```
function dequeue
    if isEmpty then
        print("Queue empty")
        item = Null
    else
        item = q[front]
        front = (front + 1) MOD maxSize
        size = size - 1
    endif
    return item
endfunction
```

Q4: In what respect is a circular queue an example of **abstraction**?

Priority queues

In some situations where items are placed in a queue, a system of priorities is used. For example an operating system might schedule jobs in order of priority, or a printer may give shorter print jobs priority over longer ones.

A **priority queue** acts like a queue in that items are dequeued by removing them from the front of the queue. However, the logical order of items within the queue is determined by their priority, with the highest priority items at the front of the queue and the lowest priority items at the back. It is therefore possible that a new item joins the queue at the front, rather than at the rear.

Q5: In what circumstances would an item join a priority queue at the front? In what circumstances would the item join the queue at the rear?

Such a queue could be implemented by checking the priority of each item in the queue, starting at the rear and moving it along one place until an item with the same or lower priority is found, at which point the new item can be inserted.

A

7-34

Exercises

1. (a) Explain why a queue may be implemented as a **circular queue**. [2]

    (b) Explain what is meant by a **dynamic data structure** and why an inbuilt dynamic data structure in a programming language may be useful in implementing a queue. [2]

    (c) Print jobs are put in a queue to be printed. The queue is implemented in an array, indexed from 0, as a circular queue which can hold 5 jobs. Jobs enter the queue in the sequence Job1, Job2, Job3, Job4, Job5. Pointers **front** and **rear** point to the first and last items in the queue respectively.

    (i) Draw a diagram to show how the print jobs are stored. Include pointers in your diagram. [3]

    (ii) Two jobs are printed and leave the queue. Another job, Job6, joins the queue.

    Draw a diagram representing the new situation. [2]

A-Level only

2. The size of some data structures is fixed when the structure is created.

    (a) State the term used to describe such data structures.

    Give **one** example of a type of data structure whose size is always fixed.

    Give **one** advantage of using a fixed size data structure. [3]

    (b) A queue data structure has two pointers called **front** and **next** which are defined as:

    front points to the first item in the queue

    next points to the next available space

    The queue is defined as a first in, first out (FIFO) data structure.

    (i) State the condition of the pointers when the queue is empty. [1]

    (ii) Write an algorithm to remove one data item from a queue. [4]

    (c) The queue may be represented by a fixed size data structure.

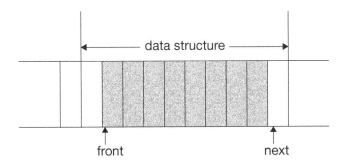

    Explain, with the aid of a diagram, what happens when attempting to add 3 data items to the queue. [5]

    OCR F453-01 Qu 5 June 2012

Chapter 35 – Lists and linked lists

Objectives

- Explain how a list may be implemented as either a static or dynamic data structure
- Show how items may be added to or deleted from a list
- **(A)** • Describe the linked list data structure
- **(A)** • Show how to create, traverse, add data to and remove data from a linked list

Definition of a list

In computer science, a **list** is an abstract data type consisting of a number of items in which the same item may occur more than once. The list is sequenced so can refer to the first, second, third,... item and we can also refer to the last element of the list.

A list is a very useful data type for a wide variety of operations, and can be used, for example, to implement other data structures such as a queue, stack or tree. Some languages such as Python have a built-in list data type, so that for example a list of numbers could be shown as

[45, 13, 19, 13, 8]

Q1: In a programming language which does not include the list data type, how could a list be implemented?

Operations on lists

Some possible list operations are shown in the following table. The list **a** is assumed to hold the values [45, 13, 19, 13, 8] initially, with the first element referred to as **a[0]**.

List operation	Description	Example	list contents	Return value
isEmpty()	Test for empty list	a.isEmpty()	[45, 13, 19, 13, 8]	False
append(item)	Add a new item to list to the end of the list	a.append(33)	[45, 13, 19, 13, 8, 33]	
remove(item)	Remove the first occurrence of an item from list	a.remove(13)	[45, 19, 13, 8, 33]	
search(item)	Search for an item in list	a.search(22)	[45, 19, 13, 8, 33]	False
length()	Return the number of items	a.length()	[45, 19, 13, 8, 33]	5
index(item)	Return the position of item	a.index(8)	[45, 19, 13, 8, 33]	3
insert(pos,item)	Insert a new item at position pos	a.insert(2,7)	[45, 19, 7, 13, 8, 33]	
pop()	Remove and return the last item in the list	a.pop()	[45, 19, 7, 13, 8]	33
pop(pos)	Remove and return the item at position pos	a.pop(1)	[45, 7, 13, 8]	19

> **Q2:** Assume that list `names` holds the values James, Paul, Sophie, Holly, Nathan. What does the list hold after each of the following consecutive operations?
>
> (i)   `names.append("Tom")`
>
> (ii)   `names.pop(3)`
>
> (iii)   `names.insert(1, "Melissa")`

Using an array

It is possible to maintain an ordered collection of data items using an array, which is a static data structure. This may be an option if the programming language does not support the `list` data type and if the maximum number of data items is small, and is known in advance.

The programmer then has to work out and code algorithms for each list operation. The empty array must be declared in advance as being a particular length, and this could be used, for example, to hold a priority queue.

Inserting a new name in the list

If the list needs to be held in sequential order in the array, the algorithm could first determine where a new item has to be added, and then if necessary, start at the end of the list and move the rest of the items along in order to make room for it.

The steps are as follows:

```
Test for list already full, print message if it is and quit
Determine where new item needs to be inserted
Starting at the end of the list, move other items along one place
Insert new item in correct place
```

> **Q3:** Suggest a different algorithm for adding a new element to a sequenced list.

> **Q4:** How could the given algorithm be adapted to insert an item in a priority queue?

Deleting a name from the list

Suppose the name Ken is to be deleted from the list shown below. The names coming after Ken in the list need to be moved up to fill the gap.

Holly	James	Ken	Nathan	Paul	Sophie	

> **Q5:** Why not simply leave the array element names[2] blank after deleting Ken?

First, items are moved up to fill the empty space by copying them to the previous spot in the array:

Holly	James	Nathan	Paul	Sophie	Sophie	

Finally the last element, which is now duplicated, is replaced with a blank.

Holly	James	Nathan	Paul	Sophie		

A-Level only

Linked lists

Definition

A linked list is a dynamic data structure used to hold an ordered sequence, as described below:

* The items which form the sequence are not necessarily held in contiguous data locations, or in the order in which they occur in the sequence

* Each item in the list is called a **node** and contains a **data field** and a next address field called a **link** or **pointer field** (the data field may consist of several subfields.)

* The data field holds the actual data associated with the list item, and the pointer field contains the address of the next item in the sequence

* The link field in the last item indicates that there are no further items by the use of a **null** pointer

* Associated with the list is a pointer variable which points to (i.e. contains the address of) the first node in the list

Operations on linked lists

In the examples which follow we will assume that the linked list is held in memory in an array of records, and that each node consists of a person's name (the data field) and a pointer to the next item in the list.

We will explore how to set up or initialise an empty list, insert new data in the correct place in the list, delete an unwanted item and print out all items in the list. We will also look at the problem of managing the free space in the list.

A node record may be defined like this:

```
type nodeType
   string name
   integer pointer
endType

dim Names[0..5] of nodeType
```

Initialising a linked list

We need to keep two linked lists; one for the actual data, and one for the free space. When a new item is added, it is put in the node pointed to by `nextfree`. When a node is deleted, it is linked into the free space list.

7-35

The array is initialised prior to entering any names, and it will consist of just one linked list of free space.

After initialisation, `nextfree` points to the first free space in the list, `Names[0]`.

A pointer named `start` will point to the first data item in the list. This will be initialised to `null`, indicating that the list is empty. The last item in the free space list also has a pointer of `null`, indicating that this is the last available free space in the list.

The array holding the linked list now looks like this:

index	name	pointer	
0		1	**start = null**
1		2	
2		3	
3		4	**nextfree = 0**
4		5	
5		null	

Figure 35.1

After the names Browning, Turner, Johnson and Cray have been added, the array will look like this:

index	name	pointer	
0	Browning	3	
1	Turner	null	**start = 0**
2	Johnson	1	
3	Cray	2	
4		5	**nextfree = 4**
5		null	

Figure 35.2

Notice that we now have two linked lists going; the list linking the nodes containing names and the list linking the free nodes.

- a pointer `start` points to the first item in the list

- `nextfree` is a pointer to the next free location in the array

- the free spaces in the array are organised as a linked list

- names can be retrieved in alphabetical order by following the links

> **Q6:** Show the state of the table and pointers after insertion of the name Allen. Write down the steps involved in inserting a new name at the front of the list, so that alphabetical sequence is maintained.

Inserting an item

We'll now work out an algorithm for inserting a name into the middle of the list. As an example, we'll insert Mortimer between Johnson and Turner. The pointers will have to be changed so that it is linked into the correct place.

After insertion of Mortimer, the list will appear as in Figure 35.3.

Names

index	name	pointer
0	Browning	3
1	Turner	null
2	Johnson	4
3	Cray	2
4	Mortimer	1
5		null

start = 0

nextfree = 5

Figure 35.3

Here are the steps:

```
store the new name Mortimer in the node pointed to by nextfree
determine, by following links, where new item should be linked in
change nextfree to point to next free location
change Mortimer's pointer to point to Turner
change Johnson's pointer to point to Mortimer
```

Diagrammatically, this is what we have done:

Before insertion:

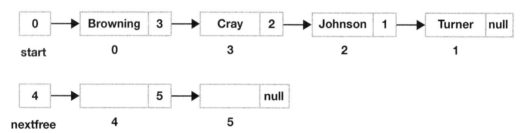

After insertion:

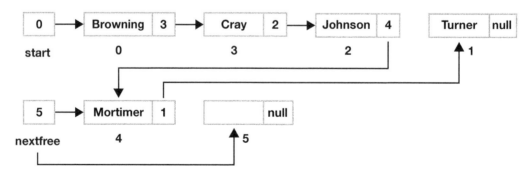

Figure 35.4

Extra steps will be needed to be added to the algorithm to cope with the special cases of inserting a name at the very front of the list (e.g. Allen), or inserting the first name into an empty list.

Before we go further and express this algorithm in more formal pseudocode, you need to make sure you clearly understand the notation used.

Names[p].name holds the name in node[p], that is, the node *pointed* to by p

Names[p].pointer holds the value of the pointer in node[p]

Q7: Look at Figure 35.4. After insertion of Mortimer, Names[2].name = Johnson, and Names[2].pointer = 4.

What is the value of

(i) Names[start].pointer?

(ii) Names[4].name?

(iii) Names[Names[3].pointer].pointer?

(iv) Names[Names[start].pointer].name?

Notice how you can 'peek ahead' using the pointers to see what name is in the next node, or even the node after that one, and so on.

This is crucial because you need to know where you have come from (the previous node), when you get to the node that has a name "greater" than the new one to be inserted.

Here's a simplified algorithm to add a new name to the list. The complications of inserting at the head of a list and dealing with a full list are dealt with in the algorithm on the next page.

The comments in the algorithm refer to inserting the name Mortimer in the linked list shown in Figures 35.2 and 35.4.

```
Names[nextfree].name = newName          //store name in next free node
p = start
follow pointers until Names[p].pointer points to a name > new name
temp = nextfree                         //put 4 in temp (Step 1)
nextfree = Names[temp].pointer          //put 5 in nextfree (Step 2)
Names[temp].pointer = Names[p].pointer  //put 1 in Mortimer's
                                        //  pointer field (Step 3)
Names[p].pointer = temp                 //put 4 in Johnson's
                                        //  pointer field (Step 4)
```

Diagramatically:

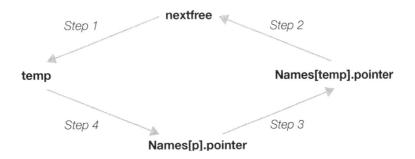

Figure 35.5

Pseudocode algorithm for inserting an item

The following algorithm copes with a full list and the special case of inserting an item at the front of the list. It also manages the free space list.

```
01    procedure AddItem(newName)
02    // check if list is full and if so, print error message
03       if nextfree == null then
04          print("List full")
05       else
06          Names[nextfree].name = newName

07          if start == null then              // empty list
08             temp = Names[nextfree].pointer   //save pointer
09             Names[nextfree].pointer = null
10             start = nextfree
11             nextfree = temp
12          else
13             p = start

14             if newName < Names[p].name then    //insert at front
                                                       of list
15                Names[nextfree].pointer = start
16                start = nextfree
17             else

18                placeFound = false // general case
19                while Names[p].pointer != null and placeFound = false
20                //peek ahead
21                   if newName >= Names[Names[p].pointer].name then
22                      p = Names[p].pointer
23                   else
24                      placefound = True
25                   endif
26                endwhile
27
28                temp = nextfree
29                nextfree = Names[temp].pointer      //update nextfree…
30                Names[temp].pointer = Names[p].pointer
31                Names[p].pointer = temp    //…and pointer in free  list
32             endif
33          endif
34    endprocedure
```

7-35

Deleting an item

Returning to the table as in Figure 36.4, shown again below, we will delete Johnson.

index	name	pointer	
0	Browning	3	
1	Turner	null	**start = 0**
2	Johnson	1	
3	Cray	2	**nextfree = 4**
4		5	
5		null	

Figure 35.6

```
follow the pointers until Johnson is found
change Cray's pointer to point to Turner
change Johnson's pointer to nextfree
change nextfree to point to Johnson
```

This is shown diagrammatically below.

Before deletion:

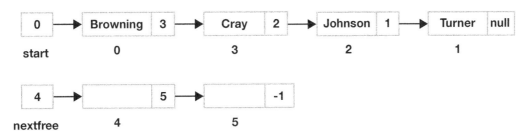

After deletion

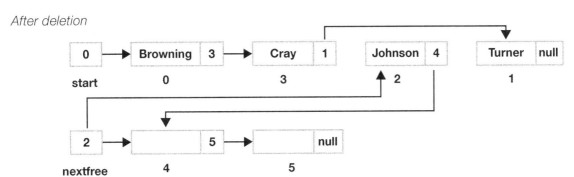

Figure 35.7

Here is the simplified algorithm:

```
p = start
follow pointers until Names[p].pointer points to the name to delete
temp = Names[p].pointer                    //put 2 in temp
Names[p].pointer = Names[temp].pointer     //put 1 in Cray's pointer
                                             field
Names[temp].pointer = nextfree             //put 4 in Johnson's pointer
                                             field
nextfree = temp                            //put 2 in nextfree
```

7-35

Q8: Draw a diagram similar to Figure 35.5 to show the steps taken to adjust the pointers. What are the special cases that the "Delete Item" algorithm will need to deal with?

Q9: Write an algorithm to count and print the number of items in the linked list **Names**.

Pseudocode algorithm for deleting an item

The following algorithm handles exceptions such as inserting into an empty list and deleting the first item in the list. It also returns the empty space to the front of the free space list.

```
01    procedure deleteItem(deleteName)
02    // check for empty list
03      if start = null then
04        print ("List is empty")
05      else
06        p = start
07        if deleteName = Names[start].name then
08          start = Names[start].pointer
09        else
10          while deleteName != Names[Names[p].pointer].name
11            p = Names[p].pointer
12          endwhile
13        endif
14        //Names[p].pointer now points to the node to be deleted
15        //adjust the pointers
16        temp = Names[p].pointer
17        Names[p].pointer = Names[temp].pointer
18        Names[temp] = nextfree
19        nextfree = temp
20      endif
21    endprocedure
```

7-35

A

198

Exercises

1. A list data structure can be represented using an array.

   The pseudocode algorithm below can be used to carry out one useful operation on a list.

   ```
   p = 1
   if ListLength > 0 then
       while p <= ListLength AND List[p] < NewItem
           p = p + 1
       endwhile
       for q = ListLength downTo p
           List[q + 1] = List[q]
       next q
   endif
   List[p] = NewItem
   ListLength = ListLength + 1
   ```

   (a) The initial values of the variables for one particular execution of the algorithm are shown in the trace table below, labelled **Table 1**.

   Draw the trace table for the execution of the algorithm. The first line is given and you will need to draw extra rows.

   Table 1

ListLength	NewItem	p	q	List [1]	[2]	[3]	[4]	[5]
4	25	-	-	18	21	42	53	

   [4]

A-Level only

   (b) Describe the purpose of the algorithm in Figure 1. [1]

   (c) A list implemented using an array is a static data structure. The list could be implemented using a linked list as a dynamic data structure instead.

   Describe **one** difference between a static data structure and a dynamic data structure. [1]

2. (a) The birds Robin, Sparrow, Blackbird, are entered, in the order given, into a linked list so that they may be processed alphabetically. Draw a diagram of this linked list. [2]

   (b) Redraw the diagram after two additional items, Chaffinch and Goldfinch, are added. [2]

   (c) Show the list implemented in an array of records, with each node holding a data item and a pointer, after the addition of the new items. [4]

   (d) Write a pseudocode algorithm to print out the birds in the list in alphabetical order. [4]

Chapter 36 – Stacks

Objectives

- Be familiar with the concept and uses of a stack
- Be able to describe the creation and maintenance of data within a stack
- **(A)** Be able to describe and apply the following operations: push, pop, peek (or top), test for empty stack, test for full stack
- **(A)** Be able to explain how a stack frame is used with subroutine calls to store return addresses, parameters and local variables

Concept of a stack

A **stack** is a Last In, First Out (**LIFO**) data structure. This means that, like a stack of plates in a cafeteria, items are added to the top and removed from the top.

Applications of stacks

A stack is an important data structure in Computing. Stacks are used in calculations, and to hold return addresses when subroutines are called. When you use the **Back** button in your Web browser, you will be taken back through the previous pages that you looked at, in reverse order as their URLs are removed from the stack and reloaded. When you use the **Undo** button in a word processing package, the last operation you carried out is popped from the stack and undone.

Implementation of a stack

A stack may be implemented as either a **static** or **dynamic** data structure.

A static data structure such as an **array** can be used with two additional variables, one being a pointer to the top of the stack and the other holding the size of the array (the maximum size of the stack).

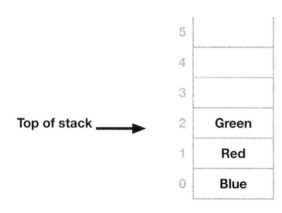

Operations on a stack

The following operations are required to implement a stack:

- push(item)   adds a new item to the top of the stack
- pop()   removes and returns the top item from the stack
- peek()   returns the top item from the stack but does not remove it
- isEmpty()   tests to see whether the stack is empty, and returns a Boolean value
- isFull()   tests to see whether the stack is full, and returns a Boolean value

Stack operation	Stack contents	Return value
s.isEmpty()	[]	True
s.push('Blue')	['Blue']	
s.push('Red')	['Blue', 'Red']	
.push('Green')	['Blue', 'Red', 'Green']	
s.isEmpty	['Blue', 'Red', 'Green']	False
s.peek()	['Blue', 'Red', 'Green']	'Green'
s.pop()	['Blue', 'Red']	'Green'
s.size()	['Blue', 'Red']	2

A-Level only

7-36

The following pseudocode implements four of the stack operations using a fixed size array.

```
function isEmpty
   if top == -1 then
      return True
   else
      return False
   endif
endfunction

function isFull
   if top == maxSize then
      return True
   else
      return False
   endif
endfunction

procedure push(item)
   if isFull then
      print("Stack is full")
   else
      top = top + 1
      s(top)= item
   endif
endprocedure
```

```
function pop
   if isEmpty then
      print("Stack is empty")
   else
      item = s(top)
      top = top - 1
      return item
   endif
endfunction
```

Q1: Write pseudocode for a "peek" function.

Q2: Show the state of the stack and stack pointer after the following operations have been performed on the stack containing ('Blue', 'Red'):
- (i)   Pop
- (ii)   Pop
- (iii)   Push('Yellow')

Some languages, such as Python, make it very easy to implement a stack using the built-in dynamic `list` data structure, with the top of the stack being the last element of the list.

The function `len(s)` can be used to determine whether the stack is empty, and if it is not, `pop()` will remove and return the top element. The built-in method `append(item)` will append or push an item onto the top of the stack (the last element of the list).

Overflow and underflow

A stack will always have a maximum size, because memory cannot grow indefinitely. If the stack is implemented as an array, a full stack can be tested for by examining the value of the stack pointer. An attempt to push another item onto the stack would cause **overflow** so an error message can be given to the user to avoid this. Similarly, if the stack pointer is -1, the stack is empty and **underflow** will occur if an attempt is made to pop an item.

Functions of a call stack

A major use of the stack data structure is to store information about the active subroutines while a computer program is running. The details are hidden from the user in all high level languages.

Holding return addresses

The **call stack** keeps track of the address of the instruction that control should return to when a subroutine ends (the **return address**). Several subroutines may be nested, so that the stack may contain several return addresses which will be popped as each subroutine completes. For example, a subroutine which draws a robot may call subroutines `drawCircle`, `drawRectangle` etc. Subroutine `drawRectangle` may in turn call a subroutine `drawLine`.

A recursive subroutine may contain several calls to itself, so that with each call, a new item (the return address) is pushed onto the stack. When the recursion finally ends, the return addresses that have been pushed onto the stack each time the routine is called are popped one after the other, each time the end of the subroutine is reached. If the programmer makes an error and the recursion never ends, sooner or later memory will run out, the stack will overflow and the program will crash.

Holding parameters

Parameters required for a subroutine (such as, for example, the centre coordinates, line colour and thickness for a circle subroutine) may be held on the call stack. Each call to a subroutine will be given separate space on the call stack for these values.

Local variables

A subroutine frequently uses local variables which are accessible and usable only within the subroutine. These may also be held in the call stack. Each separate call to a subroutine gets its own space for its local variables. Storing local variables on the call stack is much more efficient than using dynamic memory allocation, which uses **heap** space.

The stack frame

A call stack is composed of stack frames. Each stack frame corresponds to a call to a subroutine which has not yet terminated.

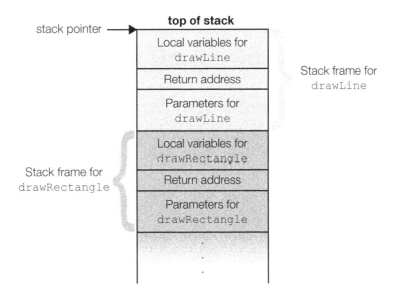

7-36

Exercises

1. A Last In, First Out (LIFO) data structure has a pointer called **top**.

    (a) What is this type of data structure known as? [1]

    (b) Name and briefly describe one type of error that could occur when attempting to add a data item or remove a data item from the data structure. [2]

    (c) Describe briefly **one** use of this type of data structure in a computer system. [2]

    (d) Write a pseudocode procedure for reversing the elements of a queue with the aid of a stack. [6]

A-Level only

Chapter 37 – Hash tables

Objectives

- **(A)** • Be familiar with a hash table and its uses
- **(A)** • Be able to apply simple hashing algorithms
- **(A)** • Know what is meant by a collision and how collisions are handled using rehashing
- **(A)** • Be familiar with the concept of a dictionary
- **(A)** • Be familiar with simple applications of a dictionary

Hashing

Large collections of data, for example customer records in a database, need to be accessible very quickly without having to look through all the records. This can be done by holding an index of the physical address on the file where the data is held. But how is the **index** created?

The answer is that a **hashing algorithm** is applied to the value in the key field of each record to transform it into an address. Normally there are many more possible keys than actual records that need to be stored. For example, if 300 records are to be stored, each having a unique 6-digit identifier or key, 1000 free spaces may be allocated to store the records.

One common hashing algorithm is to divide the key by the number of available addresses and take the remainder as the address. Using the algorithm (address = key mod 1000):

453781   would be stored at address 781

447883   would be stored at address 883

134552   would be stored at address 552

What will happen when the record with key 631552 is to be stored? This will hash to the same address as 134552 and is called a **synonym**. Synonyms are bound to occur with any hashing algorithm, and two record keys hashing to the same address is referred to as a **collision**.

A simple way of dealing with collisions is to store the item in the next available free space. Thus 134552 would be stored at address 553, assuming this space is unoccupied.

Hash table

A hash table is a collection of items stored in such a way that they can quickly be located. The hash table could be implemented as an array or list of a given size with a number of empty spaces. An empty hash table that can store a maximum of 11 items is shown below, with spaces labelled 0,1, 2,...10.

0	1	2	3	4	5	6	7	8	9	10
Empty	Empty	Empty	Empty	Empty	Empty	Empty	Empty	Empty	Empty	Empty

Now assume we wish to store items 78, 55, 34, 19 and 29 in the table using the method described above, using division by 11 and taking the remainder. Collisions are stored in the next available free slot.

First of all, calculate the hash value of each item to be stored.

7-37

A-Level only

Item	Hash value
78	1
55	0
34	1
19	8
29	7

Each of these items can now be inserted into their location in the hash table.

0	1	2	3	4	5	6	7	8	9	10
55	78	34	Empty	Empty	Empty	Empty	29	19	Empty	Empty

Q1: Which of the items has caused a collision?

Searching for an item

When searching for an item, these steps are followed:

- apply the hashing algorithm to the key field of the item

- examine the resulting cell in the list

- if the item is there, return the item

- if the cell is empty, the item is not in the table

- if there is another item in that spot, keep moving forward until either the item is found or a blank cell is encountered, when it is apparent that the item is not in the table

Other hashing algorithms

To be as efficient as possible, the hashing algorithm needs to be chosen so that it generates the least number of collisions. This will depend to some extent on the distribution of the items to be hashed.

Folding method

There are many other algorithms for determining hash values. The **folding** method divides the item into equal parts, and adds the parts to give the hash value. For example, a phone number 01543 677896 can be divided into groups of two, namely 01, 54, 36, 77, 89, 6. Adding these together, we get 263. If the table has fewer spaces than the maximum possible sum generated by this method, say 100 cells, then the extra step of dividing by 100 needs to be applied.

Q2: Using the folding method and division by 100, complete the hash table below to show where each number will be stored in a table of 100 spaces. (A sample 123456 is done for you.)
(i) 238464   (ii) 188947   (iii) 276084

Item	"Folded" value	Remainder	Location in hash table
123456	12+34+56=102	2	2
238464			
188947			
276084			

A-Level only

Hashing a string

A hash function can be created for alphanumeric strings by using the ASCII code for each character. A portion of the ASCII table is shown below:

Character	ASCII value
A	65
B	66
C	67
D	68
E	69
F	70
G	71

To hash the word CAB, we could add up the ASCII values for each letter and, if there are 11 spaces in the hash table, for example, divide by 11 and take the remainder as its hash value.

$$67 + 65 + 66 = 198 \qquad \text{Hash value} = 198 \bmod 11 = 0$$

so CAB goes in location 0 (assuming that location is empty).

Q3: (i) Using the above hashing algorithm, find the hash values of the following: BAG, TEA, EAT, GAB. (ASCII code for 'T' = 84)

(ii) What do you notice about the hash values associated with these words?

(iii) Can you suggest a modification of the hashing algorithm that may result in fewer collisions?

Collision resolution

The fuller the hash table becomes, the more likely it is that there will be collisions, and this needs to be taken into account when designing the hashing algorithm and deciding on the table size. For example, the size of the table could be designed so that when all the items are stored, only 70% of the table's cells are occupied.

Rehashing is the name given to the process of finding an empty slot when a collision has occurred. The rehashing algorithm used above simply looks for the next empty slot. It will loop round to the first cell if the table of the end is reached. A variation on this would be to look at every third cell, for example (the "plus 3" rehash). Alternatively, the hash value could be incremented by 1, 3, 5, 7... until a free space is found.

Different hashing and rehashing methods will work more efficiently on different data sets – the aim is to minimise collisions.

Uses of hash tables

Hash tables are primarily used for efficient lookup, so that for example an index would typically be organised as a hash table. A hash table could be used to look up, say a person's telephone number given their name, or vice versa. They can also be used to store data such as user codes and encrypted passwords that need to be looked up and verified quickly.

Hash tables are used in the implementation of the data structure called a **dictionary**, which is discussed below. A dictionary is a useful data structure for implementing **graphs**, introduced in the next chapter.

7-37

Dictionaries

A dictionary is an abstract data type consisting of associated pairs of items, where each pair consists of a **key** and a **value**. It is a built-in data structure in Python and Visual Basic, for example. When the user supplies the key, the associated value is returned. Items can easily be amended, added to or removed from the dictionary as required.

In Python, dictionaries are written as comma-delimited pairs in the format key:value and enclosed in curly braces. For example:

```
IDs = {342:'Harry', 634:'Jasmine', 885:'Max',571:'Sheila'}
```

Operations on dictionaries

It is possible to implement a dictionary using either a static or a dynamic data structure. The implementation needs to include the following operations:

- Create a new empty dictionary

- Add a new `key:value` pair to the dictionary

- Delete a `key:value` pair from the dictionary

- Amend the value in a `key:value` pair

- Return a value associated with key k

- Return `True` or `False` depending on whether key is in the dictionary

- Return the length of the dictionary, i.e. the number of `key:value` pairs

An interactive Python session is shown below:

```
>>> IDs = {342:'Harry', 634:'Jasmine', 885:'Max', 571:'Sheila'}
>>> IDs
{634: 'Jasmine', 571: 'Sheila', 885: 'Max', 342: 'Harry'}
>>> IDs[885]
'Max'
>>> IDs[333] = 'Maria'
>>> IDs
{634: 'Jasmine', 571: 'Sheila', 885: 'Max', 342: 'Harry', 333: 'Maria'}
>>> IDs[885] = 'Maxine'
>>> IDs
{634: 'Jasmine', 571: 'Sheila', 885: 'Maxine', 342: 'Harry', 333:
'Maria'}
>>> del IDs[885]
>>> IDs
{634: 'Jasmine', 571: 'Sheila', 342: 'Harry', 333: 'Maria'}
>>> 634 in IDs
True
>>> len(IDs)
4
```

Note that the pairs are not held in any particular sequence. The key is hashed using a hashing algorithm and placed at the resulting location in a hash table, so that a fast lookup is possible.

7-37

A

A-Level only

Exercises

1. Student records held by a school are stored in a database which organises the data in files using hashing.

   (a) In the context of storing data in a file, explain what a hash function is. [1]

   (b) The system allows for a maximum of 1000 unique 6-digit integer student IDs in the file holding current student records. Give an example of a hashing function that could be used to find a particular record. Ignore collisions. [2]

2. A bank has a number of safety deposit boxes in which customers can store valuable documents or possessions. The details of which box is rented by a customer with a particular account number are held in a dictionary data structure. Sample entries in the dictionary are:

   {0083456: 'C11', 0154368: 'B74', 1178612: 'B6', 0567123: 'A34'}

   (a) What value will be returned by a lookup operation using the key 1178612? [1]

   (b) The dictionary is implemented using a hash table, using the algorithm

   accountNumber mod 500

   What value is returned by the hashing function when it is applied to account number 0093421? [1]

   (c) What is the maximum number of entries that can be made in the dictionary? [1]

   (d) (i) Explain what is meant by a collision. [1]

   (ii) Give an example of how a collision might occur in this scenario, using sample account numbers. [2]

   (iii) Describe **one** way of dealing with collisions in the hash table. [1]

7-37

A

Chapter 38 – Graphs

Objectives

- (A) • Be aware of a graph as a data structure used to represent complex relationships
- (A) • Be familiar with typical uses for graphs
- (A) • Be able to explain the terms: graph, weighted graph, vertex/node, edge/arc, undirected graph, directed graph
- (A) • Know how an adjacency matrix and an adjacency list may be used to represent a graph
- (A) • Be able to compare the use of adjacency matrices and adjacency lists

Definition of a graph

A graph is a set of **vertices** or **nodes** connected by **edges** or **arcs**. The edges may be one-way or two way. In an **undirected graph**, all edges are bidirectional. If the edges in a graph are all one-way, the graph is said to be a **directed graph** or **digraph**.

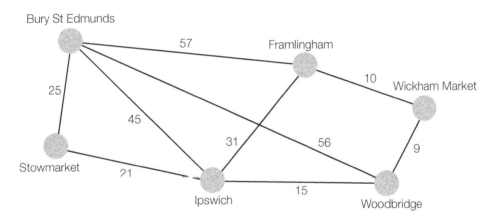

Figure 38.1: An undirected graph with weighted edges

The edges may be **weighted** to show there is a cost to go from one vertex to another as in Figure 38.1. The weights in this example represent distances between towns. A human driver can find their way from one town to another by following a map, but a computer needs to represent the information about distances and connections in a structured, numerical representation.

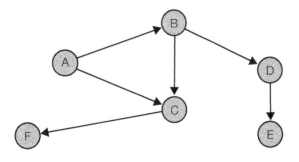

Figure 38.2: A directed, unweighted graph

7-38

Implementing a graph

Two possible implementations of a graph are the **adjacency matrix** and the **adjacency list**.

The adjacency matrix

A two-dimensional array can be used to store information about a directed or undirected graph. Each of the rows and columns represents a node, and a value stored in the cell at the intersection of row i, column j indicates that there is an edge connecting node i and node j.

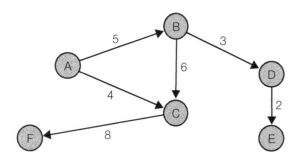

	A	B	C	D	E	F
A		5	4			
B			6	3		
C						8
D					2	
E						
F						

In the case of an **undirected graph**, the adjacency matrix will be symmetric, with the same entry in (0,1) as in (1,0), for example.

An unweighted graph may be represented with 1s instead of weights, in the relevant cells.

Q1: Draw an adjacency matrix to represent the weighted graph shown in Figure 38.1.

Advantages and disadvantages of the adjacency matrix

An adjacency matrix is very convenient to work with, and adding an edge is very simple. However, a sparse graph with many nodes but not many edges will leave most of the cells empty, and the larger the graph, the more memory space will be wasted. Another consideration is that using a static two-dimensional array, it is harder to add or delete nodes.

The adjacency list

An adjacency list is a more space-efficient way to implement a sparsely connected graph. A list of all the nodes is created, and each node points to a list of all the adjacent nodes to which it is directly linked. The adjacency list can be implemented as a list of dictionaries, with the key in each dictionary being the node and the value, the edge weight.

The graph above would be represented as follows:

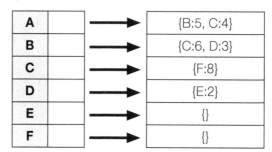

A	→	{B:5, C:4}
B	→	{C:6, D:3}
C	→	{F:8}
D	→	{E:2}
E	→	{}
F	→	{}

The unweighted graph in Figure 38.2 would be represented as shown below, with the adjacency list containing lists of nodes adjacent to each node. A dictionary data structure is not required here as there are no edge weights.

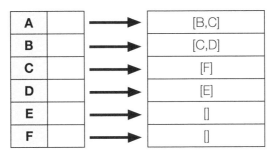

The advantage of this implementation is that is uses much less memory to represent a sparsely connected graph.

Q2: Draw an adjacency list to represent the unweighted graph shown in Figure 38.2, but assuming this time that it is undirected.

Traversing a graph

There are two ways to traverse a graph so that every node is visited.

- A **depth-first** traversal
- A **breadth-first** traversal

Depth-first traversal

In this traversal, we go as far down one route as we can before backtracking and taking the next route.

Consider the following graph:

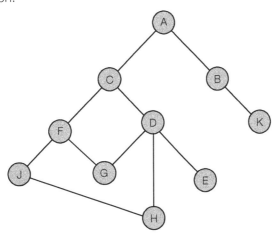

Figure 38.3

Starting at A, we can either go left or right. We will choose to go left whenever there is a choice of routes.

We visit C, F, J, H, D, G. We have already visited F so we have reached the end of this path. Back up to D and visit E. Now we must retrace our steps via D, H, J, F, C, to A, and go down the alternative route to B and K.

A-Level only

Nodes were visited in the order A C F J H D G E B K.

This sequence involved some choices, so is not unique. Another depth-first route would be

A C D E H J F G B K.

Q3: Find another route that visits all nodes in a depth-first search.

Breadth-first search

With a breadth-first traversal, we visit all the neighbours of a node, and then all the neighbours of the first node visited, all the neighbours of the second node and so on, before moving further away from the start node.

Consider the graph below:

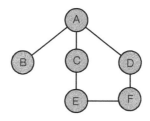

Figure 38.4

Starting at A, we visit B, then C, then D (or we could have started by visiting C or D).

Then we move to B, which has no neighbours, so we back up to A and go to C. From C, we visit E before returning to A. Next, we go to D and visit F. All nodes have now been visited, in the order A B C D E F.

Q4: Find another route that visits all nodes in a breadth-first search.

Q5: Write down a possible route through the graph in Figure 38.3 using a breadth-first search.

Applications of graphs

Graphs may be used to represent, for example:

*   computer networks, with nodes representing computers and weighted edges representing the bandwidth between them

*   roads between towns, with edge weights representing distances, rail fares or journey times

*   tasks in a project, some of which have to be completed before others

*   web pages and links (see Google's PageRank algorithm in Section 5)

7-38

A

A-Level only

Exercises

1. The figure below shows an adjacency matrix representation of a directed graph (digraph).

From \ To	A	B	C	D	E
A	0	5	3	10	0
B	0	0	1	8	0
C	0	0	0	7	6
D	0	0	0	0	4
E	0	0	0	0	0

(a) Draw a diagram of the directed graph, showing edge weights. [3]

(b) Draw an adjacency list representing this graph. [3]

(c) Give **one** advantage of using an adjacency matrix to represent a graph, and **one** advantage of using an adjacency list. Explain the circumstances in which each is more appropriate. [4]

2. An undirected graph is shown below.

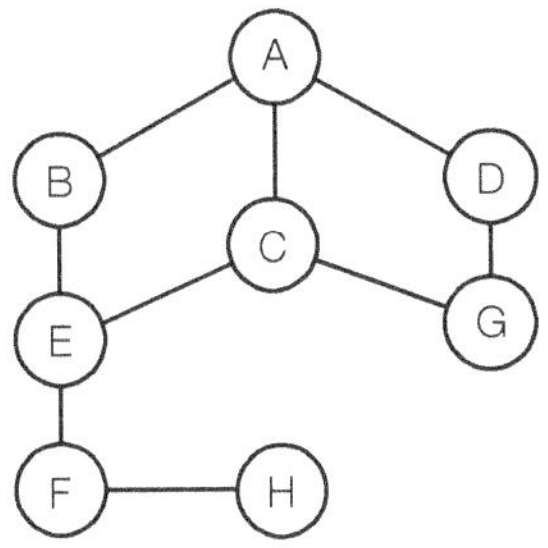

(a) Complete the adjacency matrix below to represent this graph. [4]

	A	B	C	D	E	F	G	H
A	0	1	0	1	0	0	0	0
B	1	0	0	0	1	0	0	0
C	1	0	0	0	1	0	1	0
D	1	0	0	0	0	0	1	0
E	0	1	1	0	0	1	0	0
F	0	0	0	0	1	0	0	1
G	0	0	1	1	0	0	0	0
H	0	0	0	0	0	1	0	0

(b) List the nodes in the order in which they would be visited using

(i) a depth-first search [3]

(ii) a breadth-first search [3]

7-38

A

A-Level only

Chapter 39 – Trees

Objectives

Ⓐ • Define a binary tree as a rooted tree in which each node has at most two children

Ⓐ • Create and traverse a binary tree

Ⓐ • create, search and traverse a binary search tree

Concept of a tree

Trees are a very common data structure in many areas of computer science and other contexts. Like a tree in nature, a **rooted tree** has a root, branches and leaves, the difference being that a tree in computer science has its root at the top and its leaves at the bottom.

Typical uses for rooted trees include:

• manipulating hierarchical data, such as folder structures or moves in a game

• making information easy to search (see binary tree search below)

• manipulating sorted lists of data

Generations of a family may be thought of as having a tree structure:

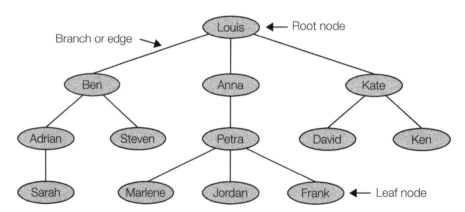

The tree shown above has a **root node**, and is therefore defined as a **rooted tree**. Here are some terms used in connection with rooted trees:

Node: The nodes contain the tree data

Edge: An edge connects two nodes. Every node except the root is connected by exactly one edge from another node

Root: This is the only node that has no incoming edges

Child: The set of nodes that have incoming edges from the same node

Parent: A node is a parent of all the nodes it connects to with outgoing edges

Subtree: The set of nodes and edges comprised of a parent and all descendants of the parent. A subtree may also be a leaf

Leaf node: A node that has no children

Q1: Identify the leftmost subtree, the parent of Frank and the children of Kate. How many parent nodes are there in the tree? How many child nodes?

Note that a rooted tree is a special case of a **connected graph**. A node can only be connected to one parent node, and to its children. It is described as having has no **cycles** because there can be no connection between children, or between branches, for example from Ben to Anna or Petra to Kate.

A binary search tree

A **binary tree** is a rooted tree in which each node has a maximum of two children. A **binary search tree** holds items in such a way that the tree can be searched quickly and easily for a particular item, new items can be easily added, and the whole tree can be printed out in sequence. A binary search tree is a typical use of a rooted tree.

Constructing a binary search tree

Suppose the following list of numbers is to be inserted into a binary tree, in the order given, in such a way that the tree can be quickly searched.

17, 8, 4, 12, 22, 19, 14, 5, 30, 25

The tree is constructed using the following algorithm:

Place the first item at the root. Then for each item in the list, visit the root, which becomes the current node, and branch left if the item is less than the value at the current node, and right if the item is greater than the value at the current node. Continue down the branch, applying the rule at each node visited, until a leaf node is reached. The item is then placed to the left or right of this node, depending on whether it is less than or greater than the value at that node.

Following this algorithm, 17 is placed at the root. 8 is less than 17, so is placed at a new node to the left of the root.

4 is less than 17, so we branch left at the root, branch left at 8, and place it to the left.

12 is less than 17, so we branch left at the root, branch right at 8, and place it to the right.

The final tree looks like this:

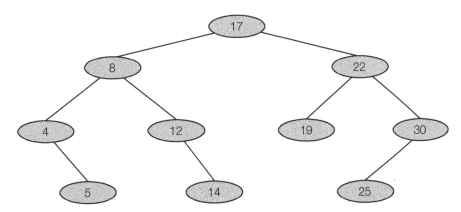

To search the tree for the number 19, for example, we follow the same steps.

19 is greater than 17, so branch right.

19 is less than 22, so branch left. There it is!

A-Level only

Q2: (a) Which nodes will be visited when searching for the number 14?

(b) Which nodes will be visited when searching for the number 21, which is not in the tree?

(c) Where will new nodes 10 and 20 be inserted?

Traversing a binary tree

There are three ways of traversing a tree:

- Pre-order traversal

- In-order traversal

- Post-order traversal

The names refer to whether the root of each sub-tree is visited before, between or after both branches have been traversed.

Pre-order traversal

Draw an outline around the tree structure, starting to the left of the root. As you pass to the left of a node (where the red dot is marked), output the data in that node.

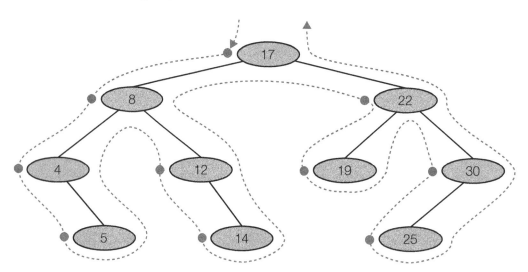

The nodes will be visited in the sequence 17, 8, 4, 5, 12, 14, 22, 19, 30, 25

A pre-order traversal may be used to produce prefix notation, used in functional programming languages. A simple illustration would be a function statement, x = sum a,b rather than x = a + b, in which the operation comes before the operands rather than between them, as in infix notation.

In-order traversal

Draw an outline around the tree structure, starting to the left of the root. As you pass underneath a node (where the red dot is marked), output the data in that node.

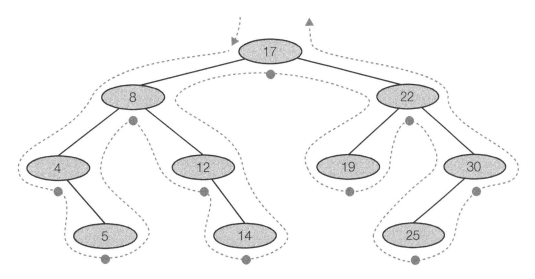

The nodes will be visited in the sequence 4, 5, 8, 12, 14, 17, 19, 22, 25, 30.

The in-order traversal visits the nodes in sequential order.

Q3: Construct a binary search tree to hold the names Mark, Stephanie, Chigozie, Paul, Anne, Hanna, Luke, David, Vincent, Tom. List the names, in the order they would be checked, to find David.

Q4: List the names in the order they would be output when an in-order traversal is performed.

Post-order traversal

Draw an outline around the tree structure, starting to the left of the root. As you pass to the right of a node (where the red dot is marked), output the data in that node.

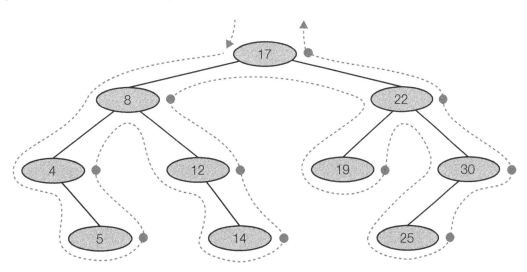

The nodes will be visited in the sequence 5, 4, 14, 12, 8, 19, 25, 30, 22, 17.

Implementation of a binary search tree

A binary search tree can be implemented using an array of records, with each node consisting of:

- left pointer
- data item
- right pointer

Alternatively, it could be held in a list of tuples, or three separate lists or arrays, one for each of the pointers and one for the data items.

The numbers 17, 8, 4, 14, 22, 19, 12, 5, 30, 25 used to construct the tree above could be held as follows:

	left	data	right
tree[0]	1	17	4
tree[1]	2	8	6
tree[2]	-1	4	7
tree[3]	-1	14	-1
tree[4]	5	22	8
tree[5]	-1	19	-1
tree[6]	-1	12	3
tree[7]	-1	5	-1
tree[8]	9	30	-1
tree[9]	-1	25	-1

For example, the left pointer in tree[0] points to tree[1] and the right pointer points to tree[4]. The value -1 is a 'rogue value' which indicates that there is no child on the relevant side (left or right).

Q5: Show how the search tree below could be implemented in an array with left and right pointers.

Names were inserted in the tree in the following order: Monkey, Topi, Ostrich, Giraffe, Hippo, Zebra, Buffalo, Cheetah, Rhino, Baboon, Jackal

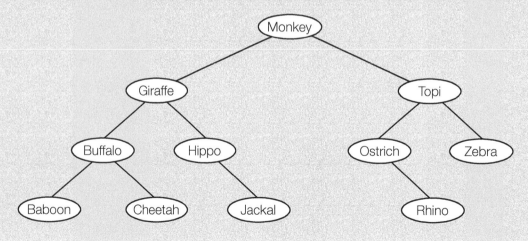

Tree traversal algorithms

We have looked at three tree traversal algorithms: in-order, pre-order and post-order. The pseudocode algorithm for each of these traversals is **recursive**. If you have not yet covered recursion, you may like to leave the pseudocode algorithms to be covered at a later date.

The algorithm for an in-order traversal is

```
traverse the left subtree
visit the root node
traverse the right subtree
```

Example of in-order traversal

An algebraic expression is represented by the following binary tree. It could be represented in memory as, for example, three 1-dimensional arrays or as a list with each list element holding the data and left and right pointers to the left and right subtrees. The value of the root node is stored as the first element of the list.

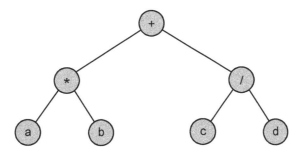

Figure 39.1

Suppose this data is held as shown below:

	left	data	right
tree[0]	1	+	2
tree[1]	3	*	4
tree[2]	5	/	6
tree[3]	-1	a	-1
tree[4]	-1	b	-1
tree[5]	-1	c	-1
tree[6]	-1	d	-1

In pseudocode:

```
procedure inorderTraverse(p)
   if tree[p].left != -1 then
      inorderTraverse(tree[p].left)
   endif
   print(tree[p].data)
   if tree[p].right != -1 then
      inorderTraverse(tree[p].right)
   endif
endprocedure
```

7-39

A-Level only

The routine is called with a statement `inorderTraverse(0)`

Tracing through the algorithm, the nodes are output in the order **a * b + c / d**

Use of in-order traversal algorithm

An in-order traversal is used with a binary search tree, to perform an efficient search for any item.

Algorithm for post-order traversal

The algorithm for a post-order traversal is

```
traverse the left subtree
traverse the right subtree
visit the root node
```

In pseudocode:

```
procedure postorderTraverse(p)
   if tree[p].left != -1 then
      postorderTraverse(tree[p].left)
   endif
   if tree[p].right != -1 then
      postorderTraverse(tree[p].right)
   endif
   print(tree[p].data)
endprocedure
```

The nodes are output in the sequence **a b * c d / +**. This is the sequence in which algebraic expressions are written using **Reverse Polish Notation**, which is used by compilers to evaluate expressions.

Algorithm for pre-order traversal

The algorithm for a pre-order traversal is

```
visit the root node
traverse the left subtree
traverse the right subtree
```

In pseudocode:

```
procedure preorderTraverse(p)
   print(tree[p].data)
   if tree[p].left != -1 then
      preorderTraverse(tree[p].left)
   endif
   if tree[p].right != -1 then
      preorderTraverse(tree[p].right)
   endif
endprocedure
```

A pre-order traversal may be used for producing a prefix expression from an expression tree such as the one shown in Figure 39.1. Prefix is used in some compilers and calculators.

Exercises

1. Data may be stored as a binary tree.

    (a) Show how the following data may be stored as a binary tree for subsequent processing in alphabetic order by drawing the tree. Assume that the first item is the root of the tree and the rest of the data items are inserted into the tree in the order given,

    Data items: magpie, robin, chaffinch, linnet, thrush, blackbird, fieldfare, skylark, pigeon. [3]

    (b) Show how the data could be represented using three one-dimensional arrays. [3]

    (c) List the order that the nodes would be visited using

    (i) a pre-order traversal [2]

    (ii) an in-order traversal [2]

    (iii) a post-order traversal [2]

2. In what order should the following tree be traversed so that each section and subsection is printed in the correct sequence? [1]

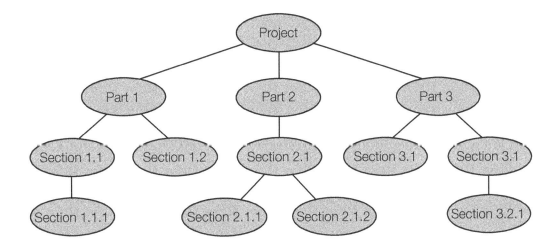

7-39

A

221

Section 8

Boolean algebra

In this section:

8

Chapter 40 – Logic gates and truth tables

Objectives

- Construct a truth table for a variety of logic gates
- Be familiar with drawing and interpreting logic gate circuit diagrams involving multiple gates
- Complete a truth table for a given logic gate circuit
- Write a Boolean expression for a given logic gate circuit
- Draw an equivalent logic gate circuit for a given Boolean expression
- Define problems using Boolean logic

Binary logic

At the most elementary level, an electronic device can only recognise the presence or absence of current or voltage. Either electricity is present or it isn't. This is a switch – on or off, true or false, 1 or 0. With a computer's semiconductor, the voltage at the input and output terminals is measured and is either high or low; 1 or 0. Computers comprise billions of these switches and manipulating these sequences of ONs and OFFs can change individual bits.

Electronic logic gates can take one or more inputs and produce a single output. This output can become the input to another gate and a complicated cascaded sequence of logic gates can be implemented to form a circuit in, for example, the CPU.

8-40

Simple logic gates and truth tables

There are a number of different logic gates that are each designed to perform a different operation in terms of output. We will look at NOT, AND, OR and XOR gates.

Each of these gates may be represented by a truth table showing the output for each possible input or combination of inputs. The four gates are shown below. Inputs are usually given algebraic letters such as A, B and C and output is usually represented by P or Q.

NOT gate (negation)

The NOT gate is represented by the symbol below and inverts the input. The small circle denotes an inverted input.

Using 1s and 0s as inputs to a gate, its operation can summarised in the form of a **truth table**.

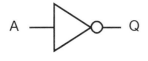

Q = NOT A

Input A	Output Q
0	1
1	0

The Boolean algebraic expression is written: Q = ¬A where ¬ represents NOT.

AND gate (conjunction)

Q = A AND B

Input A	Input B	Output Q
0	0	0
0	1	0
1	0	0
1	1	1

The Boolean expression for AND is written: Q = A ∧ B where ∧ represents AND.

The truth table reflects the fundamental property of the AND gate: the output of A AND B is 1 only if input A and input B are both 1.

OR gate (disjunction)

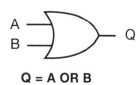

Q = A OR B

Input A	Input B	Output Q
0	0	0
0	1	1
1	0	1
1	1	1

The Boolean expression for OR is written: Q = A ∨ B where ∨ represents OR.

XOR gate (exclusive disjunction)

The XOR (*pronounced ex-or*) gate stands for exclusive OR, meaning that the output will be true if one or other input is true, but not both. Compare this to the OR gate, which will accept two true inputs as true also.

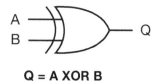

Q = A XOR B

Input A	Input B	Output Q
0	0	0
0	1	1
1	0	1
1	1	0

The Boolean algebraic expression is written: Q = A ⊻ B where the ⊻ represents XOR, and is the equivalent of Q = (A ∧ ¬B) ∨ (¬A ∧ B). This gate is similar to the OR gate but excludes the condition where A and B are both true. XOR is referred to as exclusive OR, and OR is sometimes referred to as inclusive OR.

Creating logic gate circuits

Multiple logic gates can be connected to produce an output based on multiple inputs.

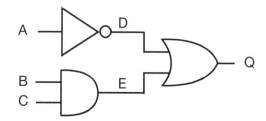

This circuit can be represented by the expression Q = ¬A ∨ (B ∧ C)

or alternatively as Q = (NOT A) OR (B AND C)

The equivalent truth table is shown below:

Input A	Input B	Input C	D = ¬ A	E = B ∧ C	Output Q = D ∨ E
0	0	0	1	0	1
0	0	1	1	0	1
0	1	0	1	0	1
0	1	1	1	1	1
1	0	0	0	0	0
1	0	1	0	0	0
1	1	0	0	0	0
1	1	1	0	1	1

Q1: Draw a truth table for the following circuit:

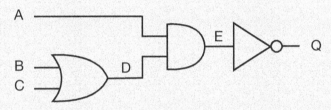

Q2: Show, by drawing a truth table for P = (A ∧ ¬B) ∨ (¬A ∧ B), that P = Q, where Q = A ⊻ B.

Q3: Write the Boolean expression Q = ¬ ((A ⊻ B) ∧ C) using AND, OR, NOT, XOR instead of symbols. Draw the corresponding logic circuit.

Q4: Write the Boolean expression represented by the logic diagram below, using AND, OR and NOT instead of symbols. Then write the same expression using symbols. What is the output if A, B and C are all True?

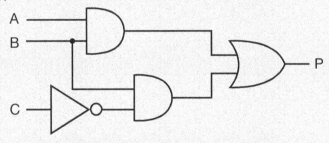

Defining problems using Boolean logic

We can define problems in terms of Boolean logic.

Example 1

A boiler has two sensors, a pressure sensor and a temperature sensor. If either the temperature (T) or the pressure (P) is too high, a valve (V) will close.

This can be expressed as $V = T \lor P$ or alternatively as V = T OR P

The table representing these conditions could be drawn as follows:

Input	Binary value	Condition
T	1	Temperature too high
	0	Temperature not too high
P	1	Pressure too high
	0	Pressure not too high

Example 2

A chemical process has a sensor to detect a dangerous situation, in which case it sounds an alarm (A). The alarm is sounded if:

    either   temperature >= 100°C AND rotator is OFF

    or   PH > 6 AND temperature < 100°C

A table can be drawn to represent these conditions as Boolean values.

Input	Binary value	Condition
T	1	Temperature >= 100°C
	0	Temperature < 100°C
R	1	Rotator ON
	0	Rotator OFF
P	1	PH > 6
	0	PH <= 6

The conditions can be written as

    $A = (T \land \lnot R) \lor (P \land \lnot T)$ or alternatively as A = (T AND NOT R) OR (P AND NOT T)

Now the logic circuit for this process can be drawn as follows:

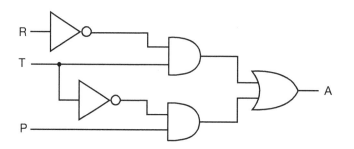

Q5: Draw the truth table for this alarm system.

Exercises

1. (a) Complete the following truth table for the XOR logic gate.

Input A	Input B	Output Q
0	0	
0	1	
1	0	
1	1	

[1]

   (b) Draw logic circuits for the following Boolean expressions:

      (i)   Q = A ⊻ B ∨ ¬B   [3]

      (ii) Q = ¬A ∧ B ∨ C   [3]

      (iii) Q = ¬(A ∨ B) ∨ (A ∧ C)   [3]

2. The figure below shows a logic circuit.

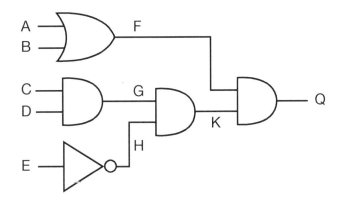

   (a) Write the equivalent Boolean expression.   [4]

   (b) What are the values of F, G, H, K and Q if A, B, C and D and E are all equal 1?   [5]

3. Three sensors A, B and C are used to monitor a process. A signal X is output from the circuit.

   X has the value 1 if either of the following conditions are met:

      Sensor A outputs 1 AND sensor B outputs 0

      Sensor B outputs 1 OR sensor C outputs 0

   Draw a logic circuit to represent these conditions.   [5]

8-40

Chapter 41 – Simplifying Boolean expressions

Objectives

A • Use the following rules to derive or simplify statements in Boolean algebra:
  o de Morgan's Laws
  o commutation
  o association
  o distribution
  o absorption
  o double negation

• Write a Boolean expression for a given logic gate circuit, and vice versa

A-Level only

de Morgan's laws

Augustus de Morgan (1806-1871) was a Cambridge Mathematics professor who formulated two theorems or laws relating to logic. These laws can be used to manipulate and simplify Boolean expressions. Although his theoretical work had little practical application in his lifetime, it became of major significance in the next century in the field of digital electronics, in which TRUE and FALSE can be replaced by ON and OFF or the binary numbers 0 and 1.

Using de Morgan's laws, any Boolean function can be converted to one which uses only NAND functions or only NOR functions, and these can be further converted to an expression using all NAND functions or all NOR functions.

Thus, any integrated circuit can be built from just one type of logic gate. This is an advantage in manufacturing where costs can be kept down by using only one type of gate.

de Morgan's first law

$$\neg(A \lor B) = \neg A \land \neg B$$

The truth of this is clear from the Venn diagram on the right. Suppose we have a variable X defined by

$$X = \neg(A \lor B)$$

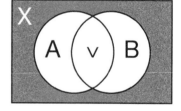

Looking at the Venn diagram, $A \lor B$ is represented by the white area. Since X is not in $A \lor B$, it consists of all the grey area. This can be defined as everything not in A and not in B, i.e.

$$X = \neg A \land \neg B$$

Q1: Complete the following truth table to show that $\neg(A \lor B) = \neg A \land \neg B$

A	B	¬A	¬B	A ∨ B	¬(A ∨ B)	¬A ∧ ¬B
0	0					
0	1					
1	0					
1	1					

de Morgan's second law

$$\neg(A \wedge B) = \neg A \vee \neg B$$

Again, looking at the Venn diagram on the right, if

$$X = \neg(A \wedge B)$$

X cannot be in the white area, so must be in the red, orange, or grey areas. That is, X is either not in A, or not in B, or not in either. This is the definition of

$$X = \neg A \vee \neg B$$

Q2: Complete the following truth table to show that $\neg(A \wedge B) = \neg A \vee \neg B$

A	B	¬A	¬B	A ∧ B	¬(A ∧ B)	¬A ∨ ¬B
0						
0						
1						
1						

To implement each of de Morgan's laws, follow the three steps:

Complement both terms in the expression, e.g. A, B

Change AND to OR and OR to AND

Complement the result

Rules of Boolean algebra

In addition to de Morgan's laws, there are several identities or "rules" which will help you to simplify Boolean expressions. The most useful are listed below.

General rules

1. $X \wedge 0 = 0$
2. $X \wedge 1 = X$
3. $X \wedge X = X$
4. $X \wedge \neg X = 0$
5. $X \vee 0 = X$
6. $X \vee 1 = 1$
7. $X \vee X = X$
8. $X \vee \neg X = 1$

Commutative rule

9. $X \wedge Y = Y \wedge X$
10. $X \vee Y = Y \vee X$

8-41

A-Level only

Associative rules

11. $X \wedge (Y \wedge Z) = (X \wedge Y) \wedge Z$

12. $X \vee (Y \vee Z) = (X \vee Y) \vee Z$

Distributive rules

13. $X \wedge (Y \vee Z) = (X \wedge Y) \vee (X \wedge Z)$

14. $(X \vee Y) \wedge (W \vee Z) = (X \wedge W) \vee (X \wedge Z) \vee (Y \wedge W) \vee (Y \wedge Z)$

Absorption rules

15. $X \vee (X \wedge Y) = X$

16. $X \wedge (X \vee Y) = X$

Double negation

17. $X = \neg \neg X$

Example 1

Use de Morgan's laws and the laws of Boolean algebra to simplify the following Boolean expression:

$$Q = \neg(\neg(X \wedge \neg Y) \wedge (\neg Y \vee \neg Z))$$

Answer: $Q = \neg(\neg(X \wedge \neg Y) \wedge \neg(Y \wedge Z))$ (using de Morgan's second law)

$\quad = (X \wedge \neg Y) \vee (Y \wedge Z)$ (using de Morgan's first law)

Example 2

Use de Morgan's laws to simplify $A \wedge B \vee \neg A \vee \neg B$

Answer: Put brackets between the parts of the expression separated by $\wedge$ (OR)

$(A \wedge B) \vee (\neg A \vee \neg B)$

$= (A \wedge B) \vee \neg(A \wedge B)$ (using de Morgan's first law)

$= 1$ (using Rule 8 above)

Q3: Use de Morgan's laws to simplify $\neg A \vee \neg B \vee \neg(A \vee B)$

Example 3

Use Boolean algebra to show that $(A \vee B) \wedge (A \vee C) = A \vee B \wedge C$

Answer:
$(A \vee B) \wedge (A \vee C) = (A \wedge A) \vee (B \wedge A) \vee (A \wedge C) \vee (B \wedge C)$ (Distributive law)

$= A \vee (B \wedge A) \vee (A \wedge C) \vee (B \wedge C)$ (since $A \wedge A = A$

$= A \vee (A \wedge B) \vee (A \wedge C) \vee (B \wedge C)$ (commutative law)

$= A \vee (A \wedge C) \vee (B \wedge C)$ (Absorption Law)

$= A \vee (B \wedge C)$ (Absorption Law)

Q4: Draw a truth table to show that $(A \vee B) \wedge (A \vee C) = A \vee (B \wedge C)$

Example 4

A single output Q is produced from three inputs X, Y and Z. Q is 1 only if X and Y are 1, or Z is 1 and Y is 0.

Write the Boolean expression to represent this circuit.

Answer: There are two separate logic gates involved here: X ∧ Y, Z ∧ ¬Y.

The output from these two gates are input to an OR gate.

Q = (X ∧ Y) ∨ (Z ∧ ¬Y)

Represent this equation diagrammatically using a combination of AND, OR and NOT gates.

Answer:

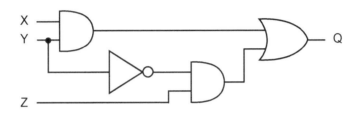

Example 5

Write the Boolean expression corresponding to the following logic circuit.

Answer: A ∨ ¬(B ∧ C)

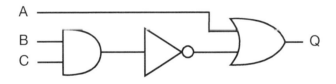

8-41

A

Exercises

1. (a) Write a Boolean expression for P in the logic circuit shown in Figure 1.   [1]

    (b) Write a Boolean expression for R.   [1]

    (c) Draw the truth table for the logic circuit.   [3]

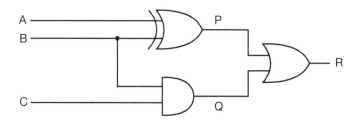

Figure 1

A-Level only

2. Simplify the Boolean expressions below.

    (i)   A ∨ B ∧ (A ∨ ¬B)   [3]

    (ii) ¬(A ∧ B) ∧ (¬A ∨ B) ∧ (¬B ∨ B)   [4]

3. (a) State the names of the logic gates represented by each of the truth tables below.   [2]

Input A	Input B	Output
0	0	0
0	1	0
1	0	0
1	1	1

Logic gate name:

Input A	Input B	Output
0	0	0
0	1	1
1	0	1
1	1	0

Logic gate name:

    (b) Simplify the following Boolean expressions.

    (i)   B ∧ (A ∨ ¬A)   [1]

    (ii) A ∧ B ∨ B   [1]

    (iii) (A ∨ ¬B) ∧ (A ∨ B)   [4]

    (c) Draw a logic circuit for the following Boolean expression:

    Q = A ∧ B ∨ ¬(A ∧ C)   [3]

8-41

232

Chapter 42 – Karnaugh maps

Objectives

- Simplify Boolean expressions using Karnaugh maps

Introduction

A Karnaugh map provides an alternative way of simplifying Boolean expressions which is often easier than using Boolean algebra for those involving up to three or four variables. It is similar to a truth table and allows us to easily detect groupings of expressions with common factors.

The two-variable problem

The figure below shows the correspondence between a truth table and a Karnaugh map.

A	B	P
0	0	a
0	1	b
1	0	c
1	1	d

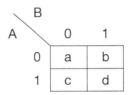

The values inside the squares are copied from the output column of the truth table, so there is one square in the Karnaugh map for every row in the truth table. Suppose we have the following truth table:

Input A	Input B	Output Q
0	0	0
0	1	0
1	0	0
1	1	1

The corresponding Karnaugh map is

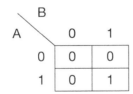

For example, when A = 0 and B = 0, the output is 0. When A = 1 and B = 1, the output is 1.

8-42

Example 1

Use a Karnaugh map to simplify the expression Q = ¬A ∧ ¬B ∨ A ∧ ¬B ∨ ¬A ∧ B

Group the expression into three sub-expressions separated by ∨.

Q = (¬A ∧ ¬B) ∨ (A ∧ ¬B) ∨ (¬A ∧ B)

Draw a blank Karnaugh map and fill in a 1 for the first sub-expression ¬A ∧ ¬B. Then insert a 1 for the second sub-expression A ∧ ¬B. Finally add a 1 for the sub-expression ¬A ∧ B

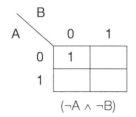
(¬A ∧ ¬B)

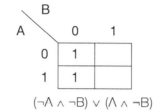
(¬A ∧ ¬B) ∨ (A ∧ ¬B)

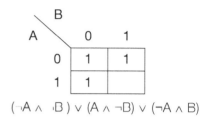
(¬A ∧ ¬B) ∨ (A ∧ ¬B) ∨ (¬A ∧ B)

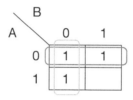

8-42

Now make groupings of 1, 2, or 4 ones, which can be overlapping. Each grouping should be as large as possible – in this case, the two groupings each consist of two squares.

The pink group represents NOT A, and the blue group represents NOT B. Therefore the whole expression represents Q = NOT A OR NOT B, or in alternative notation, ¬A ∨ ¬B.

This is the simplification of the expression Q = ¬A ∧ ¬B ∨ A ∧ ¬B ∨ ¬A ∧ B

Q1: Draw a Karnaugh map representing A ∧ B ∨ A ∧ ¬B, and hence simplify the expression.

The three-variable problem

With three variables, each column can represent a combination of two variables.

Example 2

Represent the expression ¬A ∨ ¬B ∨ A ∧ B ∧ ¬C in a Karnaugh map, and hence simplify the expression.

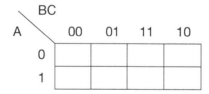

Note: The order of terms along the top is not random: they are arranged so that each subsequent term reflects a change in only one variable. They are not in numerical sequence of 00, 01, 10, 11.

The choice of whether to put A on its own, and group B and C together, or choose a different pair, and put for example C as the column heading and AB as the row heading, is not important, and will produce the same groupings.

First, divide the expression into sub-expressions, bracketing between the ∨ (OR) symbols, giving

(¬A) ∨ (¬B) ∨ (A ∧ B ∧ ¬C)

As before, we can now start filling in the table one step at a time, representing each sub-expression in turn.

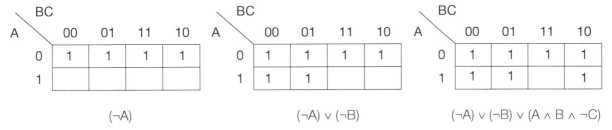

| | (¬A) | | (¬A) ∨ (¬B) | | (¬A) ∨ (¬B) ∨ (A ∧ B ∧ ¬C) |

The next step is to identify the largest groups of 1, 2 4 or 8 ones.

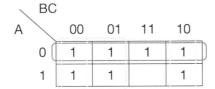

Notice that the green group has "wrapped around" and is counted as one group representing ¬C.

These three groups together represent ¬A ∨ ¬B ∨ ¬C.

This is the simplification of the expression.

8-42

Q2: Use a Karnaugh map to simplify the expression (A ∧ C) ∨ (¬A ∧ B) ∨ (B ∧ C)

Example 3

Use a Karnaugh map to simplify the expression (¬ A ∧ B) ∨ (B ∧ ¬ C) ∨ (B ∧ C) ∨ (A ∧ ¬ B ∧ ¬ C)

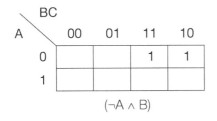

(¬A ∧ B)   (¬A ∧ B) ∨ (B ∧ ¬C)

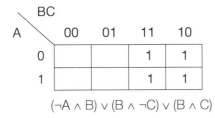

(¬A ∧ B) ∨ (B ∧ ¬C) ∨ (B ∧ C)   (¬A ∧ B) ∨ (B ∧ ¬C) ∨ (B ∧ C) ∨ (A ∧ ¬B ∧ ¬C)

BC				
A	00	01	11	10
0			1	1
1	1		1	1

Here, the group outlined in green "wraps around" but is still a single group. The expression simplifies to

B ∨ (A ∧ ¬C)

Q3: Simplify the same expression as above, (¬ A ∧ B) ∨ (B ∧ ¬ C) ∨ (B ∧ C) ∨ (A ∧ ¬ B ∧ ¬ C), but this time use a Karnaugh map with the following headings:

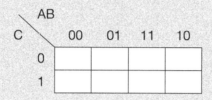

AB				
C	00	01	11	10
0				
1				

The four-variable problem

With four variables, each row or column represents a combination of two variables.

Example 4

Represent the expression A ∨ (A ∧ ¬ B ∧ C ∧ D) in a Karnaugh map, and hence simplify the expression.

CD				
AB	00	01	11	10
00				
01				
11	1	1	1	1
10	1	1	1	1

CD				
AB	00	01	11	10
00				
01				
11	1	1	1	1
10	1	1	1	1

This simplifies to A.

Summary of the Karnaugh map method

1. Construct the Karnaugh map step by step, placing 1s in the squares for each sub-expression separated by an OR symbol (∨)

2. Group any octet (8 squares)

3. Group any quad (4 squares that have not already been grouped, making sure to use the minimum number of groups

4. Group any pair which contains a 1 adjacent to only one other 1 which is not already in a group

5. Group any isolated 1s which are not adjacent to any other 1s.

6. Form the OR sum of all the terms generated by each group.

8-42

Exercises

1. A Karnaugh map is shown below.

AB \ CD	00	01	11	10
00	0	0	0	0
01	0	0	0	0
11	1	1	1	1
10	0	0	0	0

What Boolean expression does this map show?   [1]

2. A Karnaugh map is shown below.

AB \ CD	00	01	11	10
00	0	1	0	0
01	0	1	0	0
11	1	1	1	1
10	1	1	1	1

What Boolean expression does this map show?   [2]

3. Use Karnaugh maps in the format given below to simplify the following expressions:

    (a) (B ∧ C) ∨ (A ∧ C) ∨ (A ∧ B) ∨ (A ∧ ¬B ∧ ¬C)   [3]

    (b) (¬A ∧ B) ∨ (B ∧ ¬C) ∨ (B ∧ C)   [3]

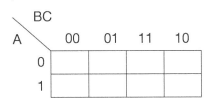

4. Use a Karnaugh map to simplify the following expression.

    (¬ A ∧ ¬B ∧ C ∧ D) ∨ (¬A ∧ B ∧ C ∧ D) ∨ (A ∧ B ∧ C ∧ D) ∨ (A ∧ ¬B ∧ C ∧ D)

        ∨ (A ∧ B ∧ ¬C ∧ ¬D) ∨ (A ∧ B ∧ ¬C ∧ D) ∨ (A ∧ B ∧ C ∧ ¬D)   [4]

Chapter 43 – Adders and D-type flip-flops

Objectives

A • Recognise and trace the logic of the circuits of a half adder and a full adder

A • Construct the circuit for a flip-flop

A • Be familiar with the use of the edge-triggered D-type flip-flop as a memory unit

Performing calculations using gates

With the right combination of gates, it is possible to output the result of a binary addition or subtraction including the value of any carry bit as a second output.

Half adders

A half adder can take an input of two bits and give a two-bit output as the correct result of an addition of the two inputs.

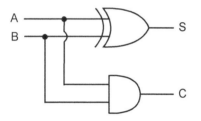

A		B		S	C
0	+	0	=	0	0
0	+	1	=	1	0
1	+	0	=	1	0
1	+	1	=	0	1

This is shown by the diagram above and represented by the truth table where S represents the sum and C represents the carry bit. S can be given as $S = A \veebar B$, and C as $C = A \wedge B$. Although a flip-flop can output the value of a carry bit, it only has two inputs so it cannot use the carry from a previous addition as a third input to a subsequent addition in order to add n-bit numbers.

Full adders

A full adder combines two half adders to add three bits together including the two inputs A and B, and a carry bit C. The logic gate circuit below illustrates how two half adders have been connected with an additional OR gate to output the carry bit.

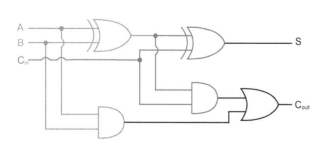

A		B		C_{in}		S	C_{out}
0	+	0	+	0	=	0	0
0	+	0	+	1	=	1	0
0	+	1	+	0	=	1	0
0	+	1	+	1	=	0	1
1	+	0	+	0	=	1	0
1	+	0	+	1	=	0	1
1	+	1	+	0	=	0	1
1	+	1	+	1	=	1	1

Now the Boolean logic becomes $S = A \veebar B \veebar C_{in}$, and $C_{out} = (A \wedge B) \vee (C_{in} \wedge (A \veebar B))$.

8-43

Concatenating full adders

Multiple full adders can be connected together. Using this construct, n full adders can be connected together in order to input the carry bit into a subsequent adder along with two new inputs to create a concatenated adder capable of adding a binary number of n bits.

The four-bit adder is an example of a standard component that can be used in many applications involving arithmetic operations.

$$
\begin{array}{cccccc}
 & 0^{C_3} & 1^{C_2} & 1^{C_1} & & \\
 & 0^{A_3} & 0^{A_2} & 1^{A_1} & 1^{A_0} & 3 \\
+ & 1^{B_3} & 0^{B_2} & 1^{B_1} & 1^{B_0} & 11 \\
\hline
= & 1^{S_3} & 1^{S_2} & 1^{S_1} & 0^{S_0} & 14
\end{array}
$$

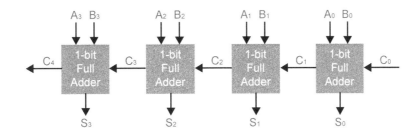

Q1: What would be the output S_4 from a fifth adder connected to the diagram above if the inputs for A_4 and B_4 were 0 and 1? What would be the output C_5?

D-type flip-flops

A flip flop is an elemental **sequential logic circuit** that can store one bit and flip between two states, 0 and 1. It has two inputs, a control input labelled D and a clock signal.

The **clock** or **oscillator** is another type of sequential circuit that changes state at regular time intervals. Clocks are needed to synchronise the change of state of flip flop circuits.

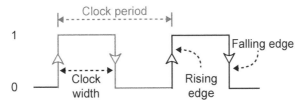

The **D-type flip-flop** (D stands for Data or Delay) is a positive **edge-triggered flip-flop**, meaning that it can only change the output value from 1 to 0 or vice versa when the clock is at a rising or positive edge, i.e. at the beginning of a clock period.

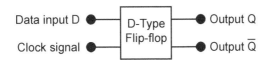

When the clock is not at a positive edge, the input value is held and does not change. **The flip-flop circuit is important because it can be used as a memory cell to store the state of a bit.**

8-43

A-Level only

Output Q only takes on a new value if the value at D has changed at the point of a clock pulse. This means that the clock pulse will freeze or 'store' the input value at D until the next clock pulse. If D remains the same on the next clock pulse, the flip-flop will hold the same value.

The use of a D type flip flop as a memory unit

A flip flop comprises several NAND (or AND and OR) gates and is effectively 1-bit memory. To store eight bits, eight flip-flops are required. **Register memories** are constructed by connecting a series of flip-flops in a row and are typically used for the intermediate storage needed during arithmetic operations. Static RAM is also created using D-type flip-flops. Imagine trying to assemble 16GB of memory in this way!

The graph below illustrates how the output Q only changes to match the input D in response to the rising edge on the clock signal. Q therefore delays, or 'stores' the value of D by up to one clock cycle.

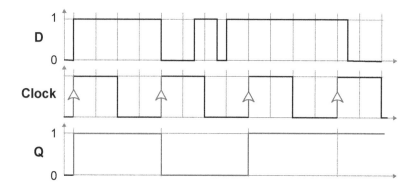

8-43

Q2: Show the output Q for the input D in the figure below.

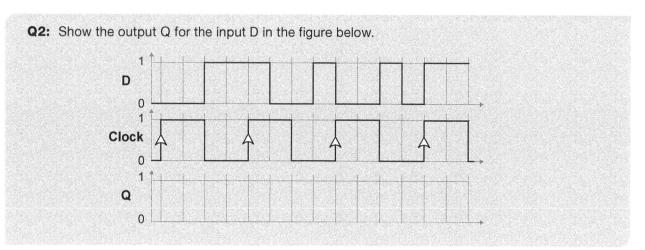

Ⓐ

Exercises

1. A half-adder is used to find the sum of the addition of two binary digits.

   (a) Complete the diagram below to construct a half adder circuit. [3]

   (b) Complete the following truth table for a half adder's outputs S and C.

A	B	S	C

   [2]

   (c) How does a full adder differ from a half adder in terms of its inputs? [2]

2. An edge-triggered D-type flip-flop can be used as a memory cell to store the value of a single bit. The following graph shows the clock cycle and the input signals applied to D.

   (a) Label each rising edge on the diagram below. [1]

   (b) Draw the flip-flop's output Q on the graph. [4]

   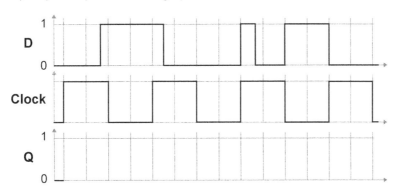

8-43

A

241

Section 9

Legal, moral, ethical and cultural issues

In this section:

9

Chapter 44 – Computing related legislation

Objectives

- Be aware of computing related legislation, including:

  o The Data Protection Act 1998

  o The Computer Misuse Act 1990

  o The Copyright Design and Patents Act 1988

  o The Regulation of Investigatory Powers Act 2000

- Understand that developments in digital technologies have enabled massive transformations in the capacity of organisations to monitor behaviour, amass and analyse personal information

Introduction

The rapidly changing field of computing and worldwide communications poses particular challenges to legislators.

Countries have different laws, and it is sometimes hard to prove in which country an offence was committed, and equally hard to trace the offender or to prosecute.

New applications in computing are constantly being invented and with them, new ways of committing offences for which there is no legislation. Legislators have to balance the rights of the individual with the need for security and protection from terrorist or criminal activity. Many countries, for example, have enacted legislation restricting or banning the use of strong cryptography.

9-44

Computing related legislation

Legislation relating to privacy can be broadly categorised into laws intended to protect personal privacy and those which have been passed in the interests of national security, crime detection or counter-terrorism.

Some laws relate specifically to computing, for example:

- the Data Protection Act (1998) which is designed to ensure that personal data is kept accurate, up-to-date, safe and secure and not used in ways which would harm individuals

- the Computer Misuse Act, which makes it an offence to access or modify computer material without permission

- The Regulation of Investigatory Powers Act 2000

Other laws such as the Copyright, Designs and Patents Act (1988) have a more general application, covering the intellectual property rights of many types of work including books, music, art, computer programs and other original works.

The Data Protection Act 1998

The Data Protection Act says that anyone who stores personal details must keep them secure. Companies with computer systems that store any personal data must have processes and security mechanisms designed into the system to meet this requirement.

- The act includes a number of principles:
- data must be processed fairly and lawfully
- data must be adequate, relevant and not excessive
- data must be accurate and up to date
- data must not be retained for longer than necessary
- data can only be used for the purpose for which it was collected
- data must be kept secure
- data must be handled in accordance with people's rights
- data must not be transferred outside the EU without adequate protection

All data users must register with the Data Commissioner.

> **Q1:** How concerned are you about misuse of your personal data? Are you aware of how your social profile may be used by future employers?

The Computer Misuse Act 1990

The Computer Misuse Act has three main principles, primarily designed to prevent unauthorised access or 'hacking' of programs or data.

The Computer Misuse Act (1990) recognised the following new offences:

- Unauthorised access to computer material
- Unauthorised access with intent to commit or facilitate a crime
- Unauthorised modification of computer material
- Making, supplying or obtaining anything which can be used in computer misuse offences

> **Q2:** Describe some behaviours which would be illegal under this Act. Find some examples of the application of the Computer Misuse Act (e.g. www.computerevidence.co.uk/Cases/CMA.htm)

The Copyright Designs and Patents Act 1988

This Act is designed to protect the creators of books, music, video and software from having their work illegally copied.

The Act makes it illegal to use, copy or distribute commercially available software without buying the appropriate licence. When a computer system is designed and implemented, licensing must be considered in terms of which software should be used. If you use commercial software called for example TestSoft to create a series of multiple choice tests called ReviseHistory, it may not be permissible to sell your finished product without paying TestSoft a fee for every copy you sell.

Similarly, if your school buys a copy of ReviseHistory, they may not be permitted to install it on more than one computer without buying a multi-user licence for a certain number of users.

9-44

If you buy a music CD or pay to download a piece of music, software or a video, it is illegal to

- pass a copy to a friend

- make a copy and then sell it

- use the software on a network, unless the licence allows it

The software industry can take some steps to prevent illegal copying of software:

- The user must enter a unique key before the software is installed

- Some software will only run if the CD is present in the drive

- Some applications will only run if a special piece of hardware called a 'dongle' is plugged into a USB port on the computer

However, although a piece of software such as an applications package, game or operating system is protected, **algorithms** are not eligible for protection. If you come up with a much better sorting algorithm than anyone else, for example, you cannot stop others from using it.

The Regulation of Investigatory Powers Act 2000

This Act regulates the powers of public bodies to carry out surveillance and investigation, and covers the interception of communications. It was introduced to take account of the growth of technology, the Internet and strong encryption, and additions have been made regularly between 2003 and 2010, with the latest draft bill put before Parliament in November 2015.

The Act:

- enables certain public bodies to demand that an ISP provide access to a customer's communications in secret

- enables mass surveillance of communications in transit

- enables certain public bodies to demand ISPs fit equipment to facilitate surveillance

- enables certain public bodies to demand that someone hand over keys to protected information

- allows certain public bodies to monitor people's Internet activities

- prevents the existence of interception warrants and any data collected with them from being revealed in court

9-44

Analysing personal information

According to the head of a 2006 Royal Academy study into surveillance, Google is within a few years of having sufficient information to be able to track the exact movements and intentions of every individual, via Google Earth and other software they are developing.

It is predicted that small computers will become embedded in everything from clothes to beermats. Consequently, we will be interfacing with computers in everything we do, from meeting chip-wearing strangers to entering smart buildings or sitting on a smart sofa, and each of these interfaces will end up on a Google database.

It is a vision of a world without privacy.

Already, Google collects and stores data about millions of emails every day. Here are some extracts from the information they post on their website, which users must agree to if they wish to use Google software.

To be consistent with data protection laws, we're asking you to take a moment to review key points of Google's Privacy Policy. This isn't about a change that we've made - it's just a chance to review some key points.

Data we process when you use Google

• When you search for a restaurant on Google Maps or watch a video on YouTube, for example, we process information about the activity - including information like the video you watched, device IDs, IP addresses, cookie data and location.

• We also process the kind of information described above when you use apps or sites that use Google services like ads, Analytics and the YouTube video player.

Why we process it

We process this data for the purposes described in our policy, including to:

• Help our services deliver more useful, customised content such as more relevant search results;

• Improve the quality of our services and develop new ones;

• Deliver ads based on your interests, including things like searches you've done or videos you've watched on YouTube;

• Improve security by protecting against fraud and abuse; and

• Conduct analytics and measurement to understand how our services are used.

9-44

Organisations, including governments and security agencies, collect huge amounts of data about private citizens, often supplied by Internet companies such as Google, as well as by telephone companies.

With the aim of detecting terrorist or other illegal activities, the US Government collects, stores and monitors metadata about all electronic communications in the US. **Metadata** includes information such as the telephone number called, date, time and duration of call.

In one month in 2013, the unit collected data on more than 97 billion emails and 124 billion phone calls from around the world. Edward Snowden is a famous 'whistle-blower' who informed the world about these practices.

Q3: Why do some people object to this data being collected and stored? What are the arguments for and against organisations collecting such data?

Case Study: Edward Snowden

In April 2013, Guardian journalist Glenn Greenwald and Academy Award-winning documentary film director and producer Laura Poitras met in the Marriott Hotel in New York to discuss an initial contact with an anonymous "whistle-blower". Seated in the hotel restaurant, Laura Poitras asked Glenn to either remove the battery from his cell phone or leave it in the hotel room. "It sounds paranoid," she said, "but the government has the capability to activate cell phones and laptops remotely as eavesdropping devices. Turning off the phone or laptop does not defeat the capability; only removing the battery does."

The anonymous source had refused to email any details of what material he had to offer until Glenn installed PGP on his computer. PGP, which stands for "Pretty Good Privacy" is a sophisticated tool to prevent online communications from being hacked. The encryption codes are so lengthy and random that it would take years to decrypt a communication. But it was complicated to install and it took Glenn several months to get round to it, before he was eventually talked through the process online by his anonymous contact. Only then did he receive information from his source about a program called PRISM, which allowed America's National Security Agency (NSA) to collect private communications from the world's largest Internet companies, including Facebook, Google, Yahoo, Microsoft, Apple, YouTube, AOL and Skype.

The first document that Glenn opened was a training manual to teach analysts about the new surveillance capabilities. It told analysts how they could query, for example, particular email addresses or telephone numbers and what data they would receive in response.

What did the source hope to achieve by exposing the secret surveillance practices of the NSA?

"I want to spark a worldwide debate about privacy, Internet freedom, and the dangers of state surveillance," he stated. "I'm not afraid of what will happen to me. I've accepted that my life will be over from my doing this. I'm at peace with that. I know it's the right thing to do."

9-44

The next step was for Glenn and Laura to travel to Hong Kong to meet the whistleblower – Edward Snowden, a 29-year-old who had worked since 2005 as a technical expert for the CIA, NSA and its sub-contractors, making around $200,000 in salary and bonuses. He had travelled to Hong Kong in May, staying in a hotel under his own name, figuring he was safer there than staying in the US when news of the leaked documents broke.

"I watched NSA tracking people's Internet activities as they typed. I became aware of just how invasive US surveillance capabilities had become. I realised the true breadth of this system. And almost nobody knew it was happening.

"For many kids, the Internet is a means of self-actualisation. It allows them to explore who they are and who they want to be, but that works only if we're able to be private and anonymous, to make mistakes without them following us. I worry that mine will be the last generation to enjoy that freedom. I do not want to live in a world where we have no privacy and no freedom, where the unique value of the Internet is snuffed out."

On 6th June 2013, the first of many articles was published by the Guardian.

NSA collecting phone records of millions of Verizon customers daily

Exclusive: Top secret court order requiring Verizon to hand over all call data shows scale of domestic surveillance under President Obama.

The order, signed by Judge Roger Vinson, compels Verizon to produce to the NSA electronic copies of "all call detail records or 'telephony metadata' created by Verizon for communications between the United States and abroad" or "wholly within the United States, including local telephone calls".

As journalist Glenn Greenwald painstakingly sifted through the mountain of information provided by Snowden, he was shocked at the extent of the American surveillance operation. It included the NSA's tapping of Internet servers, satellites, underwater fibre-optic cables, local and foreign telephone systems and personal computers. A list of individuals targeted for particularly invasive forms of spying included terrorist and criminal suspects, democratically elected leaders of many countries in Europe including France and Germany, and ordinary American citizens.

The documents leaked by Snowden revealed that the literal aim of the US Government was to collect, store, monitor and analyse metadata about all electronic communications by everybody in the world.

Exercises

1. Do you think Edward Snowden was right to reveal the secret documents to which he had access, being legally forbidden to do so under the US Espionage Act 1917? Justify your answer. [4]

2. The FBI and NSA have been protesting about losing surveillance capabilities—through greater encryption of the Internet—since the 1990s. In China, the manufacture, use, sale, import, or export of any item containing encryption without prior government approval may lead to administrative fines, the seizure of equipment, confiscation of illegal gains, and even criminal prosecution.

   Give arguments for and against a policy of making it illegal for individuals and organisations to use strong encryption in their online communications. [4]

3. The *Data Protection Act 1998* sets out eight principles for the protection of privacy in data collection, handling and distribution. Name two of these principles and explain how each serves to protect privacy. [4]

4. What Act provides intellectual property protection for software? What actions are illegal under this Act? [3]

References:

Andrew Keen, "The Internet is not the Answer", Atlantic Books, London, 2015

Glenn Greenwald, "No Place to Hide: Edward Snowden, the NSA and the Surveillance State", McLelland and Stewart, 2014

Luke Harding, "The Snowden files: The Inside Story of the World's Most Wanted Man", Vintage Books, 2014

Websites:

http://www.theguardian.com/world/2013/jun/06/nsa-phone-records-verizon-court-order

https://www.youtube.com/watch?v=5yB3n9fu-rM

http://www.nybooks.com/articles/archives/2013/nov/21/snowden-leaks-and-public/

9-44

Chapter 45 – Ethical, moral and cultural issues

Objectives

- Discuss the individual (moral), social (ethical) and cultural opportunities and risks of digital technology:
  - computers in the workforce
  - automated decision making
  - artificial intelligence
  - environmental effects
  - analysis of personal information
- Understand the real and potential impact that digital technology has on employment, the distribution of wealth and the lives of millions of people
- Discuss the environmental effects of computers

The economic impact of the Internet

The Internet has its origins in the 1960s with ARPANET, the first North American wide area network. In 1974, two engineers called Bob Kahn and Vint Cerf devised a protocol for linking up individual networks into what they termed the Internet – the "internetworking of networks".

In the 1980s Tim Berners-Lee, working for CERN in Geneva, invented, or designed, the World Wide Web. He wrote his initial Web proposal in March 1989 and in 1990 built the first Web browser, called WorldWideWeb. His vision was that "all the bits of information in every computer in CERN, and on the planet, would be available to me and to anyone else. There would be a single global information space."

Berners-Lee had little interest in money and gave away his technology for nothing, but one of the most significant consequences of his invention was a complete reshaping of the economy throughout the world. Has it created jobs, or simply created the "1% economy" in which the top Internet companies like Amazon, Google, Facebook, Instagram and others have accumulated huge wealth at the expense of thousands of workers?

Amazon

Amazon started as an online bookstore in 1994 but soon diversified into DVDs, software, video games, toys, furniture, clothes and thousands of other products. In 2013 the company turned over $75 billion in sales, and it now accounts for 65% of all digital purchases of book sales. As a consequence of their domination, in 2015 there were fewer than 1,000 independent bookstores in Britain, one third less than in 2005. Where a bookshop employs 47 people for every $10 million in sales, Amazon employs 14 to generate the same revenue.

eBay

eBay, essentially an electronic platform bringing together buyers and sellers of goods, grew from a user base of 41,000 trading goods worth $7.2 million in 1995, to 162 million users trading goods worth $227.9 billion in 2014.

Google

In 1996, Larry Page and Sergey Brin, two Stanford University Computer Science postgraduate students, created Google. There were already several successful search engines like Yahoo and AltaVista on the market, but Page and Brin came up with a game-changing algorithm, which they called PageRank, for determining the relevance of a Web page based on the number and quality of its incoming links. The idea was that you could estimate the importance of a Web page by the number and status of other web pages that link to it. Every time you make a search, the Google search engine becomes more knowledgeable and thus more useful. Even more valuable to Google is the fact that Google learns more about you every time you search.

By 1998, Google was getting 10,000 queries every day. By 1999, they were getting 70 million daily requests. Their next step was to figure out how to make money out of their free technology, and they came up with AdWords, which enabled advertisers to place keyword-associated ads down the right hand side of the page. The image below shows what comes up when a user in Dorchester searches for "Paintball", with the nearest companies, sponsored advertisements and a map with their locations appearing on the right of the screen.

By 2014, Google had joined Amazon as a winner-takes-all company, with 1.5 billion daily searches and revenues of $50 billion.

Computers in the workforce

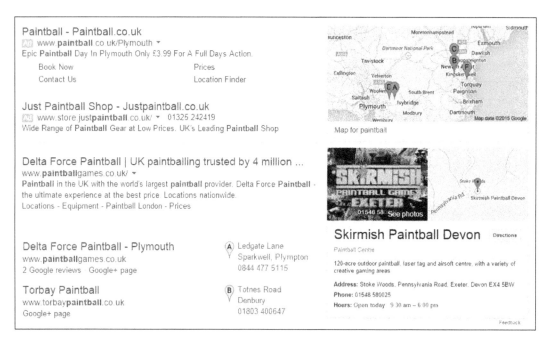

A 2013 paper by Carl Benedikt Frey and Michael Osborne entitled "*The future of Employment: how susceptible are jobs to computerisation?*" estimates that 47% of total US employment is at risk. They examine the impact of future computerisation on more than 700 individual occupations, and note the shifting of labour from middle-income manufacturing jobs to low-income service jobs which are less susceptible to computerisation. At the same time, with falling prices of computing, problem-solving skills are becoming relatively productive, explaining the substantial employment growth in occupations involving cognitive tasks where skilled, well-educated labour has a comparative advantage.

Thus there is a polarization of labour, with growing employment in high-income cognitive jobs and low-income manual labour, and the disappearance of middle-income occupations. Driverless cars developed by Google are an example of how computerisation is no longer confined to routine manufacturing tasks. The possibility of drones delivering your parcels is no longer in the realms of science fiction. In the 10 jobs that have a 99% likelihood of being replaced by software and automation within the next 25 years, the authors include tax preparers, library assistants, clothing factory workers, and photographic process workers.

In fact, jobs in the photographic industry have already all but vanished. In 1989, when Tim Berners-Lee invented the World Wide Web, Kodak employed 145,000 people in research labs, offices and factories in Rochester US and had a market value of $31 billion. In 2013 the company filed for bankruptcy and Rochester became virtually a ghost town.

Meanwhile, in 2010, a young entrepreneur called Kevin Systrom started up Instagram, which enabled users to create photos on their smartphones with filters to give them, for example, a warm, fuzzy glow.

An Instagram moment

9-45

Twenty-five thousand iPhone users downloaded the app when it launched on 6th October 2010. A month later, Systrom's Instagram had a million members. By early 2012, it had 14 million users and by November, 100 million users, with the app hosting 5 billion photos. But when Systrom sold Instagram to Facebook for a billion dollars in 2012 (less than two years after the startup), Instagram still only had thirteen full-time employees working out of a small office in San Fransisco. It is a good example of a service that is not providing any jobs at all in the winner-takes-all economics of the digital marketplace.

User generated content

In his book "The Cult of the Amateur", Andrew Keen argues that *"MySpace and Facebook are creating a youth culture of digital narcissism; open-source knowledge-sharing sites like Wikipedia are undermining the authority of teachers in the classroom, the YouTube generation are more interested in self-expression than in learning about the outside world; the cacophony of anonymous blogs and user-generated content is deafening today's user to the voices of informed experts and professional journalism; kids are so busy self-broadcasting themselves on social networks that they no longer consume the creative work of professional musicians, novelists, or filmmakers."*

Keen asserts that a thriving music, video and publishing economy is being replaced by the multi-billion dollar monopolist YouTube. The traditional copyright-intensive industries accounted for almost 510 billion euros in the European Union during the period 2008-2010, and generated 3.2% of all jobs, amounting to more than 7 million jobs. What will happen if large numbers of these jobs disappear?

Algorithms and ethics

Computer scientists and software engineers who devise the multitude of algorithms used by YouTube, Facebook, Amazon and Google, and by organisations from banks and Stock Exchanges to the Health Service and the police, have significant power and therefore the responsibility that goes with it. In some US cities, algorithms determine whether you are likely to be stopped and searched on the street. Banks use algorithms to decide whether to consider your application for a mortgage or a loan. Algorithms are applied to decision-making in hiring and firing, healthcare and advertising. It has been reported, for example, that some algorithms which decide what advertisements are shown on your browser screen classify web users into categories which include "probably bipolar", "daughter killed in car crash", "rape victim", and "gullible elderly"[i]. Did the programmer who wrote that algorithm have any qualms about his work?

When algorithms prioritise, they "bring attention to certain things at the expense of others"[ii].

Facebook's 'News Feed' product filters posts, stories and activities undertaken by friends. Content for the Newsfeed is selected or omitted according to a ranking algorithm which Facebook, with its billion-plus user base, continually develops and tests to show users the content they will be most interested in. But it has been suggested that these social interactions may influence people's emotions and state of mind; the emotions expressed by friends via online social networks may influence our own moods and behaviour[iii]. Clearly, then, those who devise the ranking algorithms potentially have the ability to influence the emotional state of people using Facebook.

Should computer scientists consider the institutional goals of a prospective employer, or the social worth of what they do, before accepting a job? Phillip Rogway, Professor of Computer Science at the University of California, found that on a Google search of deciding among job offers, not one suggested that this was a factor [iv].

9-45

Driverless cars

The prospect of large numbers of self-driving cars on our roads raises ethical questions about the morality of automated decision making and different algorithms which could be used in the face of causing "unavoidable harm" - who gets harmed and who gets spared[v].

(a) The car can stay on course and kill several pedestrians, or swerve and kill one passer-by

(b) The car can stay on course and kill one pedestrian, or swerve and kill its passenger

(c) The car can stay on course and kill several pedestrians, or swerve and kill its passenger

The MIT Technology Review asked: "Should different decisions be made when children are on board, since they both have a longer time ahead of them than adults, and had less say in being in the car in the first place? If a manufacturer offers different versions of its moral algorithm, and a buyer knowingly chose one of them, is the buyer to blame for the harmful consequences of the algorithm's decisions?"

One of the commonly held principles that form a commonly held set of pillars for moral life is the obligation not to inflict harm intentionally; in medical ethics, the physician's guiding principle is "Do no harm". Going further, the moral duties of all scientists, including computer scientists, should also include trying to promote the common good.

Artificial intelligence

As digital technologies are used in more and more areas of our lives, spreading into our offline environments through the so-called 'Internet of things', previously inert objects are expected to become networked and start making decisions for us. Algorithms will allow the refrigerator to decide what food needs replacing, a door will decide who to let in. Should your door call the police if the door is opened by someone without a tracking device? Should your house report a child who screams excessively to the Social Services?

Environmental effects of computers

Environmental issues include the carbon footprint and waste products that result from manufacturing computer systems, but this is often outweighed by the positive effects on the environment of using computerised systems to manage processes that might otherwise generate more pollution.

Considerations may include:

- Does a computer system mean that people can work from home and therefore drive less?

- Has computer technology led to a "throw-away society", with huge waste dumps of unwanted products which are thrown away rather than repaired or upgraded?

- Is working at home more environmentally friendly than everyone working in a big office, in terms of heating and lighting?

- Do computer-managed engines work more efficiently? Create less pollution and use less fuel?

9-45

Computers and waste

The pace of technology is so rapid that computers, mobile phones and handheld-devices that seemed so desirable a few short years ago are now discarded without a thought for the latest must-have piece of equipment. Are they recyclable or are they simply contributing to a huge mountain of waste, containing dangerous chemical elements which leach into water supplies in third world countries?

Electronic waste processing, Agbogbloshie, Ghana

Exercises

1. Some of the jobs likely to disappear over the next decade owing to computerisation include manufacturing jobs, clerical jobs and even service jobs, where people will be replaced by robots. Give examples of other jobs which may be lost owing to computerisation. What will be the social effects of the job losses? [7]

2. Decisions are often made about us on the basis of algorithms of which we may be completely unaware. Car insurance premiums are calculated based largely on your age, experience, address, occupation and vehicle details. Health insurance premiums are affected by age, occupation, personal and parental medical histories. Are the algorithms that calculate these premiums fair? Discuss how the algorithms used embed moral and/or cultural values. State with reasons who benefits from the decisions made by these algorithms and whether anyone is harmed. [4]

3. Computers have had a considerable impact on our environment. Describe an environmental problem to which the industry contributes and what measures individuals can take to help solve this problem. [4]

9-45

References

(i) Naughton, John, The Guardian (2015, December 6) "Algorithm writers need a code of conduct" www.theguardian.com/commentisfree/2015/dec/06/algorithm-writers-should-have-code-of-conduct

(ii) Centre of Internet & Human Rights (2015) "The ethics of Algorithms: from radical content to self-driving cars". Retrieved from www.gccs2015.com/sites/default/files/documents/ Ethics_Algorithms-final%20doc.pdf

(iii) Kramer, Adam et al (2014, March 25) "Experimental evidence of massive-scale emotional contagion through social networks". Retrieved from http://www.pnas.org/content/111/24/8788.full

(iv) Rogway, Phillip (2015, December 12) "The Moral Character of Cryptographic Work". Retrieved from http://web.cs.ucdavis.edu/~rogaway/papers/moral-fn.pdf

(v) Owano, Nancy (2015 October 24) "When self-driving cars drive the ethical questions". Retrieved from http://techxplore.com/news/2015-10-self-driving-cars-ethical.html

Chapter 46 – Privacy and censorship

Objectives

- Discuss the cultural opportunities and risks of digital technology relating to:
  - censorship and the Internet
  - the monitoring of behaviour
  - piracy and offensive communications
  - layout, colour paradigms and character sets

Trolls on the Internet

Trolls, cyber-bullying and misogyny have become a fact of everyday life on the Internet. It wasn't supposed to be this way – the Internet was going to inspire a generation to voice a broad diversity of opinion and empower those who traditionally had no voice.

After the 2010-11 Arab Spring, many people argued that the social media networks were helping to overthrow dictatorships and empower the people. But the Arab Spring deteriorated into vicious religious and ethnic civil wars, culminating in the rise of the so-called ISIS, which uses social networks to post atrocities and radicalise impressionable young people.

Feminist writers and journalists, academics like Mary Beard and political campaigner Caroline Criado-Perez, who petitioned the Bank of England to create a bank note featuring Jane Austen's face, receive hundreds of death threats, rape threats and other offensive communications for no other reason than that they are women who have dared to appear on the media. Thousands of other women and teenage girls are victims of similar trolling on the Internet. Savage bullying on various social networking sites has led to several tragic cases of suicide.

The Internet has brought great benefits, but all of us have a responsibility to use it wisely and well.

9-46

Censorship and the Internet

Internet censorship is the control or suppression of what can be accessed, viewed or published on the Internet. It may be carried out by governments or by private organisations in response to government regulators. Individuals and organisations may censor certain websites for moral, religious or business reasons, or from fear of intimidation or legal consequences. For example, websites containing copyright infringements, harassment or obscene material may be censored.

The extent of censorship varies from country to country, and many of the issues associated with Internet censorship are similar to traditional censorship of newspapers, books, films, etc. It is more difficult to censor Internet information in one particular country, since the information can generally be found on websites hosted outside the country. In some countries such as North Korea and Cuba, the government has total control over all Internet-connected computers, and can therefore enforce censorship.

Most people agree that there needs to be some form of censorship on the Internet; in a 2012 Internet Society survey, 71% of respondents agreed that "censorship should exist in some form on the Internet".

Q1: Do you agree that there should be some form of censorship on the Internet?

Case study 1: Online abuse

In 2016, comments on the Guardian newspaper website regularly exceeded 70,000 per day. Journalists put their names to all the articles they write, and regular columnists frequently have their photograph accompanying the column. One consequence of this is that gender and race appear to be key factors in attracting abuse. In a study of almost 70 million comments posted on the Guardian website, it was found that eight of the top ten Guardian Opinion writers most likely to attract abusive or off-topic comments below their articles were women, while the other two were black men. As well as the gender and race of the author, other factors appeared to be significant: one of the women was Jewish, one was Muslim and two were lesbian, while one of the two men was gay.

Despite white men forming the majority of Guardian Opinion writers, the 10 columnists attracting the least abuse or off-topic comments were all men (nine of them white).

One female journalist writing about a demonstration outside an abortion clinic was told "You are so ugly that if you got pregnant I would drive you to the abortion clinic myself". A British Muslim woman writing about Islamophobia was told to "marry an ISIS fighter and then see how you like that!"

As one journalist said, "Even if I tell myself the abuse doesn't mean anything, it has a toll on me. It has an emotional effect, it takes a physical toll. And over time, it builds up." Another said "Imagine going to work every day and walking through a gauntlet of 100 people saying "You're stupid", "You're terrible", "I can't believe you get paid for this".

In April 2016 it was reported that Google, Facebook and Twitter were talking to organisations around the world to organise a global counter-speech movement against the violent misogyny, racism, threats, intimidation and abuse that flood social media platforms.

9-46

Q2: Do you think that net firms should do more to halt trolls? Would this be an unwanted prevention of free speech?

Case study 2: Monitoring content on the Guardian website

Almost every website, whether it be a newspaper or personal blog, has struggled with comments. A really good comment "informs its readers, corrects authors and provides worthwhile insights in a polite and constructive manner". Other comments fall into the category of rants, bile, insults and trolling.

The majority of comments are civil and productive, and engaging with comments is part of a journalists' work. Many factors affect the success of commenting at news sites: topic, user anonymity, scale, site culture, moderation, journalists' engagement and attitudes, and management support.

Newspapers such as The Guardian employ a team of moderators to read comments and block or delete offensive ones. One moderator in April 2016 described how over the past five years he has read millions of comments and blocked tens of thousands. Moderation is about not letting anyone's agenda ruin the conversation or ranting about irrelevant issues, as well as blocking trolls.

An irony of successful discussion forums is that their success begets their failure. They get too big and attract spammers, scammers and trolls.

Q3: The media scholar Clay Shirky encapsulated the problem of managing discussion forums by saying "Comment systems can be good, big, cheap – pick two". What did he mean by this?

Monitoring behaviour

We are all used to our movements and behaviour being caught on camera, in town and on the roads. CCTV cameras are used for security purposes, crime prevention and detection. They are used to record drivers speeding, turning or parking illegally or driving the wrong way up a one-way street.

Employers may monitor employee behaviour on the Internet, recording what sites are visited during working hours and how much time is spent on them.

And, of course, you can use wearable technology to monitor your own behaviour – how many steps you have taken during the day, your heart rate during a run, the time you took to swim 100 metres.

Layout, colour paradigms and character sets

Websites designed in one country are viewable all over the world, so if they are intended for an international viewership, it is a good idea to give consideration to layout, colour and character sets.

Layout

Most websites are designed based on the US layout containing a linear structure of information with multiple blocks of text that a western reader is likely to skim over. With Japanese websites, for example, the preference is to include less information per page which, as a whole, is easier to absorb without fear of missing something. In the West, where text is read from left to right, menus are commonly placed on the left. In other countries, where Arabic script, for example, is read from right to left, menus and other page features might more logically appear mirrored in comparison with western versions of the same page.

Maps are a good example of the use of cultural or nationalistic bias reflected in layout. A world map is frequently shown with the country where it was created appearing in the centre.

9-46

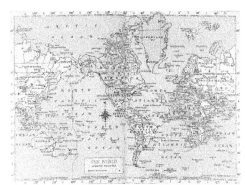

Map1: The Americas in the centre

Map 2: Australasia in the centre

Colour paradigms

Around the world, the way that different cultures see and describe colours varies dramatically. In general, blue is considered the safest colour choice around the world, since it has many positive associations. In North America and Europe, blue represents trust, security, and authority, and is considered to be soothing and peaceful. However, it can also represent depression, loneliness, and sadness (hence having "the blues").

In Western cultures, green represents luck, nature, freshness, spring, environmental awareness, wealth, inexperience, and jealousy (the "green-eyed monster"). In Indonesia, green has traditionally been forbidden, whereas in Mexico, it's a national colour that stands for independence. In the Middle East, green represents fertility, luck, and wealth, and it's considered the traditional colour of Islam. In Eastern cultures, green symbolizes youth, fertility, and new life, but it can also mean infidelity. In fact, in China, green hats for men are taboo because it signals that their wives have committed adultery!

In Western cultures, orange represents autumn, harvest, warmth, sunshine. In Hinduism, saffron (a soft orange colour) is considered auspicious and sacred. In Eastern cultures, orange symbolizes love, happiness, humility, and good health.

Look up http://www.shutterstock.com/blog/the-spectrum-of-symbolism-color-meanings-around-the-world to see the symbolism of other colours in countries around the world.

Character sets

A character set is the mapping of a collection of characters to specific bit sequences or codes. The collection can increase in number dependent on the maximum number of bits allocated to each character. ASCII uses only seven bits allowing for 128 characters whereas Unicode (UTF-16) has been developed to represent over a million characters including those of most languages, and symbols used in mathematical, scientific and musical notation. Unicode and ASCII is covered in more detail in Chapter 29.

9-46

Exercises

1. Networking sites frequently feature angry, violent or inaccurate content.

   Should Facebook, Twitter, Ask.com and others take responsibility for content posted on their sites? What sort of content should be allowed? Would it be possible to develop software to facilitate such a task? Discuss. [5]

2. "Honest and law-abiding citizens have nothing to fear from the distribution of their personal data." Do you agree with this statement? Give reasons for your view and a reason why someone else might not agree with you. [5]

3. A University is debating whether to offer a course on writing malware such as viruses, worms and Trojan horses. Discuss the ethical issues involved in this decision, and whether or not you think they should run the course. [5]

References

Andrew Keen, "The Cult of the Amateur", Nicholas Brealey Publishing, 2007, 2008

Andrew Keen, "The Internet is not the Answer", Atlantic Books, London, 2015

Carl Benedict Frey and Michael Osborne, "The Future of employment: How susceptible are jobs to computerisation?" http://www.oxfordmartin.ox.ac.uk/downloads/academic/The_Future_of_Employment.pdf

Section 10

Computational thinking

In this section:

10

Chapter 47 – Thinking abstractly

Objectives

- Understand the nature of and need for abstraction

- Describe the differences between an abstraction and reality

- Devise an abstract model for a variety of situations

Computational thinking

What is **computational thinking**? It is *not* about following an algorithm in one's head to carry out a mathematical task like adding ten numbers. Rather, it is about thinking how a problem can be solved. This involves two basic steps:

- Formulate the problem as a computational problem – in other words, state it in such a way that it is potentially solvable using an algorithm

- Try to construct an algorithm to solve the problem

A computational thinker will not be satisfied with any old algorithm, though; it must be a 'good' solution – that is, a *correct* and *efficient* solution. A programmer needs to be able to show that a solution is correct and efficient by using logical reasoning, test data and user feedback.

Clearly, then, computational thinking is a vital skill for a programmer, and in fact it is not possible to be a programmer without it. It includes the ability to think logically and to apply the tools and techniques of computing to thinking about, understanding, formulating and solving problems.

Computing has been called the **automation of abstractions**, so let's move on to talk about abstraction.

Abstraction

Representational abstraction can be defined as a *representation arrived at by removing unnecessary details*.

Here are some examples of abstraction.

- Any computer model, say of the environment, a new car or a flight simulator, is an abstraction.

- If you are planning to write a program for a game involving a bouncing ball, you will need to decide what properties of the ball to take into account. If it's bouncing vertically rather than, say, on a snooker table, gravity needs to be taken into account. How elastic is the ball? How far and in what direction will it bounce when it hits an edge? What you are required to do is build an abstract model of a real-world situation, which you can simplify; remembering, however, that the more you simplify, the less likely it becomes that the model will mimic reality.

- A builder who is planning to build 100 houses on a new estate may use a physical model of the new estate, or in the first instance, a plan on paper or on a computer screen. In either case the model will be greatly simplified. All the houses may appear identical in the model. They may lack windows, doors or chimneys. All the trees in the model may be of identical size, colour and shape.

- The map of the London Underground is a simple model of the actual geography of the Tube stations.

The map tells you what line each station is on and which other lines each station is connected to. It is very useful for a person travelling around London, but of very little use to an engineer who is planning where to dig tunnels for a proposed new line.

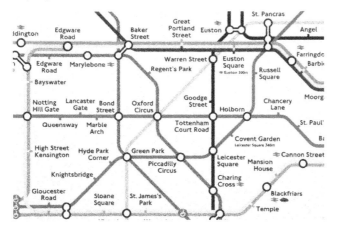

All of these models contain different types of abstraction which are used in programming. In programming, abstraction is concerned with the distinction between what a program unit does and how it does it.

Abstraction applied to high level programming languages

Abstraction is the most important feature of high level programming languages such as Python, C#, Java and hundreds of other languages written for different purposes. To understand why, we need to look at different generations of programming language.

- The first generation of language was **machine code** – programmers entered the binary 0s and 1s that the computer understands. Writing a program to solve even a short, simple problem was a tedious, time-consuming task largely unrelated to the algorithm itself.

- The second generation was an improvement; mnemonic codes were used to represent instructions. But as you saw in Chapter 14, it is still an enormously complex task to write an assembly language program and what's more, if you want to run the program on a different type of computer, it has to be completely rewritten for the new hardware.

- The third generation of languages, starting with BASIC and FORTRAN in the 1960s, used statements like X = A + 5, freeing the programmer from all the tedious details of where the variables X and A were stored in memory, and all the other fiddly implementation details of exactly how the computer was going to carry out the instruction.

Finally, programmers could focus on the problem in hand rather than worrying about irrelevant technological details, and that is a good example of what abstraction is all about.

10-47

Abstraction by generalisation

There is a famous problem dating back more than 200 years to the old Prussian city of Königsberg. This beautiful city had seven bridges, and the inhabitants liked to stroll around the city on a Sunday afternoon, making sure to cross every bridge at least once. Nobody could figure out how to cross each bridge once and once only, or alternatively prove that this was impossible, and eventually the Mayor turned to the local mathematical genius Leonhard Euler.

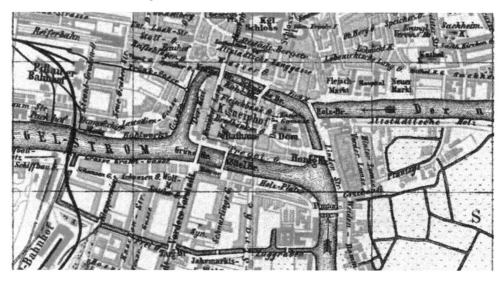

The map of 18th century Königsberg

10-47

Euler's first step was to remove all irrelevant details from the map, and come up with an abstraction:

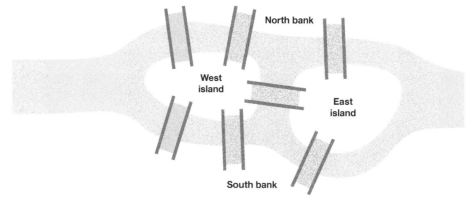

To really simplify it, Euler represented each piece of land as a circle and each bridge as a line between them.

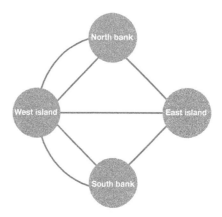

What he now had was a **graph**, with **nodes** representing land masses and **edges** (lines connecting the nodes) representing the bridges. Now that Euler had his graph, how could he solve the problem?

He did not want to try every possible solution; he realised that this was just a particular instance of a more general problem and he wanted to find a solution that was applicable to similar problems. He noticed a critical feature of the puzzle: since each bridge could be crossed only once, each node had to have an even number of connections, because you must enter and leave a node by a different edge. The only exceptions are the start and end node, since you don't have to enter a start node or leave the end node.

All the nodes in this graph have an odd number of edges, so it is therefore impossible!

Euler had laid the foundation of **graph theory**, which you met in Chapter 38, with more in Chapter 63.

By abstracting the problem, Euler made possible the solution of innumerable related problems. Not only does it apply to different cities with different numbers of bridges, it applies to many other problems with similar requirements.

Abstraction by generalisation, as illustrated above, is a grouping by common characteristics to arrive at a hierarchical relationship of the "is a kind of" type. Thus Euler's problem is a particular instance of graph theory.

This type of abstraction is very common in object-oriented programming. A class of object, say an Animal, will be defined with its own attributes such as gender and whether it is carnivore or vegetarian, and its own behaviours, methods or procedures such as move, sleep, eat, etc. Other objects such as Dog, Cat, Mouse and so on may be defined as subclasses of Animal - they all share common characteristics which are defined in the Animal class, but have their own attributes and behaviours as well. In other words Dog "is a kind of" Animal, as are Cat and Mouse.

10-47

> **Q1:** Use abstraction by generalisation to continue the sequence 1,4,9,16... What is the 50th number in the sequence?

Data abstraction

A similar idea is that of **data abstraction**.

The details of how data are actually represented are hidden. For example, when you use integers or real numbers in a program, you are not interested in how these numbers are actually represented in the computer.

In a higher level language, it is possible to create **abstract data types** such as queues, stacks and trees. The abstract data type, for example a queue, is a logical description of how the data is viewed and the operations that can be performed on it. For example, elements can be added to the rear of the queue and removed from the front. The queue may have a maximum size that cannot be exceeded. The programmer using this data structure, however, is concerned only with the operations such as AddToQueue or RemoveFromQueue and does not need to know how the data structure is implemented using, for example, an array and pointers to the front and rear of the queue.

Exercises

1. "Representational abstraction is a representation arrived at by removing unnecessary details."

   Describe what this means in relation to a computer program which allows the user to enter a starting address **A** and a destination address **B** and returns a map of the route, the number of miles and the estimated journey time it will take to travel by car from **A** to **B**. [5]

   ▼ Suggested routes

   M25   **213 mi, 3 hours 43 mins**
   ○ In current traffic: 3 hours 47 mins

2. Explain how **abstraction** could be used in a game program in which the player has to collect treasure in a cave and avoid being eaten by a monster. [5]

10-47

Chapter 48 – Thinking ahead

Objectives

- Identify the inputs and outputs for a given situation
- Determine the preconditions for devising a solution to a problem
- Understand the need for reusable program components
- **(A)** Understand the nature, benefits and drawbacks of caching

Computational problems

At its most abstract level, a computational problem can be represented by a simple diagram:

Input is the information relevant to the problem, which could for example be passed as parameters to a subroutine.

Output is the solution to the problem, which could be passed back from a subroutine.

A clear statement of exactly what the inputs and outputs of a problem are is a necessary first step in constructing a solution.

10-48

Example 1: Determine whether a given item is present in a list

On the face of it, this is a simple problem. But do we know exactly what the inputs are? For example, is the list sorted? Are the items numeric or alphabetic? What about the output – are we expecting it to be simply True or False, or should the output give the position in the list of the item if it is found?

The problem needs to be formally defined, stating the inputs and outputs. This can be done as follows:

Name: ScarchList

Inputs: A list of strings $S = (s_1, s_2, s_3 \dots s_n)$
A target string t

Outputs: A Boolean variable b

Now we can write pseudocode for the function `SearchList`:

```
function SearchList(s, t)
   found = False
   n = 0
   while found == False AND n < len(s)
     if t == s[n] then
        found = True
     else
          n = n + 1
     endif
   endwhile
   return found
endfunction
```

265

> **Q1:** Write a pseudocode algorithm which initialises a list of string items, asks the user to enter an item to search for, calls the above function `SearchList` and prints an appropriate message depending on whether the function returns True or False.

Specifying preconditions

Suppose that a pseudocode algorithm has been written to find the maximum of a list of numbers.

```
function maxInt(listInt)
  maxNumber = listInt[0]
  for i = 1 to len(listInt) - 1
    if listInt[i] > maxNumber then
      maxNumber = listInt[i]
    endif
  next i
  return maxNumber
endfunction
```

If the function is called with an empty list, it will crash on the statement

```
maxNumber = listInt[0]
```

In order to make sure the function never crashes, either the function must test for an empty list, or a **precondition** must be specified with the documentation for the function.

Name:	maxInt
Inputs:	A list of integers listInt = $(k_1, k_2, k_3 \ldots k_n)$
Outputs:	An integer maxInt
Precondition:	length of listInt > 0

> **Q2:** Specify the input, output and any preconditions for a function `sqrt(n)` which finds the square root of an integer or floating point number.

Advantages of specifying preconditions

- Specifying preconditions as part of the documentation of a subroutine ensures that the user knows what checks, if any, must be carried out before calling the subroutine.

- If there are no preconditions, then the user can be confident that necessary checks will be carried out in the subroutine itself, thus saving unnecessary coding. The shorter the program, the easier it will be to debug and maintain.

- Clear documentation of inputs, outputs and preconditions helps to make the subroutine **reusable**. This means that it can be put into a library of subroutines and called from any program with access to that library.

The need for reusable program components

The Windows DLL (Dynamic Link Library) is an example of a package of reusable program components. Programming languages have libraries of functions to perform common functions, from printing to finding a square root to generating a random number.

10-48

In a large project, programmers may create their own libraries of reusable components. If, for example, abstract data structures such as queues, stacks or trees are used, routines to traverse, add to or delete from these data structures may be required in many different modules making up the whole project. Clearly, having components which have already been written, debugged and thoroughly tested will save time in completing the project.

A-Level only

Nature and benefits of caching

Caching is another aspect of thinking ahead, this time done automatically by the operating system rather than the programmer. Caching is the temporary storage of program instructions or data that have been used once and may be needed again shortly. The last few instructions of a program may be stored in cache memory for quick retrieval.

Web caching, i.e. the storing of HTML pages and images recently looked at, is another example of caching. This gives fast access to pages that have been recently looked at (and may be returned to) and saves having to download pages again, using up bandwidth unnecessarily.

Ⓐ

Exercises

1. Explain the benefits of specifying inputs, outputs and preconditions in the documentation for a subroutine which will be saved in a library of subroutines for importing into many programs. [6]

2. Give **two** examples of reusable program components in a programming language with which you are familiar. [2]

10-48

A-Level only

3. Explain what is meant by **caching** and give an example of when it is used in a computer system. [2]

Ⓐ

Chapter 49 – Thinking procedurally

Objectives

- Identify the components of a problem
- Identify the components of a solution to the problem
- Determine the order of steps needed to solve a problem
- Identify sub-procedures necessary to solve a problem

Procedural abstraction

Computer science is, in broad terms, the study of problem-solving, and as such is also the study of **abstraction**. As we have seen, abstraction allows us to separate the **physical** reality of a problem from the **logical** view. Thus, for example, you can send an email, play music or download an image without knowing any of the detail of how these things are actually done. On the other hand, the computer engineers, technicians and system administrators who enable these things to happen have a very different view. They need to be able to control the low-level details that users are not even aware of.

Procedural abstraction means using a procedure to carry out a sequence of steps for achieving some task such as calculating a student's grade from her marks in three exam papers, buying groceries online or drawing a house on a computer screen.

Consider, for example, how you could code a program to create the plan for an estate of 100 new houses. You could use a procedure which will draw a triangle of certain dimensions and colour. The colour and dimensions are passed as arguments to the procedure, for example:

```
procedure drawTriangle(colour, base, height)
```

This procedure may be called using the statement

```
drawTriangle("red", 4.5,2.0)
```

The programmer does not need to know the details of how this procedure works. She simply needs to know how the procedure is called and what arguments are required, what data type each one is and what order they must be written in. This is called the **procedure interface**.

Similarly, there may be a procedure to build a rectangle that is defined by parameters colour, height and width, which are passed as arguments:

```
drawRectangle ("beige", 4.0, 5.0)
```

To draw a house at a given position on the screen, the programmer may write a procedure buildHouse() which uses the drawTriangle() and drawRectangle() procedures, aligns them and positions the house at a particular position on the screen. All these variables will be passed as arguments to the procedure.

Several houses could be combined to make a street. Several streets could be drawn to represent the estate.

Then, if the builder of the new estate decides to make all the houses larger, the procedure for drawing the house does not need to be changed - it is simply called with new arguments.

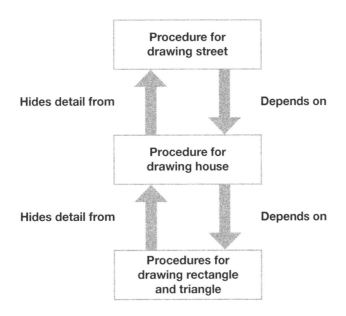

Problem decomposition

Most computational problems beyond the trivial need to be broken down into sub-problems before they can be solved. Think of any system which starts off by presenting the user with a menu of choices. Each choice will result in a different, self-contained module.

Top-down design

Top-down design is the technique of breaking down a problem into the major tasks to be performed; each of these tasks is then further broken down into separate subtasks, and so on until each subtask is sufficiently simple to be written as a self-contained **module** or subroutine. Remember that some programs contain tens of thousands, or even millions, of lines of code, and a strategy for design is absolutely essential. Even for small programs, top-down design is a very useful method of breaking down the problem into small, manageable tasks.

Advantages of problem decomposition

As well as making the task of writing the program easier, breaking a large problem down in this way makes it very much simpler to test and maintain. When a change has to be made, if each module is self-contained and well documented with inputs, outputs and preconditions specified, it should be relatively easy to find the modules which need to be changed, knowing that this will not affect the rest of the program.

Q1: Give some other advantages of writing a program as a collection of independent modules.

Hierarchy charts

A hierarchy chart is a tool for representing the structure of a program, showing how the modules relate to each other to form the complete solution. The chart is depicted as an upside-down tree structure, with modules being broken down further into smaller modules until each module is only a few lines of code (never more than a page).

10-49

Example 1

Draw a hierarchy chart for a program which calculates and prints a customer's monthly gas bill.

This can be broken down into several steps.

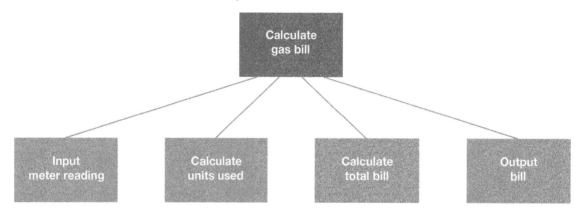

'*Calculate units used*' and '*Calculate total bill*' may now be further broken down.

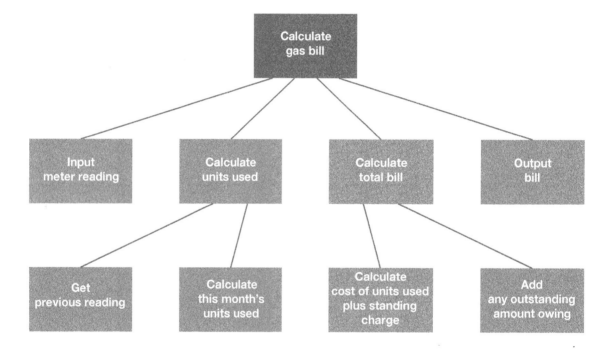

10-49

Q2: Draw a hierarchy chart for a program which asks the user which times table they would like to be tested on, and then displays five questions, getting the user's answer each time and telling them whether they were right or wrong. If they are wrong, the correct answer is displayed.

Exercises

1. Using local rather than global variables in subroutines is one way of helping to make a program easy to maintain.

   (a) Explain why this is the case. [3]

   (b) Describe briefly **three** other ways in which a program can be made easy to understand and maintain. [6]

2. Draw a hierarchy chart for a quiz program which does the following:

   • asks the user 10 random multiple-choice questions from a bank of 100 questions held in a file

   • if the user gives the correct answer, gives feedback and adds 1 to the user's score

   • if they give the wrong answer, gives feedback and displays the correct answer

   • at the end of the questions, gives the score out of 10 [6]

10-49

Chapter 50 – Thinking logically, thinking concurrently

Objectives

- Identify the points where a decision has to be taken
- Determine the logical conditions that affect the outcome of a decision
- Determine how decisions affect flow through a program
- (A) • Determine which parts of a program can be tackled at the same time
- (A) • Determine the benefits and trade-offs of concurrent processing

The structured approach

The structured programming approach aims to improve the **clarity** and **maintainability** of programs. Using structured programming techniques, only three basic programming structures are used:

- sequence – one statement following another
- selection – if ... then ... else... endif and switch/case ... endswitch statements
- iteration – while ... endwhile, do... until and for ... next loops

10-50

Languages such as Python and Pascal are **block-structured languages** which allow the use of just three control structures. They may allow you to break out of a loop, but this is not recommended in structured programming. Each block should have a single entry and exit point.

Tools for designing algorithms

Flow diagrams and pseudocode are two methods or tools which are commonly used for designing algorithms. Pseudocode corresponds more closely to the iteration structures in a programming language and is generally more useful for designing algorithms of any complexity.

There are no universally accepted ways of writing pseudocode and so long as the meaning is clear, it is acceptable. OCR has its own standard way of writing pseudocode and that is used throughout this book and will be used in any exam questions involving pseudocode. Note that in this pseudocode the symbol == denotes equality in a condition. This is also how it is written in Python.

Most of the logic errors that occur in programs occur at the points where decisions have to be made, or in the conditions which affect the outcome of a decision. This applies both to selection and iterative structures.

The more algorithms you write, the more aware you will become of the places where errors are likely to occur. A useful strategy to test an algorithm is to draw a **trace table** and follow it through manually.

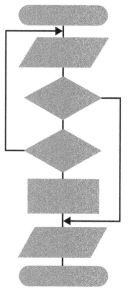

Example 1

Consider the following algorithm. It is intended to print out the number of values between a lower and upper bound entered by the user, that are divisible by either 3, 5 or both.

```
count = 0
first = input("Please enter lower bound: ")
last = input("Please enter upper bound: ")
n = first
while n <= last
   if n mod 5 == 0 then
      count = count + 1
   endif
   if n mod 3 == 0 then
      count = count + 1
   endif
   n = n + 1
endwhile
print("Values divisible by 3 or 5: ", count)
```

Q1: Suppose the user enters a lower bound of 0 and an upper bound of 15. What answer would you expect?
What will be output by the program?

There are two problems with this algorithm. The first is that it counts the value 0 as divisible by both 3 and 5, whereas the user would probably not intend 0 to be included. We have not specified that the user should enter positive integers, and this should be specified as a pre-condition to the routine.

The second problem is that any number divisible by both 3 and 5 will be counted twice. This is a logic error which needs to be corrected.

Q2: Suggest amendments to the algorithm so that it works correctly for any two positive integers entered by the user.

Example 2

Competitors playing in a chess tournament are awarded 2 points for a win, 1 point for a draw and 0 points for a loss. Each player plays 12 games.

The results for a player are held in an array of characters, with "W" representing a win, "D" representing a draw and "L" representing a loss.

Write a pseudocode algorithm for a function which returns the points score of a player. Show how the function would be called and the result output.

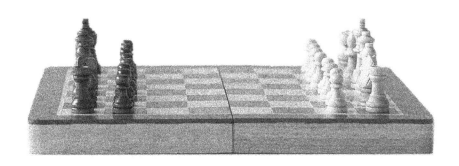

10-50

```
function calculatePoints(score)
   points = 0
   for n = 0 to len(score) - 1
      if score[n] == "W" then
         points = points + 2
      else if score[n] == "D" then
         points = points + 1
      endif
   next n
   return points
endfunction


// main program
myscore = ["W", "W", "D", "W", "W", "W", "W", "L", "D", "D", "W", "L")
result = calculatePoints(myscore)
print("Points scored: ", result)
```

Q3: What is the expected output of the program above?

A second algorithm is written to provide the administrator of the tournament with further information about the players' performance. The array names holds the name of each player in the tournament, and the array scores holds the corresponding points score for each player.

The algorithm is shown below.

```
function playerStats(names, scores)
   lowerCount = []
   for j = 0 to len(names) - 1
      count = 0
      for k = 0 to len(names) - 1
         if scores[k] < scores[j] then
            count = count + 1
         endif
      next k
      lowerCount.append((names[j], count))
   next j
   return lowerCount
endfunction

names = ["Adam", "Ben", "Carol", "Davina", "Enid", "Fred","George",
                               "Henry", "Ian", "Jane", "Keith"]
scores = [14, 3, 21, 14, 15, 10, 20, 6, 10, 12, 10]
lowerCount = playerStats (names, scores)
for n = 0 to len(names)
   print(lowerCount[n][0], lowerCount[n][1])
next n
```

10-50

In the above algorithm, the function `playerStats` returns a list of tuples called `lowerCount`. Each element of the tuple consist of a player's name and an integer `count`:

```
((names[0], count[0]), (names[1], count[1]) … (names[10], count[10]))
```

The first line output in the main program is

```
Adam 6
```

Q4: What are the second and third lines output? What is the function `playerStats` calculating?

A-Level only

Thinking concurrently

The difference between concurrent computing and parallel computing is debatable and is often taken to mean the same thing. For example, a house may have a burglar alarm system which continually monitors the front door, back door, windows, rooms upstairs and downstairs.

Q5: Is this parallel or concurrent processing?

Generally, concurrent computing is defined as being related to but distinct from parallel computing. **Parallel computing** requires multiple processors each executing different instructions simultaneously, with the goal of speeding up computations. It is impossible on a single processor.

Concurrent processing, on the other hand, takes place when several processes are running, with each in turn being given a slice of processor time. This gives the appearance that several tasks are being performed simultaneously, even though only one processor is being used. Processor scheduling algorithms are covered in Section 2, Chapter 7.

Benefits and trade-offs of concurrent processing

Concurrent processing has benefits in many situations.

- Increased program throughput – the number of tasks completed in a given time is increased
- Time that would be wasted by the processor waiting for the user to input data or look at output is used on another task
- The drawback is that If a large number of users are all trying to run programs, and some of these involve a lot of computation, these programs will take longer to complete

Benefits and trade-offs of parallel processing

- Parallel processors enable several tasks to be performed simultaneously by different processors. It can speed up processing enormously when repetitive calculations need to be performed on large amounts of data
- Graphics processors can quickly render a 3-D object by working simultaneously on individual components of the graphic
- A browser can display several web pages in separate windows and one processor may be carrying out a lengthy search or query while processing continues in other windows
- parallel processing has limitations; there is an overhead in coordinating the processors and some tasks may run faster with a single processor than with multiple processors.

10-50

A

Exercises

1. A plumber charges for parts and labour. Labour is charged at £20 per half hour or part of a half hour. The time spent is recorded as a four-digit integer, so that for example

   0120 means that 1 hour and 20 minutes labour is to be charged

   0350 means that 3 hours and 50 minutes labour is to be charged

   A variable called `duration` holds the four-digit integer representing time spent.

   (a) Write a subroutine to calculate and return the labour charge. [4]

   (b) Identify **two** local variables used in your subroutine. [2]

   (c) Show how the subroutine will be called using a parameter. [2]

2. In a vote for which of three plays produced at a theatre was most enjoyable, the total votes cast for each of plays "A", "B" and "C" have been stored in an array `totalVotes`.

   The following algorithm has been written to output the play with the most votes.

```
01 if totalVotes[0] > totalVotes[1] then
02    if totalVotes[0] > totalVotes[2] then
03       print ("Play A")
04    endif
05 else
06    if totalVotes[1] > totalVotes[2] then
07       print ("Play B")
08    else
09       print ("Play C")
10    endif
11 endif
```

   (a) In the event that an equal number of votes is cast for each play,

   (i) which lines of the algorithm will be executed? [3]

   (ii) what will be printed? [1]

   (b) Write an algorithm so that the result is always printed correctly in the event of two or three plays all receiving the same number of votes. [8]

   A-Level only

3. (a) Distinguish between parallel processing and concurrent processing. [2]

   (b) A school runs a local area network linking computers throughout the school. Describe how concurrent processing can be achieved on the network. [2]

   (c) When a class of students all try and download a piece of software at the beginning of a class, performance is affected. Explain why. [2]

10-50

Chapter 51 – Problem recognition

Objectives

A • Know what features of a problem make it soluble by computational methods

A • Categorise different types of problem and solutions

A • Explore different strategies for problem-solving

A • Understand the concept and application of the "divide and conquer" approach

Computable problems

A problem is defined as being **computable** if there is an algorithm that can solve every instance of it in a finite number of steps. Some problems may be theoretically computable, but if they take millions of years to solve, they are, in a practical sense, insoluble.

An example of such a problem is the cracking of a secure password. If you choose a password of 10 characters or more, comprising a mixture of random letters, numbers and special symbols, it will be impossible to crack. You can test the strength of your passwords on various websites.

10-51

Methods of problem solving

There are many ways of problem solving, including:

- enumeration (listing all cases)
- simulation
- theoretical approach
- creative solution

Enumeration

Theoretically, many problems and algorithmic puzzles can be solved by **exhaustive search** – trying all possible solutions until the correct one is found. Thousands of problems which were in the past insoluble have, thanks to the power of modern computers, become soluble. For example, a database of fingerprints or DNA can within a reasonable time find the identity of an individual, if his or her fingerprints or DNA are on the database.

The most important limitation of the exhaustive search strategy is its inefficiency – in general, the number of possible solutions increases exponentially as the size of the problem increases.

Consider, for example, the problem of constructing a magic square of order 3. The problem can be stated as follows:

Fill the 3 x 3 square with the integers 1 to 9 in such a way that the sum of each row, column and corner-to-corner diagonal is the same.

?	?	?
?	?	?
?	?	?

How many possibilities are there? There is a choice of 9 numbers for the first square, 8 for the second, and so on giving $9 \times 8 \times 7 \times 6 \times 5 \times 4 \times 3 \times 2 \times 1 = 362,880$ ways of arranging the 9 numbers. This is 9! (spoken 9 factorial.)

Q1: Is this a computable problem?

A magic square of 5 rows and columns has 25! solutions, and it would take a computer making 10 trillion operations per second about 49,000 years to try all the options.

There are in fact algorithms which will find solutions for magic squares of any size. This is the **theoretical approach**, which will generally find results considerably faster than a "brute force" method of solution.

Simulation

Simulation is the process of designing a model of a real system in order to understand the behaviour of the system, and to evaluate various strategies for its operation. Such problems include:

- financial risk analysis
- population predictions
- queueing problems
- climate change predictions
- engineering design problems

Simulating a system invariably makes use of **abstraction** to reduce the problem to its essentials, removing all unnecessary details. Queueing problems, for example, include problems of finding out how many checkouts are needed in a new supermarket or on a new toll road, or how many staff are needed in a software support department to man the helplines, or in a tax office to process tax returns.

Q2: How would abstraction be applied to this type of problem? What factors would be relevant, and what would be irrelevant?

Simulation can also involve building a physical model of, for example, a spacecraft, ship or wind turbine, so that its behaviour can be studied. This is obviously useful when it would be too expensive, dangerous or impractical to carry out tests on the real thing. A model can be used to evaluate performance or test outcomes.

10-51

Strategies for problem solving

In Chapter 49 we looked at decomposition as a strategy for solving large, complex problems. **Top-down design** involves breaking a large task down into several smaller tasks, which are again broken down until each one is a small, manageable subtask. This is an excellent strategy for problem-solving.

Divide and conquer

This is a very powerful technique which essentially reduces the size of the problem with every iteration. Its best-known application is the **binary search** (see Chapter 60), which halves the size of the problem with each iteration. Other problems may be tackled in this way but do not necessarily reduce the problem so fast.

Problem abstraction

Problem abstraction involves removing details until the problem is represented in a way that it is possible to solve because it reduces to one that has already been solved.

Consider the following problem: There are four knights on a 3x3 chessboard: the two white knights are at the bottom two corners, and the two black knights are at the two upper corners. The goal is to switch the knights in the minimum number of moves so that the white knights are in the upper corners and the black knights are in the bottom corners. (A knight can only move in the following manner: one or two squares horizontally or vertically, followed by two squares or one square at right angles, moving 3 squares in total.)

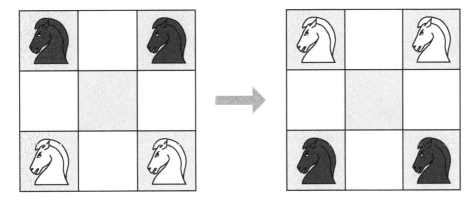

We can abstract this problem by first numbering the squares of the chessboard. 1 to 9. Now we can draw lines from 1 to 6 and 1 to 8 representing the two possible moves from square 1. Do the same for each square in turn, and you end up with the graph shown in (b). (Square 5 can't be reached with a knight's move so it is omitted from this graph.)

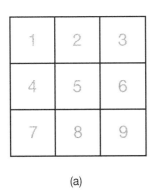

(a)

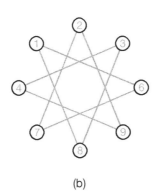

(b)

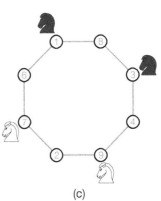

(c)

A-Level only

Figure (b) is not much help in solving the problem. Now imagine that all the vertices are joined by a single string, and rearrange the string so that the vertices form a circle – this gives us a much more revealing picture. There are only two ways to solve the puzzle in the minimum number of moves; move the knights along the edges in either a clockwise or a counter-clockwise direction until each of the knights reaches the diagonally opposite corner for the first time.

This is the "**graph unfolding**" method of solution, equivalent to a general problem that has already been solved in the same way, so is a **reduction** of the more general problem.

Q3: What is the total number of moves required to switch the knights to the opposite side of the board?

Automation

Automation in computer science deals with building and putting into action models to solve problems. For example, you could model the financial implications of running an ice-cream stand at a given venue for a week or a longer period. You have to decide on what has to be included in the model and what assumptions you are going to make. Then you have to create and implement the algorithms and execute and test the results.

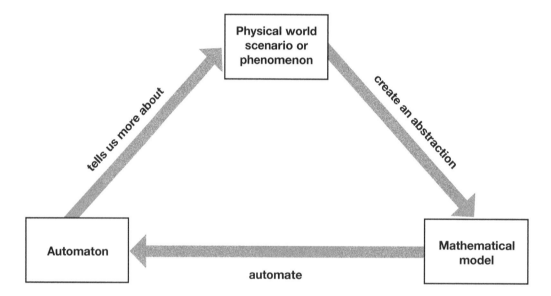

Automating the abstraction may in fact tell us more about the reality that we are modelling.

10-51

Exercises

1. A computer game is being designed to simulate cars on a race track. Abstraction has been used in the design.

    Explain how abstraction may be applied in the creation of the game. [3]

2. The goal in this problem is to place as many coins as possible at points of the 8-pointed star depicted below, according to the following rules:

    -   Each coin must first be placed on an unoccupied point and then moved along a line to an unoccupied point

    -   Once a coin has been positioned, it cannot be moved again.

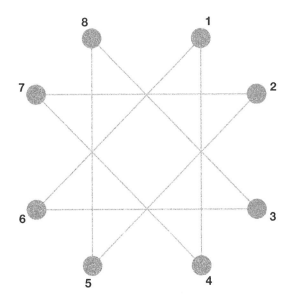

10-51

For example, you could make the following sequence of moves: 1 → 4, 2 → 5, 3 → 6, 7 → 2, 8 → 3 which places 5 coins.

What is the maximum number of coins that can be placed? [2]

Tip: Use the "graph unfolding" method of solution explained on the previous page.

A

A-Level only

Chapter 52 Problem solving

Objectives

A • Learn about and apply the following to solve problems:

- o visualisation
- o backtracking
- o data mining
- o heuristics
- o performance modelling
- o pipelining

Visualisation

The manner in which a problem is presented is often a very important factor in finding a solution. Computers work with binary numbers but humans often prefer a visual image. Consider this representation of a binary tree:

	left	data	right
tree[0]	3	Mike	1
tree[1]	2	Tara	5
tree[2]	-1	Oliver	-1
tree[3]	6	George	4
tree[4]	-1	Harriet	10
tree[5]	8	Vicky	-1
tree[6]	9	Bill	7
tree[7]	-1	Charles	-1
tree[8]	-1	Ursula	-1
tree[9]	-1	Babs	-1
tree[10]	-1	Julie	-1

Who is the parent of Harriet? Who are the children of Tara?

It is quite difficult to work out. But if we look at the tree in its graphical form, it becomes very simple.

10-52

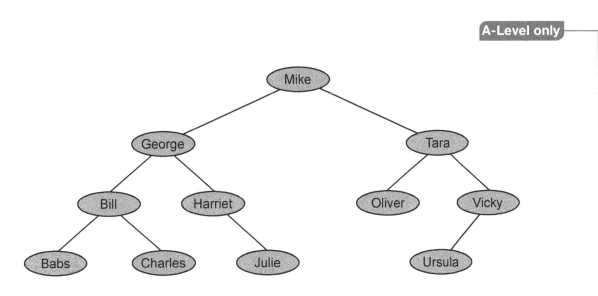

A flow diagram is a useful way of visualising an algorithm.

Q1: Suggest some other applications where an image is more useful for solving a problem than a written description or other method of presenting the information.

Backtracking

In some problems, in order to find a solution you have to make a series of decisions, but there may be cases for which:

- you don't have enough information to know which is the best choice
- each decision leads to a new set of choices
- one or more of the sequences may be a solution to the problem

Backtracking is a methodical way of trying out different sequences until you find one that leads to a solution. Solving a maze is a typical problem of this kind, and it is the technique used in a depth-first traversal of a graph, covered in Chapter 63.

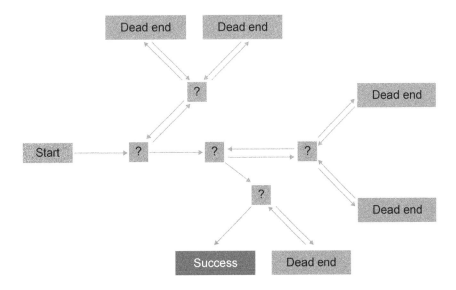

10-52

283

Data mining

Data mining is the process of digging through big data sets to discover hidden connections and predict future trends, typically involving the use of different kinds of software packages such as analytics tools. **Big data** is the term used for large sets of data that cannot be easily handled in a traditional database.

Big Data analysis is quite probably going to be the most exciting, interesting and useful field of study in the computing world over the next decade or two. We are just at the beginning of exploring its massive benefits in healthcare and medicine, business, communication, speech recognition, banking, and many other fields. Here are some questions it can answer:

- Does cellphone use increase the likelihood of cancer? With six billion cellphones in the world, there is plenty of data to analyse. (The answer turned out to be "No"!)

- How can you improve voice-translation software? By scoring the probability that a given digitised snippet of voice corresponds to a specific word. Google has made use of this data in its speech recognition software.

- How does the Bank of England find out whether house prices are rising or falling? By analysing search queries related to property.

- How can online education programmers use data collection to improve the courses offered? By studying data on the percentage of thousands of students registered who rewatched a segment of the course, suggesting it was not clear, or collecting data on wrong answers to assignments.

The term "Big Data" was first coined in the early 2000s by scientists working in fields such as astronomy and human genome projects, where the amount of data they were collecting was so massive that traditional methods of organising and analysing data, such as relational databases, could no longer be used.

Intractable problems

Some problems are termed **intractable** because although an algorithm may exist for their solution, it would take an unreasonably long time to find the solution. An example of such a problem is known as the **Travelling Salesman Problem (TSP)**, which poses the question "Given a list of towns and the distances between each pair of towns, what is the shortest possible route that the salesman can use to visit each town exactly once and return to the starting point?"

This is different from finding the shortest path from A to B. This problem has many applications in fields such as planning, logistics, the manufacture of microchips and DNA sequencing.

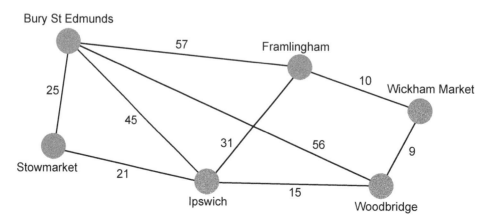

A-Level only

To solve the problem, we could look first at a **brute-force** method, testing out every combination of routes.

With just five cities, the number of possible routes is: $4! = 4 \times 3 \times 2 \times 1 = 24$.

A computer could calculate the best route in a fraction of a second.

> **Q2:** How many different routes are there for (a) 10 cities?   (b) 20 cities?   (c) 50 cities?

The problem is said to be **intractable** because it will take a long time for a fast computer to find the optimal solution for even a relatively small number of cities, and using the brute force algorithm, the problem rapidly becomes impossible to solve within a reasonable time as the number of cities increases.

Comparing time complexities

The table below shows what a huge difference there is in algorithms with different orders of time complexity for different values of n.

	10	50	100	1000
n	10	50	100	1000
$\log_2 n$	3.3	5.64	6.65	9.97
n^2	100	2500	10,000	1 million
n^3	1000	125000	1 million	1 billion
2^n	1024	A 16-digit number	A 31-digit number	A 302-digit number
$n!$	3.6 million	A 65-digit number	A 161-digit number	A very, very large number!

10-52

> **Q3:** Algorithms for problems A, B and C have time complexities $O(n^3)$, $O(2^n)$, $O(n!)$. Using the table above, which of A, B, C are tractable and which are intractable?

Intractable problems, which have no efficient algorithms to solve them, are in fact quite common; so how can solutions to these problems be found?

Heuristic methods

Not all intractable problems are equally hard, and not all instances of a given intractable problem are equally hard. Brute-force algorithms are not the only option for solving these problems. It may be quite simple to get an approximate answer, or an answer that is good enough for a particular purpose. One approach is to find a solution which has a high probability of being correct.

Another approach is to solve a simpler or restricted version of the problem, if that is possible. This may give useful insights into possible solutions.

An approach to problem solving which employs an algorithm or methodology not guaranteed to be optimal or perfect, but is sufficient for the purpose, is called a **heuristic** approach. An adequate solution may be achieved by trading optimality, completeness, accuracy or precision for speed. The objective is to find a good solution in a reasonable time frame.

A

We often apply heuristics in our everyday lives – if we want to travel from A to B we may use a route that we already know, even if it is not the best one. An employer who interviews several people for a job may see several suitable candidates, and make a decision based on two or three factors, ignoring others which may be relevant to the decision. In psychology, a heuristic is a mental shortcut that allows people to make a judgement and solve problems, while being aware that the solution may not necessarily be the optimal one.

Returning to the **Travelling Salesman Problem (TSP)**, a large number of heuristic solutions has been developed, the best of which (developed in 2006) can compute a solution within two or three percent of an optimal tour for as many as 85,000 "cities" or nodes.

Performance modelling

Performance modelling is the process of simulating different user and system loads on a computer using a mathematical approximation, rather than doing actual performance testing which may be difficult and expensive. For example, it could be used to test the performance of a network under different conditions. The output from the performance model may then be used to help with planning a new system which is suited to the requirements of an organisation.

Pipelining

Pipelining is the technique of splitting tasks into smaller parts and overlapping the processing of each part of the task. It is commonly used in microprocessors used in personal computers so that for example while one instruction is being fetched, another is being decoded and a third, executed. It basically works much like an assembly line.

10-52

Exercises

1. (a) Describe what is meant by **data mining**. [2]

   (b) Describe **two** applications which use data mining. [6]

2. Describe the key features of a **backtracking** algorithm. Give an example of a problem which can be solved using this technique. [3]

3. Explain what is meant by a **heuristic** solution to a problem. Give an example of when such a solution could be applied and why it would be an appropriate method. [4]

A

Section 11

Programming techniques

In this section:

11

Chapter 53 – Programming basics

Objectives

- Define what is meant by an algorithm and pseudocode

- Learn how and when different data types are used

- Learn the basic arithmetic operations available in a typical programming language

- Become familiar with basic string-handling operations

- Distinguish between variables and constants

What is an algorithm?

An algorithm is a set of rules or a sequence of steps specifying how to solve a problem. A recipe for chocolate cake, a knitting pattern for a sweater or a set of directions to get from A to B, are all algorithms of a kind. Each of them has **input**, **processing** and **output**.

Q1: What are the inputs and outputs in a recipe, a knitting pattern and a set of directions?

Ingredients	Method	
100g plain flour	Put flour and salt into a large mixing bowl and make a well in the centre.	
2 eggs	Crack the eggs into the middle	
300ml milk	Pour in about 50ml milk and the oil.	
1tbsp oil	Start whisking from the centre, gradually drawing the flour into the eggs, milk and oil, etc.	
Pinch salt		

In the context of programming, the series of steps has to be written in such a way that it can be translated into program code which is then translated into machine code and executed by the computer.

Using pseudocode

Whatever programming language you are using in your practical work, as your programs get more complicated you will need some way of working out what the steps are before you sit down at the computer to type in the program code. A useful tool for developing algorithms is **pseudocode**, which is a sort of halfway house between English and program statements. There are no concrete rules or syntax for how pseudocode has to be written, and there are different ways of writing most statements. We will use a standard way of writing pseudocode that translates easily into a programming language such as Python, Visual Basic or whatever procedural language you are learning.

This section does not teach you how to program in any particular programming language – you will learn how to write programs in your practical sessions – but it will help you to understand and develop your own algorithms to solve problems.

11-53

An introduction to pseudocode statements

Input/output statements

Most programs will have input and output statements to allow the user to enter data and display or print results. Here is the pseudocode for a simple example:

```
print("What is your name?")          //display text on the screen
//wait for user input and assign the value to the variable myname
myname = input()
print("Hello, ", myname)
```

This program will ask the user to input their name, and then display "Hello, Jo" or whatever name the user entered. Notice that in this pseudocode, text such as "Hello, " will be wrapped in speech marks to distinguish it from variables.

We will normally use the pseudocode

```
myname = input("What is your name?")
```

which combines the `print` and `input` statements to display the prompt "What is your name" and then waits for the user to enter text and press the ENTER key.

Comments

Note also that anything following a // will be treated as a **comment** and will have no effect on the running of the program. Comments are very important when you come to code your programs, to document the code (specifying the name, author, date written and purpose of the program, for example) and to explain how any tricky bits of the program work.

Data types

Different data types are held differently in the computer's memory so you need to use the correct data type for the task. In Section 6 the most common data types built into programming languages were listed as:

- Integer   a whole number such as -25, 0, 3, 28879
- real/float   a number with a fractional part such as -13.5, 0.0, 3.142, 100.0001
- Boolean   a Boolean variable can only take the value TRUE or FALSE
- character   a letter or number or special character typically represented in ASCII, such as a, A, %, ? or %. Note that the character "4" is represented differently in the computer from the integer 4 or the real number 4.0
- string   anything enclosed in quote marks is a string, for example "Peter", "123", or "This is a string". Either single or double quotes are acceptable.

Common arithmetic operations

The symbols +, -, * and / are used for the common arithmetic operations of addition, subtraction, multiplication and division.

e.g. Suppose the bill in a restaurant comes to £20, and you want to divide it equally among 3 or 4 friends.

```
bill = 20
billBetween4 = bill/4      will return the value 5
billBetween3 = bill/3      returns 6.666666667
```

In pseudocode you can assume that `billBetween3` will be automatically defined as a real variable and will return a value such as 6.666666667, though this may not be the case in every programming language.

The Round function

You can round this number using a function `round`.

```
billBetween3 = round(billBetween3,2)   //round to 2 decimal places
```

This will return the value 6.67.

Q2: How could you convert this answer to a string variable and assign the answer to billstring?

Exponentiation

If you want to find, for example 2^5, 5 is called the **exponent** and you need to use exponentiation. You can write this operation in pseudocode as

```
x = 2**5
```

or, using variables,

```
x = y**n
```

Integer division and finding a remainder

Sometimes you may want to perform **integer division** and find a **remainder**.

For example: Twenty apples are to be divided between 6 people. How many will each receive, and how many will be left over?

In this case you need to use the `div` operator to find the whole number of apples each person will receive. The `mod` operator will find the remainder.

These two operations are coded differently in different programming languages, but in pseudocode you could write the following statements:

```
apples = 20
applesPerPerson = 20 div 3    (written applesperPerson = 20//3 in Python)
```

This will return 6 in `applesPerPerson`.

```
applesRemaining = 20 mod 3    (written applesRemaining = 20%3 in Python)
```

This will return 2 in `applesRemaining`.

11-53

String-handling functions

Programming languages have a number of built-in string-handling methods or functions. Some of the common ones in a typical language are:

`len(string)`	Returns the length of a string
`string.find(str)`	Determines if `str` occurs in string. Returns `index` (the position of the first character in the string) if found, and `−1` otherwise. In our pseudocode we will assume that string (1) is the first element of the string, though in Python, for example, the first element is string (0)
`ord("a")`	returns the integer value of a character (97 in this example)
`chr(97)`	returns the character represented by an integer ("a" in this example)

Q3: What will be output by the following lines of code?
```
x = "Come into the garden, Maud"
y = len(x)
z = x.find("Maud")
print("x= ", x)
print("y= ",y)
print("z= ",z)
```

To **concatenate** or join two strings, use the + operator.

e.g.   "Johnny" + "Bates" = "JohnnyBates"

String conversion operations

`int("1")`	converts the character "1" to the integer 1
`str(123)`	converts the integer 123 into a string "123"
`float("123.456")`	converts the string "123.456" to the real number 123.456
`str(123.456)`	converts the real number 123.456 to the string "123.456"
`date(year,month,day)`	returns a number that you can calculate with

Example:

```
date1 = date(2015,1,18)

date2 = date(2014,12,30)

days = date1-date2

print(date1, date2, days)
```

This will output

```
2015-01-18 2014-12-30 19
```

The actual code in, for example, Python or VB will be similar but not identical. You may need to import a `datetime` library module.

Constants and variables

Some programming languages require you to declare all variables and constants before they are used in the program.

Variables are **identifiers** (names) given to memory locations whose contents will change during the course of the program; we have seen plenty of examples of these – e.g. in the statement below, the variable `myname` will change according to what the user enters.

```
myname = input("Please enter your name: ")
```

Some programming languages also allow you to define **constants**, whose value never changes while the program is being run. For example, if your program involved calculating the area of a circle, you could define `pi` at the start of the program as a constant having the value 3.14159. Or, you might hold the company phone number as a constant, declared at the start of the program as

```
const companyPhone = "01453 123456"
```

The advantage of using a constant is that in a long, complex program there is no chance that a programmer will accidentally change its value by using the identifier for a different purpose.

Some languages such as Python do not require or even allow you to define variables or constants – you just use them as and when required in the program.

Standards for variable names

Most programming languages are very flexible in the format of variable names that you can use. Typically they must start with a letter or an underscore, with the rest of the name consisting of letters, numbers or underscore. Spaces and other characters are not permitted.

You should always try to use meaningful names for variables, rather than x, y and z, as this helps to make the program easy to follow and update when required. It is also helpful, within a team of programmers, to have standards for naming variables and constants, as this will leave less room for errors and inconsistencies in the names in a large program.

Guidelines could include:

- Start all variable names with a lowercase letter

- Do not use underscores in the middle of variable names

- Use "camelCaps" to separate parts of a variable name – for example, timeInMinutes, maxTemperature

- Do not use overly long names but keep them meaningful – maxTemp is better than maximumTemperature if there is not likely to be any confusion over the meaning of max

- Use all uppercase letters for constants, which are then instantly identifiable

- When defining a class in object-oriented programming, start with an uppercase letter, with the rest of the class name lowercase

Following guidelines such as these will save a lot of time in looking through a program to see whether you called something best_score, Best_Score, bestScore or some other variation.

Exercises

1. A school keeps data about each of its pupils. State the most suitable data type for each of the following data items:

   Pupil's surname

   A single letter indicating whether they are male or female

   The amount owed for school trips

   The number of school trips they have participated in

   Whether or not the pupil is entitled to free school meals [5]

2. (a) Write pseudocode for a program which asks the user to enter the total bill for a restaurant meal, and the total number of people who had a meal. The program should add 10% to the bill as a tip, and then calculate and display to the nearest penny what each person owes, assuming the bill is evenly split. [6]

   (b) Complete the following table showing an additional **two** sets of test data, the reason for each test and the expected result. [6]

Total bill	Number of people	Reason for test	Expected result
100.00	10	Total amount exactly divisible by number of people	11.00

3. (a) Name **two** ways in which you can help to make your programs understandable to another programmer. [2]

   (b) Imagine that you have had a stall at the Summer Fayre. At the end of the day you count up the number of each 1p, 2p, 5p, 10p, 20p and 50p coins you have received.

   Write a pseudocode algorithm to allow the user to input the number of coins of each value, and to calculate and display the total takings.

   Make use of **two** ways of making the program understandable given in your answer to part (a). [6]

4. Below is an algorithm that adds VAT to the net price of an item and outputs the total price.

```
VATRATE = 20  // rate of VAT, currently 20%
NetPrice: Real  // net price is price without VAT
PriceWithVAT: Real   // total price is price including VAT
AmountOfVAT: Real  // amount of VAT to be added
NetPrice = input("Enter net price: ")
AmountOfVAT = NetPrice * VATRATE / 100
PriceWithVAT = NetPrice + AmountOfVAT
print(AmountOfVAT)
print(PriceWithVAT)
```

   (a) Write down **one** example of the following from the above algorithm:

   (i) a constant;   (ii) a variable;   (iii) a comment [3]

   (b) Suggest **three** standards for naming variables, and give **two** reasons why such standards are useful. [5]

11-53

Chapter 54 – Selection

Objectives

- Use relational operators
- Use Boolean operations AND, OR, NOT, XOR
- Use nested selection statements

Program constructs

There are just three basic programming constructs: **sequence**, **selection** and **iteration**.

Sequence is just two or more statements executed one after the other, such as

```
n = input("Please enter a number: ")
nsquared = n * n
print("The square is",nquared)
```

The second statement is an **assignment** statement in which a value is **assigned** to a variable.

In this chapter and the next, we will look at selection, iteration and recursion.

Selection

Selection statements are used to select which statement will be executed next, depending on some condition. Conditions are formulated using **relational operators**.

11-54

Relational operators

The following operators may be used in pseudocode for making comparisons:

>	greater than	<=	less than or equal
<	less than	==	equal
>=	greater than or equal	!=	not equal

Q1: Are these operators the same as the ones used in the programming language you are learning? If not, how are they different?

If ... then ... else

Selection statements can take different forms, for example:

```
if (expression1) then
   (do these statements)
endif
```

expression1 is an expression involving a relational operator such as

```
if (AGE >= 17)then
   canDrive = TRUE
endif
```

Q2: What type of variable is `canDrive`?

If `expression1` does not evaluate to TRUE, control passes to the next statement after the if statement.

Alternatively, you can specify what should happen if the condition does not evaluate to TRUE:

```
if (expression1) then
   (do these statements)
else
   (do these statements)
endif
```

For example:

```
if mark >= 50 then
   print("Pass")
else
   print("Fail")
   print("You will have to retake this test.")
endif
```

A 'nested' selection statement may have several alternatives:

```
if (expression1) then
   if (expression2) then
      (do these statements)
   else
       do these statements)
   endif
else
   (do these statements)
endif
```

Example 1

A bank offers different interest rates according to how much is in the account. There are three thresholds of £500, £3,000 and £10,000:

If `amount` less than `500`, rate = 1%

if `amount` is greater than or equal £`500` but less than £3000, rate = 1.5%

if `amount` is greater than or equal £`3000` but less than £10000, rate = 2%

If `amount` is greater than or equal £`10000`, rate is 3.5%

The selection statement can be written as follows:

```
if (amount< 500) then
   rate = 0.01
else if (amount<3000) then
   rate = 0.015
else if (amount<10000) then
   rate = 0.02
else
   rate = 0.035
endif
```

11-54

Q3: Write the above statement in a programming language.

The switch/case statement

Some programming languages support the use of a **switch** or **case** statement, an alternative structure to a nested **if** statement. It is useful when a choice has to be made between several alternatives.

Example 2

Perform different statements according to an option `choice` entered by the user.

```
switch choice:
    1      :print("You have selected option 1")
           (more statements here)
    2      :print("You have selected option 2")
           (more statements here)
    3      :print("You have selected option 3")
           (more statements here)
    else
       print("You must enter 1, 2 or 3")
    endswitch
```

Example 3

A statement to calculate the number of days in the month between 2001 and 2009 may be written:

```
switch month:
    "Jan","Mar","May","Jul","Aug","Oct","Dec": daysInMonth = 31
    "Apr","Jun","Sep","Nov":                   daysInMonth = 30
    "Feb": if year MOD 4 = 0 then
                daysInMonth = 29
           else
                daysInMonth = 28
           endif
    endswitch
```

Boolean operators AND, OR, NOT

More complex conditions can be formed using the Boolean operators AND and OR.

Example 4

```
if (a > b) AND (a > c) then
    max = a
else if (b > a) AND (b > c) then
    max = b
else
    max = c
endif
```

Q4: What does the above algorithm do?

Example 5

Write pseudocode for a program to allow the user to input the day of the week and output "Weekday" or "Weekend".

```
day = input("Enter day of week: ")
if (day = "Saturday") OR (day = "Sunday") then
   print("Weekend")
else
   print("Weekday")
```

Example 6

A tourist attraction has a daily charge for children of £5.00 on a weekday, or £7.50 on a weekend or bank holiday. Adults are charged £8.00 on weekdays and £12.00 on weekends and bank holidays.
Write pseudocode to allow the user to calculate the charge for a visitor.

```
day = input("Enter W for weekend, B for bank holiday or D for weekday: ")
visitor = input("Enter A for adult, C for child: ")
if ((day = "W") OR (day = "B")) AND (visitor = "A") then
   charge = 12.0
else if ((day = "W") OR (day = "B")) AND (visitor = "C") then
   charge = 7.5
else if (visitor = "A") then
   charge = 8.0
else
   charge = 5.0
endif
```

11-54

Notes: It is important to use brackets and to get them in the correct place to avoid any confusion over which operator is processed first. In standard Boolean logic the precedence rules make NOT highest, then AND, then OR.

The NOT operator

You can usually avoid the use of the NOT operator, replacing it with an appropriate condition. e.g.

```
NOT (a = b)     is equivalent to a != b
NOT (a < b)     is equivalent to a >= b
```

The XOR operator

XOR stands for **exclusive OR**, so that a XOR b means "either a or b but not both".

This can be implemented with a combination of AND, OR and NOT conditions:

```
(a AND NOT b) OR (NOT a AND b)
```

Note that NOT takes precedence over AND. Add extra brackets if you are in any doubt!

Exercises

1. Below is a segment of an algorithm.

```
swimTime = False
if (Membership == "Premier") then
   swimTime =  TRUE
else if ((Membership == "Adult") AND (Day == "Weekday") AND
        (Time < 1500)) OR
        ((Membership == "Adult") AND (Day == "Weekend")) then
      swimTime = TRUE
else if (Membership == "Junior") AND (Day == "Weekend") then
      swimTime = TRUE
endif
```

Write down the values of `swimTime` after the segment of the algorithm has executed for the following data:

(i)   Membership: Premier   Day: Weekday   Time: 1700

(ii)   Membership: Adult   Day: Weekday   Time: 1100

(iii)   Membership: Junior   Day: Weekday   Time: 1000

(iv)   Membership: Adult   Day: Weekend   Time: 0900

(v)   Membership: Adult   Day: Weekday   Time: 1530   [5]

2. (a) Write a pseudocode algorithm for a program which calculates the cost of carpeting a room. The carpet is supplied in a roll 4m wide. The cost of the carpet is £10 per square metre. The program should ask the user to enter the longest dimension (length) and shortest dimension (width) of the room, then calculate and display the length and width and cost of carpet that will be supplied.

You can assume that the width of the room is not more than 4m. If a width of more than 4m is entered, display an error message and quit the program.

The length could be more or less than 4m.   [5]

(b) Calculate the expected results for the following room sizes:

Length = 5, width = 3

Length = 5, width = 4

Length = 3, width = 2

Length = 3.9, width = 2

Length = 6, width = 5   [5]

Chapter 55 – Iteration

Objectives

- Understand and use three different types of iterative statement WHILE, REPEAT and FOR

Performing a loop

In the last two chapters we looked at **sequence** and **selection** statements. The third basic programming construct is **iteration**. Iteration means repetition, so iterative statements always involve performing a loop in the program to repeat a number of statements. There are three different types of loop to be considered, although some programming languages do not implement all three.

The while ... endwhile loop

A **while ... endwhile** loop has two properties:

- The expression controlling the repetition of the loop must be of type Boolean – that is, one which evaluates to True or False

- This expression is tested at the **start** of the loop

This is best explained by means of an example. Suppose you wanted to input the daily maximum temperatures for one month, calculate and output the average of these measurements.

The program has to work for any month, so when you have entered all the temperatures you will enter a 'dummy' value -100 to signify that there are no more temperatures to enter.

11-55

A first attempt at the pseudocode might look like this:

```
temp = 0              // initialise temp
totalTemp = 0         // initialise total of Temperatures
numberOfTemps = 0     // initialise number of temperatures
while temp != -100
   temp = input("Enter next temperature")
   totalTemp = totalTemp + temp
   numberOfTemps = numberOfTemps + 1
endwhile
averageTemp = totalTemp/numberOfTemps
print(averageTemp)
```

Test this algorithm with temperatures 8, 12 and -100. We can draw a trace table showing the value of the variables as they change during execution of the program.

totalTemp	numberOfTemps	temp != -100	temp	averageTemp
0	0	TRUE	8	
8	1	TRUE	12	
20	2	TRUE		

Q1: Complete the trace table. What is the average temperature calculated by this algorithm?

You should have ended up with 3 temperatures and an average temperature of -26.66667 instead of 10. The problem is that the expression controlling the loop is tested only once each time round, at the beginning of the loop, and not after each statement within the loop as it is executed. Therefore, we have to make sure that as soon as the number -100 is entered, the next thing that happens is that the Boolean expression is tested.

```
temp = 0                          // initialise temp
totalTemp = 0                     // initialise total of Temperatures
numberOfTemps = 0                 // initialise number of temperatures
temp = input("Enter first temperature")  // input first temperature
while temp != -100
   totalTemp = totalTemp + temp
   numberOfTemps = numberOfTemps + 1
   temp = input("Enter next temperature")
endwhile
averageTemp = totalTemp/numberOfTemps
print("Average temperature: ", averageTemp)
```

Note that with a **while ... endwhile** loop, if the Boolean expression is FALSE at the start, the loop will not be executed at all and control will pass straight to the next statement after **endwhile**.

Q2: What will happen if the first temperature entered is -100? Alter the algorithm to ensure that the program displays a suitable message.

The repeat ... until loop

This type of loop is very similar to the **while ... endwhile** loop, with the difference that the Boolean expression controlling the loop is written and tested at the **end** of the loop, rather than at the beginning. This means that the loop is always performed at least once.

Note: Python does not support a **repeat ... until** statement, but the same output can be achieved with a **while ... endwhile** loop.

Example 1

Write pseudocode for a program which tests someone on the squares of numbers up to 25.

```
// program to test a user on the squares of numbers
// random(a,b) generates a random integer between a and b
repeat
   num = random(1,25)
   numsquare = num * num
   answer = input("What is the square of ", num, "? ")
   if answer == numsquare THEN
      print("correct, well done")
   else
      print("No, it is ", numsquare)
   endif
   anotherGo = input("Another go? Answer Y or N: ")
until (anotherGo = "N") OR (anotherGo = "n")
```

Q3: Rewrite this algorithm using a **while … endwhile** loop. Which loop do you think is preferable for performing this task?

The for ... next loop

This type of loop is useful when you know how many iterations need to be performed. For example, suppose you want to display the two times table:

```
for count = 2 to 12
   product = 2 * count
   print("2 x ", count, " = ", product)
next count
```

The value of count starts at 2 and is incremented each time round the loop. When it reaches 12, the loop terminates and the next statement is executed.

Nested loops

Loops can be "nested" one inside another. Suppose we want to display all the multiplication tables between 2 and 12. We can do this with two FOR loops, one inside the other.

Example 2

```
for table = 2 to 12
   for count = 2 to 12
      product = table * count
      print(table, " x ", count, " = ", product)
   next count
next table
```

11-55

Q4: What will be the second line output by this algorithm?

Example 3

Use a random number generator to simulate throwing two dice to find out how many throws it takes to get a 6.

```
totalThrows = 0
answer = "y"
while (answer == "y") OR (answer == "Y")
   numberOfThrows = 0
   throw = 0
   while throw != 6
      throw = random(1,6)
      numberOfThrows = numberOfThrows + 1
      print("You threw a ", throw)
   endwhile
   print "That took ", numberOfThrows," throws"
   answer = input("Another go? (Y or y): ")
endwhile
```

Q5: What will happen if the user answers "yes" in answer to the question "Another go? (Y or y)"?

Example 4

You can count backwards as well as forwards in a **for ... next** loop. Here is a pseudocode program which uses the 'sleep' method to count down in seconds to blast-off. It starts by importing an external module called `time` which contains a built-in method sleep:

```
import time          // imports an external module
ReadyForCountdown = input("Press enter when you're ready to start")
for sec = 10, 0, step -1
   print(sec)
   time.sleep(1)    // suspends execution for 1 second
next sec
print("BLAST-OFF!")
```

Exercises

1. Write a pseudocode algorithm to allow the user to input two integers **highestNumber** and **multiplier**. The program should output the results of multiplying integers **2, 3... highestNumber** by **multiplier**.

   For example if the user enters 100 for **highestNumber** and 7 for **multiplier** the program should output the numbers 14, 21 ... 98. [5]

2. Write pseudocode for a program that asks the user which times table they would like to be tested on, and then gives them 5 random questions on this table, telling them each time whether they got the answer right or wrong. [5]

11-55

Chapter 56 – Subroutines and recursion

Objectives

- Be familiar with subroutines (functions and procedures), their uses and advantages
- Use subroutines that return values to the calling routine
- Describe the use of parameters to pass data to subroutines by value and by reference
- Contrast the use of local and global variables
- **(A)** Write and trace recursive subroutines
- **(A)** Compare recursion with an iterative approach

Types of subroutine

A subroutine is a **named block of code** which performs a specific task within a program.

Most high-level languages support two types of subroutine, **functions** and **procedures**, which are called in a slightly different way. Some languages such as Python have only one type of subroutine, namely functions.

All programming languages have 'built-in' functions which you will have already used if you have written any programs. For example, in Python:

```
myName = input("What is your name? ")
print("Hello, ", myName)
```

A subroutine is called by writing its name in a program statement. Some functions return a result, like `input` function above, and some do not return any result, like the `print` function. Notice that the first statement above combines the **print** and **input** functions; when the statement is executed, the computer will display the question "What is your name?" and wait for the user to input an answer, which will be assigned to the variable `myName`.

In languages which distinguish between functions and procedures, a **function** is called like the **input** above and always assigns a return value to a variable. A **procedure** is called by writing its name but not assigning the result to a variable, like the **print** statement above. However, as we shall see later, a procedure can still pass values back to the calling program if necessary.

In Chapter 53, we listed some string-handling functions, and we can write, for example, pseudocode such as

```
x = int("567")
```

to call the `int` function, which will convert the string "567" into an integer.

Q1: List some other functions you have used in your programs or pseudocode algorithms.

Q2: In some languages, `sqrt` is a function which returns the square root of a number. What value will be assigned to the variable `z` by the statement
```
z = sqrt(25)
```

User-written subroutines

You can write your own subroutines (functions and/or procedures) and call them from within the program as many times as needed. The subroutine first needs to be defined, typically above the code in the main program.

Example 1

Using pseudocode, write a subroutine which displays a menu of 4 options in a game.

```
procedure displayMenu // declare the subroutine
   print("Option 1: Display rules")
   print("Option 2: Start new game")
   print("Option 3: Quit")
   print("Enter 1, 2 or 3: ")
endprocedure
```

To call the subroutine from the main program, you simply write its name:

```
displayMenu
```

This subroutine always produces the same result whenever it is called; it simply displays this menu.

Example 2

Sometimes, you may want a subroutine to return a value to the main program:

```
function getChoice
   print("Option 1: Display rules")
   print("Option 2: Start new game")
   print("Option 3: Quit")
   print("Enter 1, 2 or 3: ")
   choice = input()
   return choice
endfunction
#main program starts here
option = getChoice
print("You have chosen ",option)
```

In this example, when the program is run, the first line to be executed is the first statement in the main program, `option = getChoice`. The subroutine is called, it displays the menu, gets the user's choice in `choice` and returns this to the main program using the statement `return choice`. Execution continues where it left off, at the statement `print("You have chosen ", option)`.

The subroutine is called in a slightly different way from the subroutine `displayMenu` – compare this to the two different ways in which built-in `print` and `input` subroutines are called.

```
print("What is your name?")
myName = input()
print("Hello, ",myName)
```

The `print` subroutine does not return a value, the `input` subroutine does.

Passing parameters by value and by reference

Frequently, you need to pass values or variables to a subroutine. The exact form of the subroutine interface varies with the programming language, but will be similar to the examples below:

```
procedure subroutineName(parameter1, parameter 2,...)

function subroutineName(parameter1, parameter 2,...)
```

In some programming languages, parameters may be passed in different ways. If a parameter is passed **by value**, its actual value is passed to the subroutine, where it is treated as a local variable. Changing a parameter inside the subroutine will not affect its value outside the subroutine.

All parameters are passed **by value** in Python.

In Visual Basic or Pascal, parameters may be passed by value but they may also be passed **by reference**. In this case, the address, and not the value, of the parameter is passed to the subroutine. Therefore, if the value is multiplied by three, for example, its value in the main program will reflect that change since it is referring to the same memory location.

To pass by reference in Pascal, the procedure header will specify that the relevant parameter is a variable. For example:

```
procedure abc(x, y : integer; var z : integer;)
```

Here, x and y are passed by value and z is passed by reference.

Example 3

Consider a simple subroutine which calculates the volume of a cylinder. In the main program, the user is asked to enter values for the radius and length of the cylinder. These variables are then passed as parameters to the subroutine for use in the calculation.

The values of the parameters `radius` and `length` in line 9 are passed to the subroutine where they are referred to using the identifiers `r` and `len` respectively. The order in which the parameters are written when calling the subroutine are written is important: `radius` is passed to `r`, `length` is passed to `len`. The return value `vol` is passed back to the main program, where it is assigned to `volume` in line 9.

```
1  function cylinderVolume(r,len)
2    pi = 3.142
3    vol = pi*r*r*len
4    return vol
5  endfunction

6  #main program
7  radius = input("Enter the radius of the cylinder: ")
8  length = input("Enter the length of the cylinder: ")
9  volume = cylinderVolume(radius,length)
10 print("The volume of the cylinder is ", volume)
```

Q3: Line numbers have been added to each statement of the above pseudocode for reference. Write down the statement numbers in the order in which they are executed.

Q4: Write pseudocode for a program which calls a function `addNumbers(n,m)` to add all the numbers between 5 and 10. The result should be returned to the main program and displayed.

11-56

SECTION 11 – **PROGRAMMING TECHNIQUES**

> **Q5:** Write pseudocode for a program which asks the user to enter a name and percentage mark. It then calls a subroutine which assigns a grade to the mark which it passes back to the main program, where it is printed together with the name. Grades are assigned as follows:
>
> | | |
> |---|---|
> | mark >= 80: | Distinction |
> | mark between 65-79: | Merit |
> | mark between 50 and 64: | Pass |
> | mark < 50: | Fail |

Local and global variables

Variables used in the main program are by default **global variables**, and these can be used anywhere in the program, including within any subroutines. Within a subroutine, **local variables** can be used within the subroutine, and these exist only during the execution of the subroutine. They cannot be accessed outside the subroutine and changing them has no effect on any variable outside the subroutine, even if the variable happens to have the same name as the local variable.

In Python, variables used in subroutines are local by default, unless they are declared as global in the calling program.

> **Q6:** Can you find a local variable in function `cylinderVolume(r,len)` in Example 3 above? What would happen if you tried to print its value in the main program?

11-56

The ability to declare local variables is very useful because it ensures that each subroutine is completely self-contained and independent of any global variables that have been declared in the main program.

The principle of **encapsulation** of all the variables needed in a subroutine is very important in programming. A subroutine written according to this principle can be tested independently, and used many times in many different programs without the programmer needing to know what variables it uses. Any variable in the calling program which coincidentally has the same name as a local variable declared in the subroutine will not cause an unexpected side-effect.

Example 4

```
1  procedure printNumbers(x)
2      a = 1
3      b = 2
4      c = 3
5      print("In the subroutine, a,b,c and x have values ", a,b,c,x)
6  endprocedure

7  #main program
8  a = 4
9  b = 5
10 c = 6
11 x = 10
12 print("In the main program, a,b,c and x have values ", a,b,c,x)
13 printNumbers(x)
14 print("In the main program, a,b,c and x now have values ", a,b,c,x)
```

Q7: Write down the line numbers of the statements in the order in which they are executed.

Q8: What will be the output of the program?

Q9: What will happen when the following program is run?

```
procedure printnum
  y = 20
  print("In sub num, y = ", y)
endprocedure
#main program
printnum
print("In main program, y = ", y)
```

Modular programming

When a program is short and simple, there is no need to break it up into subroutines. With a long, complex program, however, a top-down approach, in which the problem is broken down into a number of subtasks, is generally very helpful in designing the algorithm for a satisfactory solution.

Programming with subroutines

Using subroutines in a large program has many advantages:

- A subroutine is small enough to be understandable as a unit of code. It is therefore relatively easy to understand, debug and maintain especially if its purpose is clearly defined and documented

- Subroutines can be tested independently, thereby shortening the time taken to get a large program working

- Once a subroutine has been thoroughly tested, it can be reused with confidence in different programs or parts of the same program

- In a very large project, several programmers may be working on a single program. Using a modular approach, each programmer can be given a specific set of subroutines to work on. This enables the whole program to be finished sooner

- A large project becomes easier to monitor and control

A-Level only

Recursion

Definition of a recursive subroutine

A subroutine is **recursive** if it is defined in terms of itself. The process of executing the subroutine is called **recursion**. A recursive routine has three essential characteristics:

- A stopping condition or **base case** must be included which when met means that the routine will not call itself and will start to 'unwind'

- For input values other than the stopping condition, the routine must call itself

- The stopping condition must be reached after a finite number of calls

11-56

Recursion is a useful technique for the programmer when the algorithm itself is essentially recursive.

Some algorithms can be written using either recursion or iteration. Recursive routines are often much shorter, but more difficult to trace through. If a recursive routine is called a very large number of times before the stopping condition is reached, the program may crash with a "Stack overflow" error (see below, "Use of the call stack"). An iterative routine, on the other hand, has no limit to the number of times it may be called.

Example

A simple example of a recursive routine is the calculation of a factorial, where n! (read as n factorial or factorial n) is defined as follows:

If n = 0 then n! = 1

otherwise n! = n x (n-1) x (n-2) ... x 3 x 2 x 1

Thus for example 5! = 5 x 4 x 3 x 2 x 1

If we were calculating this manually, we probably calculate 5 x 4 = 20, then multiply 20 by 3 and so on. The calculation could be written as

5! = ((((5 x 4) x 3) x 2) x 1) = (((20 x 3) x 2) x 1) = ((60 x 2) x 1) = 120 x 1 = 120

This is essentially how recursion works. In pseudocode, it can be written like this:

```
function calcFactorial(n)
   if n == 0 then
      factorial = 1
   else
      factorial = n * calcFactorial(n-1)
      print(factorial)                          //LINE A
   endif
   return factorial
endfunction
```

Nothing will be printed until the routine has stopped calling itself. As soon as the stopping condition is reached, in this case n = 0, the variable `factorial` is set equal to 1, the return statement at the end of the subroutine is reached and control is passed back (for the first time, but not the last) to the next statement after the last call to calcFactorial, which is the `print` statement marked LINE A.

Q10: How many times is the `print` statement executed?
What is printed by the statement
   `print(factorial)`
when the routine is called with the statement:
   `x = calcFactorial(4)`?

Use of the call stack

In Chapter 36 the use of the **call stack** was discussed. Each time a subroutine is called, the return address, parameters and local variables used in the subroutine are held in a **stack frame** in the call stack.

Consider the following example:

```
1. procedure printList(num)
2.    num = num - 1
3.    if num > 1 then printList(num)
4.    print("At B, num = ", num)          // Line B
5. endprocedure
6. #main program
7. x = 4
8. printList(x)
9. print("At A, x =", x)                   // Line A
```

Return addresses, parameters and local variables (not used here) are put on the stack each time a subroutine is called, and popped from the stack each time the end of a subroutine is reached. At Line 8, for example, Line 9 (referred to here as Line A) is the first return address to be put on the stack with the parameter 4 when `printlist(x)` is called from the main program, with the parameter 4.

Representations of the current state of the stack each time a recursive call is made, and the subsequent "unwinding" are shown below.

The output from the program is:

At B, num = 1   (printed at Line B)

At B, num = 2   (printed at Line B)

At B, num = 3   (printed at Line B)

At A, x = 4   (printed at Line A)

Q11: Write iterative and recursive routines to sum the integers held in a list `numbers`. Show how each routine will be called.

11-56

Ⓐ

Exercises

1. (a) A program may use global and local variables.

    (i) Explain **one** difference between a global variable and a local variable. [2]

    (ii) Describe what will happen if a programmer declares a global variable and a local variable with the same name. [2]

    (b) Jo has written a computer program to produce invoices for customers of her father's plumbing business.

    To calculate the invoice total, the number of hours worked is rounded up to the next integer (e.g. 67 minutes would round up to 2 hours). This is then multiplied by the hourly rate. Finally, the cost of parts is added.

    Here are some extracts from Jo's code.

    ```
    01 REAL HourlyRate
    ...
    40 PROCEDURE Initialise
    41    HourlyRate  =  15
    42 END PROCEDURE
    ...
    60 PROCEDURE CalculateTotal
    61    INTEGER TimeInMinutes
    62    INTEGER CostOfParts
    63    INPUT TimeInMinutes
    64    INPUT CostOfParts
    65    OUTPUT TimeInMinutes DIV 60 + 1 * HourlyRate + CostOfParts
    66 END PROCEDURE
    ```

    State **one** global variable and **one** local variable in Jo's code. [2]

    (c) Line 65 contains an error.

    (i) Calculate the output of the procedure CalculateTotal if TimeInMinutes = 96 and CostOfParts = 100 using

    OUTPUT TimeInMinutes DIV 60 + 1 * HourlyRate + CostOfParts

    You **must** show your working. [2]

    (ii) Calculate the output of the procedure CalculateTotal if TimeInMinutes = 60 and CostOfParts = 0 using

    OUTPUT TimeInMinutes DIV 60 + 1 * HourlyRate + CostOfParts [1]

    (iii) Show how the procedure should be modified so that it produces the correct answer. [3]

    (d) Evaluate the extract of Jo's code. You should identify and explain the positive and negative aspects of her coding style and the implications that this will have on the maintainability of the program.

    The quality of written communication will be assessed in your answer to this question. [8]

    OCR F452-01 Qu 3 June 2012

11-56

2. The words COW, BEEF, and FORTY have all their letters written in alphabetical order. Here is an algorithm for a function which checks whether all the letters in a word are in alphabetical order.

```
01 FUNCTION IsInOrder(Word)
02    IF LENGTH(Word) = 1 THEN
03       RETURN TRUE
04    ELSE
05       FirstChar = First character in Word
06       RestOfWord = All characters in Word except the first
07       IF FirstChar > RestOfWord THEN
08          RETURN FALSE
09       ELSE
10          RETURN IsInOrder(RestOfWord)
11       END IF
12    END IF
13 END FUNCTION
```

(a) (i)   Describe what is meant by a parameter.   [2]

    (ii) Identify **one** parameter in the algorithm above.   [1]

(b) Explain the difference between the uses of the = sign in line 02 and in line 05, stating the type of operation being carried out.   [4]

(c) Line 07 compares the first character of the word with the rest of the word as shown below.

```
07  IF FirstChar > RestOfWord THEN
```

Explain why there may be a problem with the call `IsInOrder("FoRtY")`
and what can be done to avoid this problem.   [3]

(d) State what is meant by recursion, using this algorithm as an example.   [2]

(e) The algorithm is tested with the call `IsInOrder("Z")`. State the value which will be returned.

State the lines of the algorithm which will be executed.   [2]

(f) Explain what happens if the algorithm is tested with a call `IsInOrder(" ")` where the value of the argument is the empty string.   [2]

(g) Explain what happens when the algorithm is tested with the call `IsInOrder("APE")`.

You should show each call made, the lines of the algorithm executed and the return value of each call. You may use a diagram.   [6]

OCR F452-01 Qu 4 June 2012

11-56

A-Level only

3. (a) Explain briefly the main features of a recursive procedure from the programmer's point of view. Explain what is required from the system in order to enable recursion to be used. [3]

    (b) The following recursive subroutine carries out a list operation.

```
function listProcess(numList)
    if length(numlist) > 0 then
        Remove first element of numlist and store in first
        listProcess (numList)
        append first to end of numList
    endif
    return numList
endfunction
```

(i) Complete the following trace table if the list `numbers` is defined in the main program as
`numbers = [3,5,10,2]`

and the subroutine is called with the statement
`new = listProcess(numbers)`

length (numlist)	numlist				first	new
	0	1	2	3		
4	3	5	10	2	3	

[6]

(ii) Explain what the subroutine does. [1]

Chapter 57 – Use of an IDE

Objectives

- Be familiar with the use of an IDE to develop and debug a program
- Understand the purpose of testing and devise a test plan

Facilities of an IDE

When you create a program you will be using a software package that helps you write the code more easily.

This is called an **Integrated Development Environment or IDE**.

The screenshot below shows the Komodo IDE being used.

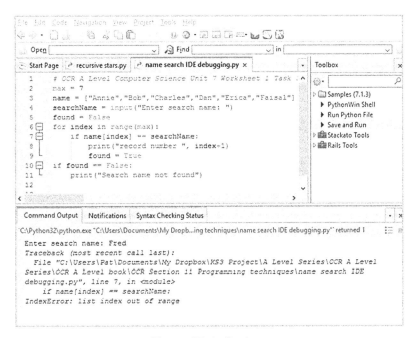

Figure 57.1: Syntax error

The IDE provides many tools to help you enter, edit, compile, test and debug your programs.

Entering a new program

In the screenshot above, you can see a menu at the top of the screen. Choosing **File, New** will present you with a blank screen to **type** your program.

The program is typed in the main window. The IDE adds line numbers for easy reference. You can **save** it using an option from the File menu. You can also **edit** your code.

11-57

Compiling and running your program

When you are ready to try out your program, it first has to be translated into machine code. This will be done using a **compiler** or **interpreter**.

Double-clicking the option **Save and Run** in the **Toolbox** on the right of the window in the Komodo IDE will **translate** the program and report any **syntax errors**.

In Figure 57.1, the interpreter has found a syntax error, and it tells you what line the error is on. There should be a double = sign on line 7, so you can correct that and run the program again by double-clicking **Save and Run** again. This time, the program starts to execute but then crashes because of a logic error, and the output is displayed in the bottom window.

```
Command Output    Notifications    Syntax Checking Status

'C:\Python32\python.exe "C:\Users\Pat\Documents\My Dropb...ing techniques\name search IDE debugging.py" returned 1

Enter search name: Edith
Traceback (most recent call last):
  File "C:\Users\Pat\Documents\My Dropbox\KS3 Project\A Level Series\OCR A Level
Series\OCR A Level book\OCR Section 11 Programming techniques\name search IDE
debugging.py", line 7, in <module>
    if name[index] == searchName:
IndexError: list index out of range
```

Figure 57.2: Logic error

Can you spot the logic error? Logic errors are usually much more difficult to find than syntax errors. The IDE has various tools to help you.

- You can set a **breakpoint** in the program which will cause the program to stop on that line, so that you can see whether it reaches that line.

- You can set a **watch** on a variable so that its value is displayed each time it changes

- You can **step through** a program a line at a time so that you can see what is happening

In this program, the variable max is the length of the list and it has been incorrectly set to 7. It should be 6. Once this has been done, it returns the correct result:

```
Command Output    Notifications    Syntax Checking Status               ▾ ✕

'C:\Python32\python.exe "C:\Users\Pat\Documents\My Dropb...ing techniques\name search IDE debugging.py" returned 0

Enter search name: Edith
Search name not found
```

Figure 57.3: Program executes correctly

Q1: Can you now deduce that the program is working correctly? If not, why not?

Q2: Suggest three more tests that could usefully be performed on the program to determine whether it works correctly for any user input.

11-57

Typical debugging options in an IDE

Debugger Command Description

This table lists common tasks and their Komodo commands.

To do this	Press this
Run a program The debugger runs until the program ends.	• **Debug Menu**: Select **Run Without Debugging** • **Windows/Linux Keyboard**: Press 'F7' • **Mac OS X Keyboard**: Press 'Meta'+'Ctrl'+'R'
Start the debugger The debugger runs until it encounters a breakpoint, or until the program ends.	• **Debug Menu**: Select **Go/Continue** • **Windows/Linux Keyboard**: Press 'F5' • **Mac OS X Keyboard**: Press 'Meta'+'>' • **Debug Toolbar**: Click the **Go/Continue** button
Step In The debugger executes the next unit of code, and then stops at the subsequent line.	• **Debug Menu**: Select **Step In** • **Windows/Linux Keyboard**: Press 'F11' • **Mac OS X Keyboard**: Press 'Meta'+'Shift'+'I' • **Debug Toolbar**: Click the **Step In** button
Step Over Like **Step In**, Step Over executes the next unit of code. However, if the next unit contains a function call, Step Over executes the entire function then stops at the first unit outside of the function.	• **Debug Menu**: Select **Step Over** • **Windows/Linux Keyboard**: Press 'F10' • **Mac OS X Keyboard**: Press 'Meta'+'Shift'+'O' • **Debug Toolbar**: Click the **Step Over** button
Step Out The debugger executes the remainder of the current function and then stops at the first unit outside of the function.	• **Debug Menu**: Select **Step Out** • **Windows/Linux Keyboard**: Press 'Shift'+'F11' • **Mac OS X Keyboard**: Press 'Meta'+'Shift'+'T' • **Debug Toolbar**: Click the **Step Out** button
Run to Cursor The debugger runs until it reaches the line where the cursor is currently located.	• **Debug Menu**: Select **Run to Cursor**. • **Windows/Linux Keyboard**: Press 'Shift'+'F10' • **Mac OS X Keyboard**: Press 'Meta'+'Ctrl'+'I'
Break Now Pause debugging an application at the current execution point. **Go/Continue** continues debugging from that point.	• **Debug Menu**: Select **Break Now** • **Debug Toolbar**: Click the **Break Now** button
Stop Stop the debugging session. **Go/Continue** restarts debugging from the beginning of the program.	• **Debug Menu**: Select **Stop** • **Windows/Linux Keyboard**: Press 'Shift'+'F5' • **OS X Keyboard**: Press 'Meta'+'Ctrl'+'P' • **Debug Toolbar**: Click the **Stop** button
Toggle breakpoint Enables, disables, or deletes a breakpoint on the current line.	• **Debug Menu**: Select **Disable/Enable Breakpoint** • **Windows/Linux Keyboard**: Press 'F9' • **Mac OS X Keyboard**: Press 'Meta'+'\'

Figure 57.4

11-57

Test strategies

There are several different test strategies used by software development companies, some of which are applicable to smaller software projects that you may have written. Test strategies are discussed in Section 3, Chapter 11.

Testing your own software

You will have implemented several algorithms in your practical sessions. Testing your solutions for correctness can be a complex and time-consuming task, but one that needs to be done thoroughly and systematically.

The purpose of testing is not to show that your program usually works correctly, if the user is careful when entering input data. *The purpose of testing is to try and uncover undetected errors*.

Devising a test plan

Your program should work correctly whatever data is input. If invalid data is entered, the program should detect and report this, and ask the user to enter valid data. Some data may be valid, but may nevertheless cause the program to crash if you have not allowed for particular values.

We need to choose test data that will test the outcome for any user input. To do this, we need to select **normal**, **boundary** and **erroneous** data.

- **normal** data is data within the range that you would expect, and of the data type (real, integer, string, etc. that you would expect. For example, if you are expecting an input between 0 and 100, you should test 1 and 99

- **boundary** data is data at the ends of the expected range – for example, test 0 and 100 to make sure that these give the expected results if the valid range is between 0 and 100

- **erroneous** data is data that is either just outside an expected range, e.g. -1, 101 or is of the wrong data type – for example, non-numeric characters when you are expecting a number to be input

For each test, you should specify the purpose of the test, the expected result and the actual result.

Example 1

The following algorithm is intended to calculate and print the average mark for each student in a class, for all the tests they have attempted:

```
// average mark
students = input("How many students? ")

for n = 1 to students
   name = input("Enter student name ")
   totalMarks = input("Enter total marks for ", name)
   numTests =  input("How many tests has this student taken? ")
   averageMark = round(totalMarks/numTests)
   print ("Average mark = ",averageMark)
next n
```

The test plan will look something like this:

Test number	Test data	Purpose of test	Expected result	Actual result
1	Number of students = 4 for tests 1-4 Jo: total marks 27, tests 3	Normal data, integer result	9	9
2	Tom: total marks 31, tests 4	Normal data, non-integer result rounded up	8	8
3	Beth: total marks 28, tests 3	Normal data, result rounded down	9	9
4	Amina: total marks 0, tests 0	No tests taken	0	Program crashes
5	Number of students abc	Test invalid data	Program terminates	

You can probably think of some other input data that would make the program crash. For example, what if the user enters 31.5 for the total marks? The program should validate all user input, so some amendments will have to be made to the program before general release!

11-57

Q3: Devise a test plan for the following program.

```
function code(message, shift)
   message = lowercase(message)
   codedMessage = ""
   for x in message
      if x in "abcdefghijklmnopqrstuvwxyz"
         num = ord(x)  # convert to ASCII value
         num = num + shift
         if num > ord("z")  # wrap if necessary
            num = num - 26
         endif
         char = chr(num) # convert back to character
         codedMessage = codedMessage + char
      else
         codedMessage = codedMessage + x
      endif
   next x
   return codedMessage
endfunction

# main program
shift = 3
msg = input("Enter your message: ")
codedMessage = code(msg,shift)
print("The encoded message is: ", codedMessage)
```

11-57

Q4: What will be the output from the algorithm if the user inputs "Hi, Jo!"?
Explain briefly the purpose of the algorithm.

Dry-running a program

A useful technique to locate an error in a program is to perform a **dry run**, with the aid of a **trace table**. As you follow through the logic of the program in the same sequence as the computer does, you note down in the trace table when each variable changes and what its value is.

Exercises

1. A Python program is run in an IDE and gives an incorrect result in the output pane, as shown:

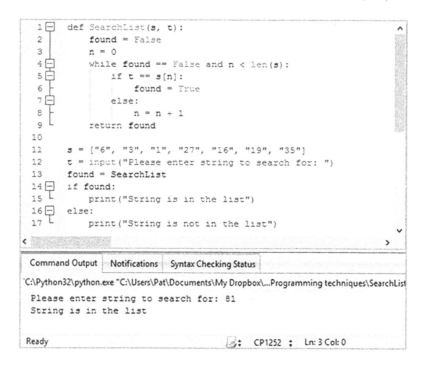

```
1   def SearchList(s, t):
2       found = False
3       n = 0
4       while found == False and n < len(s):
5           if t == s[n]:
6               found = True
7           else:
8               n = n + 1
9       return found
10
11  s = ["6", "3", "1", "27", "16", "19", "35"]
12  t = input("Please enter string to search for: ")
13  found = SearchList
14  if found:
15      print("String is in the list")
16  else:
17      print("String is not in the list")
```

| Command Output | Notifications | Syntax Checking Status |

`C:\Python32\python.exe "C:\Users\Pat\Documents\My Dropbox\...Programming techniques\SearchList`

```
Please enter string to search for: 81
String is in the list
```

Ready — CP1252 — Ln: 3 Col: 0

(a) State what the expected output is. [1]

(b) State **two** facilities an IDE might provide to help you find the error. [2]

(c) Give the line number of the line that is causing the problem and write the correct statement. [2]

(d) Apart from debugging aids, identify **three** features of an IDE that you might use when developing a program. [3]

2. Complete the trace table below to show how each variable changes when the algorithm is performed on the test data given.

```
x = 0
y = 0
z = 0
w = input
repeat
    x = x + w
    y = y + 1
    w = input
until w < 0
z = x/y
print z
```

w	x	y	z
	0	0	0
5	5	1	0

Test data: 5 7 2 2 4 -1 [5]

11-57

Chapter 58 – Use of object-oriented techniques

Objectives

A •   Be familiar with the basic concepts of object-oriented programming, such as classes, objects, methods, attributes, inheritance, encapsulation and polymorphism

Procedural programming

Programming languages have been evolving ever since the development of assembly languages. High level languages such as Basic and Pascal are known as **procedural languages**, and a program written in one of these languages is written using a series of step-by-step instructions on how to solve the problem. This is usually broken down into a number of smaller modules, and the program then consists of a series of calls to procedures or functions, each of which may in turn call other procedures or functions.

In this method of programming, the data is held in separate primitive variables such as integer or char, or in data structures such as array, list or string. The data may be accessible by all procedures in the program (**global** variables) or **local** to a particular subroutine. Changes made to global data may affect other parts of the program, either intentionally or unintentionally, and may mean other subroutines have to be modified.

A-Level only

11-58

Object-oriented programming

In object-oriented programming, the world is viewed as a collection of **objects**. An object might be a person, animal, place or event, for example. It could be something more abstract like a bank account or a data structure such as a stack or queue that the programmer wishes to implement.

An object-oriented program is composed of a number of interacting objects, each of which is responsible for its own data and the operations on that data. Program code in an object-oriented program creates the objects and allows the objects to communicate with each other by sending messages and receiving answers. All the processing that is carried out in the program is done by objects.

Object attributes and behaviours

Each object will have its own **attributes**. The attributes of a car might include its make, engine size, colour, etc. The attributes of a person could include first name, last name, date of birth.

An object has a **state**. A radio, for example, may be on or off, tuned to a particular station, set to a certain volume. A bank account may have a particular balance, say £54.20 and a credit limit of £300.

> **Q1:** What attributes might be assigned to the following objects?
> (a)   Cat
> (b)   Rectangle
> (c)   Hotel booking

An object has **behaviours**. These are the actions that can be performed by an object; for example, a cat can walk, pounce, catch mice, purr, miaow and so on.

Classes

A **class** is a blueprint or template for an object, and it defines the **attributes** and **behaviours** (known as **methods**) of objects in that class. An attribute is data that is associated with the class, and a method is a functionality of the class – something that it can do, or that can be done with it.

For example, a stock control system might be used by a bookshop for recording the items that it receives into stock from suppliers and sells to customers. The only information that the stock class will hold in this simplified system is the stock ID number, stock category (books, stationery, etc.), description, and quantity in stock.

Part of a sample definition of a class named `StockItem` is defined below. Program coding will vary according to the language used.

```
// Stock class used to model a simple stock control system,
// allowing stock to be added and sold.
class StockItem
// instance variables (properties/attributes)
   private stockID
   private category
   private description
   private qtyInStock

//A procedure may take one or more parameters. It does not return a value.
//A procedure with the name new is a constructor.
   public procedure new(aStockID, aCategory, aDescription, aQty)
      (instructions)
   endprocedure
   public procedure ReceiveStock (integer aQty)
      (instructions)
   endprocedure
   public procedure SellStock (integer aQty)
      (instructions)
   endprocedure

// A function may take one or more parameters. It returns a value.
   public  function GetQtyInStock
      (instructions)
   endfunction
endclass
```

As a general rule, instance variables or attributes are declared **private** and most methods **public**, so that other classes may use methods belonging to another class but may not see or change their attributes. This principle of **information hiding**, where a class cannot directly access the attributes of another class when they are declared private, is an important feature of object-oriented programming.

11-58

Instantiation (creating an object)

A **constructor** is used to create objects in a class. In this pseudocode, a procedure with the name `new` is a constructor.

Once the class and its constructor have been defined, and each of the methods coded, we can start creating and naming actual objects. The creation of a new object (an instance of a class) is known as **instantiation**. Multiple instances of a class can be created which each share identical methods and attributes, but the values of those attributes will be unique to each instance.

Suppose we want to create a new stock item called `book1`. The type of variable to assign to book1 has to be stated. This will be the class name, `StockItem`. The word `new` is typically used to **instantiate** (create) a new object in the class.

```
book1 = new StockItem("PT123","Book", "Computer Science", 35)
```

`book1` is called a reference type variable, or simply a reference variable. Note that this is a different type of variable from `stockID` or `qtyInStock`, which are string or integer variables.

Like primitive variables of type `integer`, `double`, `char`, `string`, reference variables are named memory locations in which you can store information. However, a reference variable does not hold the object – it holds a pointer or reference to where the object itself is stored.

A **variable reference diagram** shows in graphical form the new `StockItem` object referenced by the variable `book1`. In the diagram, reference variables are shown as circles and primitive data types (and `string` variables) are shown as rectangles.

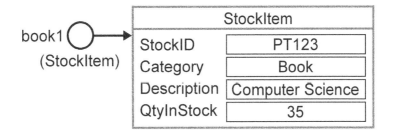

Sending messages

Messages can be categorised as either "getter" or "setter" messages. In some languages, "getter" messages are written as **functions** which return an answer, and "setter" messages as **procedures** which change the state of an object. This is reflected in the pseudocode used in this book.

The state of an object can be examined or changed by sending it a message, for example to get or increase the quantity in stock. To get the quantity in stock of `book1`, for example, you could write:

```
quantity = book1.GetQtyInStock
```

To record the sale of three book1 objects, you could write

```
book1.SellStock(3)
```

Q2: In the class definition for Radio (shown in the figure below), add the missing instance variables, and a procedure to set volume.

```
class Radio
// instance variables
   private volume
// insert more instance variables here

   public procedure new(aVolume, aStation, aSwitch)
      volume = aVolume
      station = aStation
      switch = aSwitch
   endprocedure
   ...
   public procedure setVolume(aVolume)
      (instructions)
      endprocedure
endclass
```

Q3: Write pseudocode statements to instantiate two new radio objects named `robertsRadio` and `philipsRadio`.

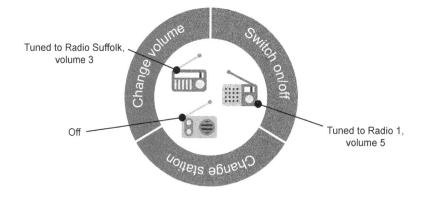

A radio modelled as a software object

Each object belongs to a class, and all the objects in the same class have the same structure and methods but they each have their own data. Objects belonging to a class are called **instances** of the class.

Encapsulation

An object **encapsulates** both its state (the values of its instance variables) and its behaviours or methods. All the data and methods of each object are wrapped up into a single entity so that the attributes and behaviours of one object cannot affect the way in which another object functions. For example, setting the `volume` of the `philipsRadio` object to 5 has no effect on any other `radio` object.

Encapsulation is a fundamental principle of object-oriented programming and is very powerful. It means, for example, that in a large project different programmers can work on different classes and not have to worry about how other parts of the system may affect any code they write. They can also use methods from other classes without having to know how they work.

11-58

Related to encapsulation is the concept of **information hiding**, whereby details of an object's instance variables are hidden so that other objects must use messages to interact with that object's state.

To change the volume of the Roberts radio, for example, a programmer might write:

```
robertsRadio.setVolume(5)
```

A programmer using the method does not need to know how this is achieved. The documentation of each method will specify the number and variable type of any arguments that need to be passed to the method, and what value, if any, is returned by the method. The attribute `volume` cannot be seen or changed directly; it can only be changed by sending a message (i.e. invoking the method).

Inheritance

Classes can **inherit** data and behaviour from a parent class in much the same way that children can inherit characteristics from their parents. A "child" class in object-oriented program is referred to as a **subclass**, and a "parent" class as a **superclass**.

For example, we could draw an inheritance hierarchy for animals that feature in a computer game. Note that the inheritance relationship in the corresponding **inheritance diagram** is shown by an unfilled arrow at the "parent" end of the relationship.

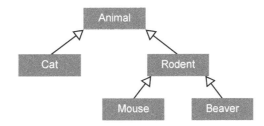

Class diagram involving inheritance

All the animals in the superclass `Animal` share common attributes such as `name` and `position`. Animals may also have common procedures (methods), such as `moveLeft`, `moveRight`. A `Cat` may have an extra attribute `size`, and an extra method `pounce`. A `Rodent` may have an extra method `gnaw`. A `Beaver` may have an extra method, `makeDam`.

Q4: What extra methods might `Mouse` have?

When to use inheritance

There is a simple rule to determine whether inheritance is appropriate in a program, called the "**is a**" rule, which requires an object to have a relationship to another object before it can inherit from the object. This rule asks, in effect, "Is object A an object B"? For example, "Is a `Cat` an `Animal`?" "Is a `Mouse` a `Rodent`?" Technically, there is nothing to stop you coding a program in which a man inherits the attributes and methods of a mouse, but this is going to cause confusion for users!

Coding inherited classes

Common behaviour can be defined in a **superclass** and inherited into a **subclass**.

The class Animal may be defined like this:

```
Class Animal
   private name
   private position
   public procedure new (aName, aPosition)
      name = aName
      position = aPosition
   endprocedure
   public procedure moveLeft(steps)
      position = position - steps
      (etc)
   endprocedure
   public function getPosition
      code for function
   endfunction
endclass
```

To code the class header for Cat, which is a subclass of Animal, in pseudocode we could write something like

```
Class Cat inherits Animal
   private size
   public procedure new(aName, aSize)
      super.new(aName)
      size = aSize
   endprocedure
endclass
```

Q5: A rodent has an extra attribute **colour**.
Write the class definition for Rodent.

Polymorphism

Polymorphism refers to a programming language's ability to process objects differently depending on their class. For example, all objects in subclasses of Animal can execute the methods moveLeft, moveRight, which will cause the animal to move one space left or right.

We might decide that a cat should move three spaces when a moveLeft or moveRight message is received, and a Rodent should move two spaces. We can define different methods within each of the classes to implement these moves, but keep the same method name for each class.

Defining a method with the same name and formal argument types as a method inherited from a superclass is called **overriding**. In the example above, the moveLeft method in each of the Cat and Rodent classes overrides the method in the superclass Animal.

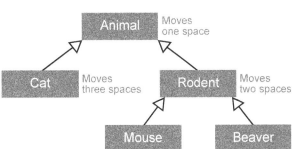

Q6: Suppose that `tom` is an instance of the `Cat` class, and `jerry` is an instance of the `Mouse` class. What will happen when each of these statements is executed?

```
tom.moveRight()
jerry.moveRight()
```

Exercises

1. A sports club keeps details of its members. Each member has a unique membership number, first name, surname and telephone number recorded. Three classes have been identified:

    ```
    Member
    JuniorMember
    SeniorMember
    ```

    The classes `JuniorMember` and `SeniorMember` are related, by single inheritance, to the class `Member`.

    (a) Draw an inheritance diagram for the given classes. [2]

    (b) Programs that use objects of the class `Member` need to create a new member, edit a member's details, delete a member's details, and show a member's details. No other form of access is to be allowed.

    Complete the definition of the attributes and the procedure `new` for the `Member` class.

    ```
    Class Member
        private memberNumber
        ...
        public procedure new(aMemberNumber, aFirstame, aSurname, aTel)
            memberNumber = aMemberNumber
        ...
        endprocedure
        ...
    endclass
    ```
    [1]

    (c) In object-oriented programming, what is meant by **encapsulation**? [1]

    (d) (i) What is meant by **instantiation** of an object? [2]

    (ii) Write a statement to create a new Member object with membership number A456, first name John, surname Bell, telephone number 07981 345987. [2]

11-58

2. (a) In an object-oriented computer game there is a class called `Crawlers`. Two subclasses of `Crawlers` are `Spiders` and `Bugs`. Draw an inheritance diagram for this. [2]

    (b) For the subclass `Spiders` suggest:

        (i) **one** attribute

        (ii) **one** method [2]

3. (a) In object-oriented programming, what is meant by **polymorphism**? [2]

    (b) An object-oriented program stores details of a class `Bird` and a subclass `Seagull`, defined as follows:

```
Class Bird
    public procedure move
        system.print("Birds can fly")
    endprocedure
endclass

Class Seabird inherits Bird
    public procedure move (override)
        system.print("Seabirds can fly and swim")
    endprocedure
    endclass
```

Two new objects are instantiated with the lines:

```
bird1 = new Bird()
bird2 = new Seabird()
```

        (i) What will be printed when the following lines are executed?

```
bird1.move
bird2.move
```
  [2]

        (ii) Explain your answer. [2]

11-58

Section 12

Algorithms

In this section:

12

Chapter 59 – Analysis and design of algorithms

Objectives

- **A** • Analyse the suitability of different algorithms for a given task and data set
- **A** • Be familiar with measures and methods to determine the efficiency of different algorithms
- **A** • Define constant, linear, polynomial, exponential and logarithmic functions
- **A** • Use Big-O notation to compare the time complexity of algorithms
- **A** • Be able to derive the time complexity of an algorithm

Comparing algorithms

Algorithms may be compared on how much time they need to solve a particular problem. This is referred to as the **time complexity** of the algorithm. The goal is to design algorithms which will run quickly while taking up the minimal amount of resources such as memory.

In order to compare the efficiency of different algorithms in terms of execution time, we need to quantify the number of basic operations or steps that the algorithm will need, in terms of the number of items to be processed.

For example, consider these two algorithms, which both calculate the sum of the first n integers.

```
function sumIntegersMethod1(n)
   sum = 0
   for i = 1 to n
      sum = sum + n
   next i
   return sum
endfunction
```

The second algorithm computes the same sum using a different algorithm:

```
function sumIntegersMethod2(n)
   sum = n * (n+1)/2
   return sum
endfunction
```

Q1: Which algorithm is more efficient? Why?

The first algorithm performs one operation (`sum = 0`) outside the loop and n operations inside the `for` loop, a total of n + 1 operations. As n increases, the extra operation to initialise sum is insignificant, and the larger the value of n, the more inefficient this algorithm is. Its **order of magnitude** or **time complexity** is basically n. The second algorithm, on the other hand, takes the same amount of time whatever the value of n. Its time complexity is a constant.

We will return to this idea later in the chapter, but first, we need to look at some of the maths involved in calculating the time complexity of different algorithms.

Introduction to functions

The order of magnitude, or time complexity, of an algorithm can be expressed as a **function** of its size.

A function maps one set of values onto another.

INPUT x

FUNCTION f:

OUTPUT f(x)

A linear function

A linear function is expressed in general terms as **f(x) = ax + c**

Values of the function $f(x) = 3x + 4$ are shown below for $x = 1, 10, 100, 10{,}000$

x	3x	4	y = f(x)
1	3	4	7
10	30	4	34
100	300	4	304
10,000	30,000	4	30,004

Notice that the constant term has proportionally less and less effect on the value of the function as the value of x increases. The only term that is significant is 3x, and f(x) increases in a straight line as x increases.

A polynomial function

A polynomial expression is expressed as **f(x) = ax^m + bx + c**

Values of the function $f(x) = 2x^2 + 10x + 50$ are shown below for $x = 1, 10, 100, 10{,}000$

x	x²	2x²	10x	50	y = f(x)
1	1	2	10	50	62
10	100	200	100	50	350
100	10,000	20,000	1,000	50	21,050
10,000	100,000,000	200,000,000	100,000	50	200,100,050

The values of b and c have a smaller and smaller effect on the answer as x increases, compared with the value of a. The only term that really matters is the term in x^2, if we are approximating the value of the function for a large value of x.

An exponential function

An exponential function takes the form **f(x) = ab^x**. This function grows very large, very quickly!

Q2: What is the value of $f(x) = 2^x$ when $x = 1$? When $x = 10$? When $x = 100$?

12-59

A logarithmic function

A logarithmic function takes the form **f(x) = a log$_n$ x**

"The logarithm of a number is the power that the base must be raised to make it equal to the number."

Values of the function f(x) = log$_2$ x are shown below for x = 1, 8, 1,024, 1,048,576.

x	y = log$_2$ x
1	0
8 (2^3)	3
1024 (2^{10})	10
1,048,576 (2^{20})	20

Permutations

The permutation of a set of objects is the number of ways of arranging the objects. For example, if you have 3 objects A, B and C you can choose any of A, B or C to be the first object. You then have two choices for the second object, making 3 x 2 = 6 different ways of arranging the first two objects, and then just one way of placing the third object. The six permutations are ABC, ACB, BAC, BCA, CAB, CBA.

> **Q3:** How many permutations are there of four objects? How many ways are there of arranging six students in a line?

The formula for calculating the number of permutations of four objects is 4 x 3 x 2 x 1, written 4! and spoken as "four factorial". (Note that 10! = 3.6 million... so don't try getting 10 students to line up in all possible ways!)

Big-O notation

Now that we have got all the maths out of the way and hopefully understood, we can study the so-called **Big-O notation** which is used to express the **time complexity**, or performance, of an algorithm. ('O' stands for 'Order'.)

The best way to understand this notation is to look at some examples.

O(1) (Constant time)

O(1) describes an algorithm that takes **constant time** (the same amount of time) to execute regardless of the size of the input data set.

Suppose array a has n items. The statement

```
length = len(a)
```

will take the same amount of time to execute however many items are held in the array.

O(n) (linear time)

O(n) describes an algorithm whose performance will grow in **linear time**, in direct proportion to the size of the data set. For example, a linear search of an array of 1000 unsorted items will take 1000 times longer than searching an array of 1 item.

O(n^2) (Polynomial time)

O(n^2) describes an algorithm whose performance is directly proportional to the square of the size of the data set. A program with two nested loops each performed n times will typically have an order of time complexity O(n^2). The running time of the algorithm grows in **polynomial time**.

12-59

O(2ⁿ) (Exponential time)

O(2^n) describes an algorithm where the time taken to execute will double with every additional item added to the data set. The execution time grows in **exponential time** and quickly becomes very large.

O(log n) (Logarithmic time)

The time taken to execute an algorithm of order O(log n) (**logarithmic time**) will grow very slowly as the size of the data set increases. A **binary search** is a good example of an algorithm of time complexity O($\log_2 n$). Doubling the size of the data set has very little effect on the time the algorithm takes to complete.

> **Q4:** A hacker trying to discover a password starts by checking a dictionary containing 170,000 words. What is the maximum number of words he will need to try out?
>
> This procedure fails to find the password. He now needs to try random combinations of the letters in the password. He starts with 6-letter combinations of a-z, A-Z.
>
> Explain why the second procedure will take so much longer than the first.

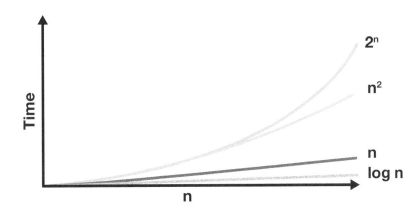

Graphs of log n, n, n², 2ⁿ

Calculating the time complexity of an algorithm

Here are two different algorithms for finding the smallest element in an array called `arrayX` of size n. Assume the index starts at 1.

The first algorithm puts the first value in the array equal to a variable called `minimum`. It then compares each subsequent item in the array to the first item, and if it is smaller, replaces minimum with the new lowest value.

```
minimum = arrayX[0]
for k = 1 to n - 1
    if arrayX[k] < minimum then
        minimum = arrayX[k]
    endif
next k
```

12-59

To calculate the time complexity of the algorithm in Big-O notation, we need to count the number of basic operations it performs. There is one initial statement, and n if statements, so the time complexity is 1 + n. However, as we have already discussed, the 1 is insignificant compared to n and this algorithm therefore executes in linear time and has time complexity O(n).

The second algorithm compares each value in the array to all the other values of the array, and if the current value is less than or equal to all the other values in the array then it is the minimum.

```
for k = 1 to n-1
    isMinimum = True
    for j = 1 to n-1
        if arrayX[k] > arrayX[j] then
            isMinimum = false
        endif
    next j
    if (isMinimum) then
        minimum = arrayX[k]
    endif
next k
```

To calculate the time complexity of this algorithm, we count the number of basic operations it performs.

There are two basic operations in the outer loop, (isMinimum = true and the final if statement) which are each performed n times. The inner loop has one basic operations performed n^2 times.

This gives us a time complexity of $2n + n^2$, but as discussed earlier, the only significant term is the one in n^2. The time complexity is therefore O(n^2).

Q5: What is the time complexity of each of the two subroutines sumIntegerMethod1 and sumIntegerMethod2 discussed at the beginning of this chapter?

Exercises

1. Assuming a is an array of n elements, compute the time complexity of the following algorithm.

    Explain how you arrive at your answer.

    ```
    duplicate = False
    for i = 0 to n - 2
      for j = i + 1 to n - 1
        if a[i] = a[j] then duplicate = True
      next j
    next i
    ```
    [3]

2. (a) Complete the following table showing values of f(n):

    [4]

n	1	2	4	8	12
$f(n) = n^2$	1	4			
$f(n) = 2^n$	2	4			
$f(n) = \log_2 n$	0	1			3.585
$f(n) = n!$	1				479,001,600

    (b) Place the following algorithms in order of time complexity, with the most efficient algorithm first. [2]

    Algorithm A of time complexity $O(n)$

    Algorithm B of time complexity $O(2^n)$

    Algorithm C of time complexity $O(\log n)$

    Algorithm D of time complexity $O(n^2)$

    Algorithm E of time complexity $O(n!)$

    (c) Explain why algorithms with time complexity $O(n!)$ are generally considered not to be helpful in solving a problem. Under what circumstances would such an algorithm be considered? [3]

12-59

Chapter 60 – Searching algorithms

Objectives

- Write and trace algorithms for linear search and binary search
- **A** • Analyse the time complexity of the linear search and binary search algorithms
- **A** • Describe and trace the binary tree search algorithm

Linear search

Sometimes it is necessary to search for items in a file, or in an array in memory. If the items are not in any particular sequence, the data items have to be searched one by one until the required one is found or the end of the list is reached. This is called a **linear search**.

The following algorithm for a linear search of a list or array `alist` (indexed from 0) returns the index of `itemSought` if it is found, –1 otherwise.

```
function linearSearch(alist,itemSought)
   index = -1
   i = 0
   found = False
   while i < length(alist) and found = False
      if alist[i] = itemSought then
         index = i
         found = True
      endif
      i = i + 1
   endwhile
   return index
endfunction
```

12-60

> **Q1:** What is the maximum number of items that would have to be examined to find a particular item in a linear search of one million items? What is the average number that would have to be searched?

A-Level only

Time complexity of linear search

We can determine the algorithm's efficiency in terms of execution time, expressed in Big-O notation. To do this, you need to compute the number of operations that the algorithm will require for n items. The loop is performed n times for a list of length n, and there are two steps in the loop (an IF statement and an assignment statement), giving a total of 3 + 2n steps (including 3 steps at the start). The constant term and the coefficient of n become insignificant as n increases in size, and the time complexity of the algorithm basically depends on *how often the loop has to be performed in the worst-case scenario*.

Therefore, the time complexity of the linear search is O(n).

A

Binary search

The binary search is a much more efficient method of searching a list for an item than a linear search, but crucially, the items in the list must be sorted. If they are not sorted, a linear search is the only option.

The algorithm works by repeatedly dividing in half the portion of the data list that could contain the required data item. This is continued until there is only one item in the list.

Consider the following ordered list where we wish to search for data item 50.

15	21	29	32	37	40	42	43	48	50	60	64	77	81	90	98

Stage 1: middle term is 43; we can therefore discard all data items less than or equal to 43. Note that the middle item of an even number of items is obtained by rounding down; the middle item of 16 items is item 8.

48	50	60	64	77	81	90	98

Stage 2: middle term is 64, so we can discard all data items greater than or equal to 64.

48	50	60

Stage 3: middle term is 50 – so we have found the data item.

Q2: Suppose we have the following sorted list:

3	5	6	8	11	12	14	15	17	18

Which one of the following is the correct sequence of comparisons when used to locate the data item 8?

(i)   12, 6, 8

(ii) 11, 5, 6, 8

Q3: Ask a friend to think of a number between 1 and 1000. Then use a binary search algorithm to guess the number. How many different guesses will you need, at most?

Q4: Look at the following data list. Which items will you examine in (a) a linear search and (b) a binary search to find the following data items?

(i)   27

(ii) 11

(iii) 60

9	11	19	22	27	30	32	33	40	42	50	54	57	61	70	78	85

12-60

Binary search algorithm

Below is an algorithm for the binary search on an array of *n* items in an array `aList`.

The ordered array is divided into three parts; a middle item, the first part of the array starting at aList[0] up to the middle item and the second part starting after the middle item and ending with the final item in the list. The middle item is examined to see if it is equal to the sought item.

If it is not, then if the middle item is greater than the sought item, the second half of the array is of no further interest. The number of items being searched is therefore halved and the process repeated until the last item is examined, with either the first or second half of the array of items being eliminated at each pass.

`first`, `last` and `midpoint` are integer variables used to index elements of the array. The variable `first` will start at 0, the beginning of the array. The variable `last` starts at `len(aList) - 1`, the last array index.

```
function binarySearch(aList, itemSought)
    found = False
    index = -1
    first = 0
    last = len(aList)-1
    while first <= last and found = False
        midpoint = Integer part of ((first + last)/2)
        if aList[midpoint] = itemSought then
            found = True
            index = midpoint
        else
            if aList[midpoint] < itemSought then
                first = midpoint + 1
            else
                last = midpoint - 1
            endif
        endif
    endwhile
    return index      #index = -1 if key not found
endfunction
```

12-60

A-Level only

Time complexity of binary search

The binary search halves the search area with each execution of the loop – an excellent example of a **divide and conquer** strategy. If we start with n items, there will be approximately n/2 items left after the first comparison, n/4 after 2 comparisons, n/8 after 3 comparisons, and $n/2^i$ after i comparisons. The number of comparisons needed to end up with a list of just one item is i where $n/2^i = 1$. One further comparison would be needed to check if this item is the one being searched for or not.

Solving this equation for i, $\qquad$ $n = 2^i$

Taking the logarithm of each side, $\qquad$ $\log_2 n = i \log_2 2$ giving $i = \log_2 n$ (since $\log_2 2 = 1$)

Therefore, the binary search is O(log n).

A

Q5: An array contains 12 numbers 5, 13, 16, 19, 26, 35, 37, 57, 86, 90, 93, 98

Trace through the binary search algorithm to find how many items have to be examined before the number 90 is found. The first row of the trace table is filled in below.

itemSought	index	found	first	upper	midpoint	aList(midpoint)
90	-1	false	0	11	5	35

Q6: What is the maximum number of items that would have to be examined to find a particular item in a binary search of one million items?

A-Level only

A recursive algorithm

The basic concept of the binary search is in fact recursive, and a recursive algorithm is given below. The procedure calls itself, eventually "unwinding" when the procedure ends. When recursion is used there must always be a condition that if true, causes the program to terminate the recursive procedure, or the recursion will continue forever.

Once again, `first`, `last` and `midpoint` are integer variables used to index elements of the array, with `first` starting at 0 and `last` starting at the upper limit of the array index.

```
function binarySearch(aList, itemSought, first, last)
   if last < first then
      return -1
   else
      midpoint - integer part of (first + last) / 2
      if aList[midpoint] > itemSought then
         // itemSought is in first half of list
         return binarySearch(aList, itemSought, first, midpoint-1)
      else
         if aList[midpoint] < itemSought then
            // itemSought is in second half of list
            return binarySearch(aList, itemSought,  midpoint+1, last)
         else
            // itemSought has been found
            return midpoint
         endif
      endif
   endif
endfunction
```

Q7: What condition(s) will cause a value to be returned from the subroutine to the calling program?

12-60

Binary tree search

The recursive algorithm for searching a binary tree is similar to the binary search algorithm above, except that instead of looking at the midpoint of a list, or a subset of the list, on each pass, half of the tree or subtree is eliminated each time its root is examined.

In the tree below, a maximum of four nodes has to be examined to find a value or return "not found".

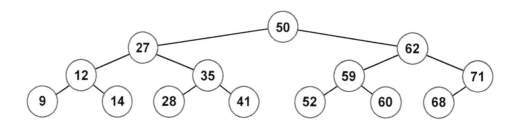

```
function binarySearchTree(itemSought,currentNode)
   if currentNode = None then
      return False
   else
      if itemSought = item at currentNode then
         return True
      else
         if itemSought < item at currentNode then
            if left child exists then
               return binarySearchTree (itemSought, left child)
            else
               return False
            endif
            if right child exists then
               return binarySearchTree(itemSought, right child)
            else
               return False
            endif
         endif
      endif
   endif
endfunction
```

Time complexity of binary tree search

Like the binary search, the number of items to be searched is halved with each pass through the algorithm. The time complexity is the same as the binary search, i.e. O(log n).

Exercises

1. (a) Data structures may be described as static or dynamic.

    (i)   State the meaning of the term static.

    (ii) State one type of data structure that is always considered static.

    (iii) State the meaning of the term dynamic.

    (iv) Give one disadvantage of using a dynamic data structure.   [4]

    (b) The list of positive even numbers up to and including 1000 is

        2, 4, 6, … 500, 502, … 998, 1000

    An attempt is to be made to find the number 607 in this list.

    Use the values given to show the first three stages for:

    (i)   a binary search   [3]

    (ii) a serial search   [3]

    (iii) Explain the difference between binary searching and serial searching.   [2]

    (iv) State one advantage and one **disadvantage** of a binary search compared with
          a serial search.   [2]

    OCR F453/01 Qu 5 June 2014

    12-60

2. The binary search method can be used to search for an item in an ordered list.

    (a) A list in alphabetical order contains 150 names.

    What is the maximum number of names that would need to be accessed to determine if a
    particular name appears in the list?   [1]

    A-Level only

    (b) Which of the following is the order of time complexity of the binary search method?

        $O(\log_2 n)$ $O(n)$ $O(n^2)$ [1]

    A

Chapter 61 – Bubble sort and insertion sort

Objectives

- Be able to describe the bubble sort and insertion sort algorithms
- Be able to trace the bubble sort and insertion sort algorithms

Sorting algorithms

Sorting is a very common task in data processing, and frequently the number of items may be huge, so using a good algorithm can considerably reduce the time spent on the task. There are many different sorting algorithms and we will start by looking at a simple but inefficient example.

Bubble sort

The Bubble sort is one of the most basic sorting algorithms and the simplest to understand. The basic idea is to bubble up the largest (or smallest) item to the end of the list, then the second largest, then the third largest and so on until no more swaps are needed.

Suppose you have an array of n items:

- Go through the array, comparing each item with the one next to it. If it is greater, swap them.
- The last element of the array will be in the correct place after the first pass
- Repeat n-2 times, reducing by one on each pass the number of elements to be examined

12-61

Q1: How do you swap two items in an array?

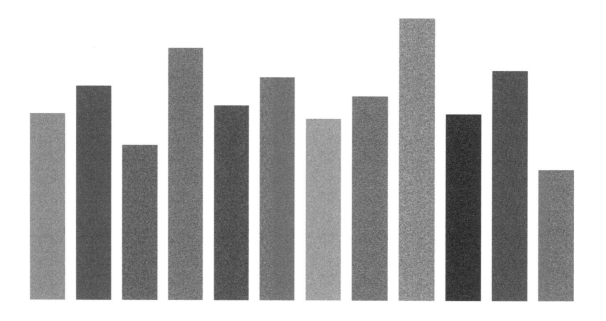

Example 3 Working through the Bubble sort algorithm

The figure below shows how the items change order in the first pass, as the largest item 'bubbles' to the end of the list. Each time an item is larger than the next one, they change places.

Pass 1

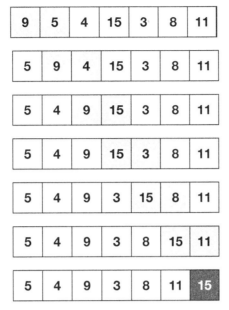

After the first pass, the largest item is in the correct place at the end of the list. On the second pass, only the first six numbers are checked.

Pass 2

11 and 15 in the correct place; so only the first five numbers are checked.

Pass 3

9, 11 and 15 in the correct place; so only the first four numbers are checked.

Pass 4

8, 9, 11 and 15 in the correct place; so only the first three numbers are checked.

Pass 5

Finally, the first two numbers are checked and swapped

Pass 6

Notice that in this case, no numbers were swapped on Pass 5. Therefore Pass 6 was not necessary. In order to avoid performing unnecessary passes on a list that is already in sequence, a *flag* may be set and tested on each pass so that if no swaps are made, no more unnecessary passes are made through an already sorted list. This is shown in Example 2 on the next page.

12-61

Example 1

Write a pseudocode algorithm for a bubble sort to sort the numbers 9, 5, 4, 15, 3, 8, 11 into ascending sequence. Print the numbers after each of the 6 passes through the list.

```
numbers = [9, 5, 4, 15, 3, 8, 11]
numItems = len(numbers)          // get number of items in the array
for i = 0 to numItems - 2
   for j = 0 to(numItems - i - 2)
      if numbers [j] > numbers[j + 1]
         // Swap the names in the array
         temp = numbers[j]
         numbers[j] = numbers[j + 1]
         numbers[j + 1] = temp
      endif
   next j
   print (numbers)
next i
```

If you run this program, the output is

[5, 4, 9, 3, 8, 11, 15]

[4, 5, 3, 8, 9, 11, 15]

[4, 3, 5, 8, 9, 11, 15]

[3, 4, 5, 8, 9, 11, 15]

[3, 4, 5, 8, 9, 11, 15]

[3, 4, 5, 8, 9, 11, 15]

The last pass through the list was not necessary.

Example 2

Amend the algorithm so that no unnecessary passes are made though the list.

```
numbers = [9, 5, 4, 15, 3, 8, 11]
numItems = len(numbers)          // get number of items in the array
flag = True                      // indicates when a swap is made
while i < (numItems - 1) and (flag = True)
   flag = False
   for j = 0 to numItems - i - 2
      if numbers [j] > numbers[j + 1]
         // Swap the names in the array
         temp = numbers[j]
         numbers[j] = numbers[j + 1]
         numbers[j + 1] = temp
         flag = True
      endif
   next j
   i = i + 1
endwhile
print(numbers)
```

Insertion Sort

This is a sorting algorithm that sorts one data item at a time. It is rather similar to how you might sort a hand of cards. The algorithm takes one data item from the list and places it in the correct location in the list. This process is repeated until there are no more unsorted data items in the list. Although more efficient than the bubble sort, it is not as efficient as the merge sort or quick sort.

Example 4 Insertion sort

The same list of numbers is sorted into ascending order using an insertion sort:

9, 5, 4, 15, 3, 8, 11

We leave the first item at the start of the list		9	5	4	15	3	8	11
5 is now inserted into the sorted list	1st pass	5	9	4	15	3	8	11
4 is now inserted into the sorted list	2nd pass	4	5	9	15	3	8	11
15 is now inserted into the sorted list (it stays where it is)	3rd pass	4	5	9	15	3	8	11
3 is now inserted into the sorted list	4th pass	3	4	5	9	15	8	11
8 is now inserted into the sorted list	5th pass	3	4	5	8	9	15	11
11 is now inserted into the sorted list	6th pass	3	4	5	8	9	11	15

On each pass, the current data item is checked against those already in the sorted list (shaded in the diagram). If the data item being compared in the sorted list is larger than the current data item, it is now shifted to the right. This continues to happen until we reach a data item in the sorted list which is smaller than the current data item.

For example, at the 5th pass 8 is compared with 15, and since it is smaller, 15 is shifted right.

8 is compared with 9, and 9 is shifted right.

8 is compared with 5, and as it is larger, it is inserted into the free space.

5th pass in summary:

8 is removed from the list temporarily	3	4	5	9	15		11
Since 15 > 8, it is shifted to the right	3	4	5	9		15	11
Since 9 > 8, it is shifted to the right	3	4	5		9	15	11
Since 5 < 8, 8 is inserted back into the sorted list	3	4	5	8	9	15	11

12-61

Algorithm for insertion sort

Here is the algorithm for a procedure to do an insertion sort :

```
procedure insertionSort(alist)
   n = len(alist)
   for index = 1 to n - 1
      currentvalue = alist[index]
      position = index
      while position > 0 and alist[position - 1] > currentvalue
         alist[position] = alist[position - 1]
         position = position - 1
      endwhile
      alist[position] = currentvalue
   next index
endprocedure

// main program
alist = [9,5,4,15,3,8,11]
insertionSort(alist)
print("sorted list ", alist)
```

Q2: The following list of names is to be sorted into alphabetical sequence using an insertion sort.
George, Jane, Miranda, Ahmed, Sophie, Bernie, Keith.

(a)   What is the first name to be moved? What will the list look like after this name is moved?

(b)   What is the second name to be moved? What will the list look like after this name has been moved?

12-61

A-Level only

Time complexity of bubble and insertion sorts

The bubble sort requires close to n passes through the list, with each pass requiring a maximum of n – 1 swaps. It is of order $O(n^2)$.

The insertion sort also has two nested loops and so has time complexity $O(n^2)$. However, if the list is already almost sorted, the time complexity is reduced to close to $O(n)$.

A

Exercises

1. (a) A bubble sort is performed on the following list:

    3, 5, 8, 17, 12, 15, 18, 23, 1

    (i)   Describe how a bubble sort works.   [3]

    (ii)   What is the sequence of the list after the first pass is completed?   [1]

    (iii) How many passes through the list will be required to sort the items into ascending numerical sequence?   [1]

    (b) An insertion sort is performed on the same list as in part (a).

    (i)   Describe how an insertion sort works.   [3]

    (ii)   What is the sequence of the list after the first pass is completed?   [1]

    (iii) What is the average time complexity of the insertion sort?   [1]

Chapter 62 – Merge sort and quick sort

Objectives

A • Understand and be able to trace the merge sort and quick sort algorithms

Merge sort

The merge sort uses a **divide and conquer** approach. The list is successively divided in half, forming two sublists, until each sublist is of length one. The sublists are then sorted and merged into larger sublists until they are recombined into a single sorted list. The basic steps are:

- Divide the unsorted list into *n* sublists, each containing one element

- Repeatedly merge sublists to produce new sorted sublists until there is only one sublist remaining. This is the sorted list.

The merge process is shown graphically below for a list in the initial sequence 5 3 2 7 9 1 3 8.

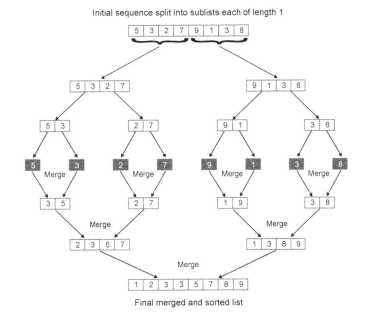

Final merged and sorted list

The list is first split into sublists each containing one element.

The merge process merges each pair of sublists into the correct sequence. Taking for example two lists: `leftlist = [2,3]` and `rightlist = [1,3]`, the merge process works like this:

1. Compare the first item in `leftlist` with the first element in `rightlist`

2. If item in `leftlist` < item in `rightlist`, add item from `leftlist` to `mergedlist` and read the next item from `leftlist`

3. Otherwise, add item from `rightlist` to `mergedlist` and read the next item from `rightlist`

4. Once one list is empty, any remaining items are copied into the merged list

5. Repeat from Step 2 until all items are in `mergedlist`

The process is then repeated for each pair of sublists until the lists are merged into the final sorted list.

12-62

An algorithm for the merge sort is given below.

```
procedure mergesort(mergelist)
   if len(mergelist) > 1 then
      mid = len(mergelist) div 2      // performs integer division
      lefthalf = mergelist[:mid]      // left half of mergelist into
                                         lefthalf
      righthalf = mergelist[mid:]     // right half of mergelist into
                                         righthalf
      mergesort(lefthalf)
      mergesort(righthalf)
      i = 0
      j = 0
      k = 0
      while i < len(lefthalf) and j < len(righthalf)
         if lefthalf[i] < righthalf[j] then
            mergelist[k] = lefthalf[i]
            i = i + 1
         else
            mergelist[k] = righthalf[j]
            j = j + 1
         endif
         k = k + 1
      endwhile
      while i < len(lefthalf)          // check if left half has
                                          elements not merged
         mergelist[k] = lefthalf[i]    // if so, add to mergelist
         i = i + 1
         k = k + 1
      endwhile
      while j < len(righthalf)         // check if rt half has elements
                                          not merged
         mergelist[k] = righthalf[j]   // if so, add to mergelist
         j = j + 1
         k = k + 1
      endwhile
   endif
endprocedure
// ****** main program ******
mergelist = [5, 3, 2, 7, 9, 1, 3, 8]
mergesort(mergelist)
print(mergelist)
```

Q1: The following list of numbers is to be sorted using a merge sort.

[54, 36, 66, 78, 64, 19, 42, 44, 51, 89, 72, 62, 22, 67, 81, 79]

Which answer below shows the first two lists to be merged?

a. [44] and [51]

b. [54] and [36]

c. [54, 36] and [66, 78]

d. [19, 36, 42, 44, 54, 64, 66, 78] and [22, 51, 62, 67, 72, 79, 81, 89]

Q2: Draw a graphical representation of how a list [5, 3, 9, 4, 2, 6, 1] is first split into halves until each sublist contains zero or one items, and then the sublists are merged to become the sorted list.

Time complexity of merge sort

The merge sort is another example of a divide and conquer algorithm, but in this case, there are n sublists to be merged, so the time complexity has to be multiplied by a factor of n.

The time complexity is therefore O(nlog n).

Space complexity

The amount of resources such as memory that an algorithm requires, known as the **space complexity**, is also a consideration when comparing the efficiency of algorithms. The bubble sort, for example, requires n memory locations for a list of size n. The merge sort, on the other hand, requires additional memory to hold the left half and right half of the list, so takes twice the amount of memory space.

Quick sort

The quick sort algorithm, like the insertion sort, uses a Divide and Conquer algorithm to quickly reduce the size of the problem, but without using the additional storage required by the merge sort.

The steps in the quick sort are as follows:

1. Select a value called the **pivot value**. There are different ways to choose the pivot value but we will choose the first item in the list. The actual position where the pivot value belongs in the final sorted list, called the **split point**, will be used to divide the list for subsequent calls. In the list shown below, 9 is the first pivot value.

9	5	4	15	3	8	11

2. Divide the remainder of the list into two partitions

   - all elements less than the pivot value must be in the first partition

   - all elements greater than the pivot value must be in the second partition

(The order of the elements in each partition is not significant in this explanation. It will become clearer in the explanation of the detailed procedure.)

3. 3 and 15 are now the pivots in the left and right partitions. Recursively repeat the process.

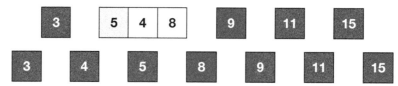

The list is now in sequence.

The detailed procedure

Below is a more detailed description of how the pivots are found at each point.

Locate two position markers called leftmark and rightmark at the beginning and end of the remaining items in the list (positions 1 and 6 in the figure). The goal of the partitioning process is to move items that are on the wrong side of the pivot value while also converging on the split point.

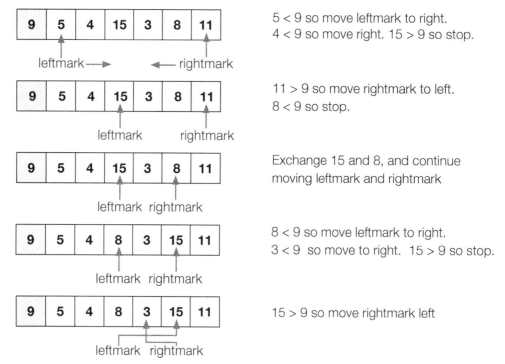

Rightmark and leftmark have now crossed over, so we stop. The position of rightmark is now the split point. The pivot value is exchanged with the contents of the split point and the pivot value is now in place.

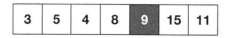

All the items to the left of the split point are less than the pivot value, and all the items to the right of the split point are greater than the pivot value. The list can now be divided at the split point and the quick sort invoked recursively on the two halves.

348

The quick sort algorithm

The quick sort algorithm shown below is recursive, repeatedly dividing the list at the split point until each half is of length 1, at which point the list is sorted. Most of the work is done in the partition function, which finds the split point.

```
function partition(alist, start, end)
   pivot = alist[start]
   leftmark = start + 1
   rightmark = end
   done = False
   while done = False
      while leftmark <= rightmark and alist[leftmark] <= pivot
         leftmark = leftmark + 1
      endwhile
      while alist[rightmark] >= pivot and rightmark >= leftmark
         rightmark = rightmark - 1
      endwhile
      if rightmark < leftmark
         done = True
      else
         // swap the list items
         temp = alist[leftmark]
         alist[leftmark] = alist[rightmark]
         alist[rightmark] = temp
      endif

   // swap the pivot with alist[rightmark]
   temp = alist[start]
   alist[start] = alist[rightmark]
   alist[rightmark] = temp
   return rightmark
endfunction

function quicksort(alist, start, end)
   if start < end
      // partition the list
      split = partition(alist, start, end)
      // sort both halves
      quicksort(alist, start, split-1)
      quicksort(alist, split+1, end)
   endif
   return alist
endfunction

alist = [9, 5, 4, 15, 3, 8, 11]
sortedList = quicksort(alist,0,len(alist)-1)
print(sortedList)
```

12-62

A-Level only

Advantages and disadvantages of the quick sort algorithm

The quicksort algorithm is extremely fast. If the partition always occurs in the middle of the list, there will be log n divisions in a list of length n, and each of the n items needs to be checked against the pivot value to find the split point. It therefore has time complexity O(n log n).

Another advantage is that it does not need additional memory, like the merge sort.

A disadvantage is that if the split points are not near the middle of the list, but are close to the start or end of the list, the division will be very uneven. If the split point is, for example, the first item in the sequenced list, the division results in a list of 0 items and a list of n-1 items. The list of n-1 items divides into 0 items and n-2 items and so on. The resulting time complexity is $O(n^2)$.

If the list is very large, and recursion continues too long, it may cause stack overflow and the program will crash.

Summary of sort algorithms

- **Bubble sort** is the slowest of the sorts, with time complexity $O(n^2)$

- **Insertion sort** is $O(n^2)$ but if the list is already almost sorted, this reduces to $O(n)$

- **Merge sort** is O(n log n) but requires additional memory space for the merging process

- **Quick sort** is generally the fastest sort, but is dependent on using a pivot that is not close to the smallest or largest elements of the list. There are several methods for selecting a pivot to ensure this does not happen. It has average time complexity O(n log n). It does not require additional memory space.

Exercises

1. (a) There are many methods of sorting a set of records into ascending order of key.
        What factors would you consider in deciding which of these methods is the most suitable
        for a particular application?   [2]

    (b) The merge sort algorithm has time complexity O(n log n). For a list of 1,024 items in
        random sequence, is this algorithm more or less efficient than a sort algorithm of time
        complexity $O(n^2)$? Explain your answer.   [3]

2. Explain briefly the steps in

    (a) the merge sort algorithm   [4]

    (b) the quick sort algorithm   [4]

12-62

Chapter 63 – Graph-traversal algorithms

Objectives

- **(A)** • Be able to trace depth-first and breadth-first algorithms
- **(A)** • Describe typical applications of each

Graph traversals

There are two ways to traverse a graph so that every node is visited. Each of them uses a supporting data structure to keep track of which nodes have been visited, and which node to visit next.

- A **depth-first** traversal uses a **stack**, which is implemented automatically during execution of a recursive routine to hold local variables, parameters and return addresses each time a subroutine is called. Alternatively, a non-recursive routine could be written and the stack maintained as part of the routine.

- A **breadth-first** traversal uses a **queue**.

Depth-first traversal

In this traversal, we go as far down one route as we can before backtracking and taking the next route.

The following recursive subroutine dfs is called initially from the main program, which passes it a graph, defined here as an **adjacency list** (see Chapter 38) and implemented as a dictionary with nodes A, B, C, ... as keys, and neighbours of each node as data. Thus if "A" is the current vertex, graph["A"] will return the list ["B","D","E"] with reference to the algorithm below and the graph overleaf.

The calling program also passes an empty list of visited nodes and a starting vertex.

Check the graph in Step 1 on the next page to verify that it corresponds to the nodes and their neighbours. There are different ways of drawing the graph but logically they should all be equivalent!

```
GRAPH = { "A":["B","D","E"],    "B":["A","C","D"], "C":["B","G"],
          "D":["A","B","E","F"],   "E":["A","D"] ,    "F":["D"], "G":["C"]}
visitedList = [] // an empty list of visited nodes


function dfs(graph, currentVertex, visited)
   append currentVertex to list of visited nodes
   for vertex in graph[currentVertex]  // check neighbours
      if vertex not in visited then
         dfs(graph, vertex, visited)   // recursive call
      // stack will store return address, parameters and local variables
      endif
   next vertex
   return visited
endfunction


#main program
traversal = dfs(GRAPH, "A", visitedList)
print("Nodes visited in this order: ", traversal)
```

12-63

It is easiest to understand how this works by looking at the graphs below. This shows the state of the **stack** (here it just shows the current node when a recursive call is made), and the contents of the **visited** list. Each visited node is coloured dark blue.

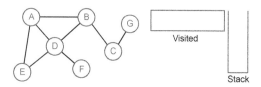

1. Start the routine with an empty stack and an empty list of visited nodes.

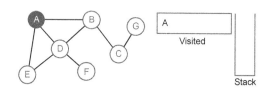

2. Visit A, add it to the visited list. Colour it to show it has been visited.

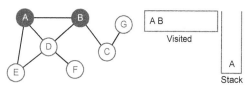

3. Push A onto the stack to keep track of where we have come from and visit A's first neighbour, B. Add it to the visited list. Colour it to show it has been visited.

4. Push B onto the stack and from B, visit the next unvisited node, C. Add it to the visited list. Colour it to show it has been visited.

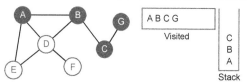

5. Push C onto the stack and from C, visit the next unvisited node, G. Add it to the visited list. Colour it to show it has been visited.

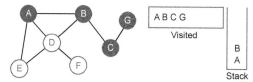

6. At G, there are no unvisited nodes so we backtrack. Pop the previous node C off the stack and return to C

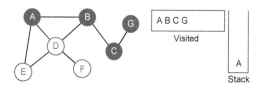

7. At C, all adjacent nodes have been visited, so backtrack again. Pop B off the stack and return to B.

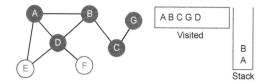

8. Push B back onto the stack to keep track of where we have come from and visit D. Add it to the visited list. Colour it to show it has been visited.

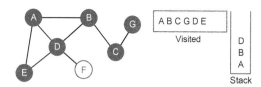

9. Push D onto the stack and visit E. Add it to the visited list. Colour it to show it has been visited.

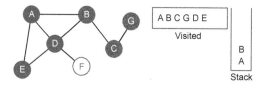

10. From E, A and D have already been visited so pop D off the stack and return to D.

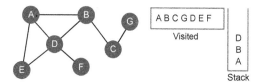

11. Push D back onto the stack and visit F. Add it to the visited list. Colour it to show it has been visited.

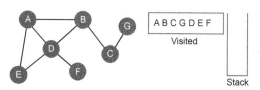

12. At F, there are no unvisited nodes so we pop D, then B, then A, whose neighbours have all been visited. The stack is now empty which means every node has been visited and the algorithm has completed.

12-63

Breadth-first traversal

With a breadth first traversal, starting at A we first visit all the nodes adjacent to A before moving to B and repeating the process for each node at this 'level', before moving to the next level. Instead of a stack, a queue is used to keep track of nodes that we still have to visit. Nodes are coloured pale blue when queued and dark blue when dequeued and added to the list of nodes that have been visited.

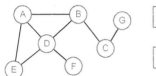

1. Append A to the empty queue at the start of the routine. This will be the first visited node.

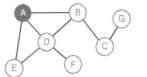

2. Dequeue A and mark it by colouring it dark blue. Add it to the visited list.

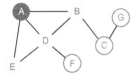

3. Queue each of A's adjacent nodes B, D and E in turn, Colour each node pale blue to show it has been queued.

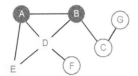

4. We've now finished with A, so dequeue the first item in the queue, which is B. Mark it by colouring it dark blue and add it to the visited list.

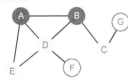

5. Queue B's remaining neighbour C. Colour it pale blue to show it has been queued.

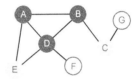

6. B's neighbours are all coloured, so dequeue the first item in the queue, which is D. Mark it by colouring it dark blue and add it to the visited list.

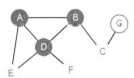

7. D's adjacent node E has already been queued and coloured. Add D's adjacent node F to the queue. Colour it pale blue to show it has been queued.

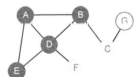 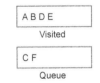

8. Dequeue the first item, E. Mark it by colouring it dark blue and add it to the visited list.

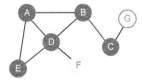

9. E's neighbours are all coloured, so dequeue the next item, C. Mark it by colouring it dark blue and add it to the visited list.

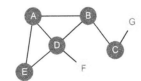

10. Add C's adjacent node G to the queue and colour it pale blue to show it has been queued.

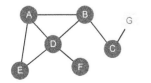

11. C's neighbours are all coloured now, so dequeue F, mark it by colouring it dark blue and add it to the visited list.

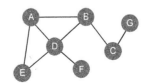

12. Finally, dequeue G, mark it by colouring it dark blue and add it to the visited list. The queue is now empty and all the nodes have been visited.

12-63

Note that we need to distinguish between a *dequeued* vertex that is added to the visited list and whose neighbours we are examining, which we colour dark blue, and *neighbours* of the current vertex, which we put in the queue and colour pale blue to show they have been queued but not visited.

Pseudocode algorithm for breadth-first traversal

The following algorithm assumes you are starting from a vertex `currentVertex`. The queue q is a dynamic data structure implemented for example as a list. A second list called `visitedNodes` holds the nodes that have been visited. Colours Black, Grey and White are more traditional in this algorithm than Dark Blue, Pale Blue and white so are used here – the diagrams are clearer in colour!

The breadth-first traversal is an iterative, rather than a recursive routine. The first node ('A' in this example), is appended to the empty queue as soon as the subroutine is entered. A Python definition of the graph as a dictionary is given below for interest, but is not directly used in the pseudocode, as implementations will vary in different languages.

```
GRAPH = {
   "A": {"colour": "White", "neighbours": ["B", "D", "E"]},
   "B": {"colour": "White", "neighbours": ["A", "D", "C"]},
   "C": {"colour": "White", "neighbours": ["B", "G"]},
   "D": {"colour": "White", "neighbours": ["A", "B", "E", "F"]},
   "E": {"colour": "White", "neighbours": ["A", "D"]},
   "F": {"colour": "White", "neighbours": ["D"]},
   "G": {"colour": "White", "neighbours": ["C"]}
   }

function bfs(graph, vertex)
   queue  = []           // an empty queue
   visited = []          // an empty list of visited nodes
   enqueue vertex
   while queue not empty
      dequeue item and put in currentNode
      set colour of currentNode to "Black"
      append currentNode to visited
      for each neighbour of currentNode
         if colour of neighbour = "White" then
            enqueue neighbour
            set colour of neighbour to "Grey"
         endif
      next neighbour
   endwhile
   return visited
endfunction

// main
visited = bfs(GRAPH, "A")
print ("List of nodes visited: ", visited)
```

12-63

Applications of depth-first search

Applications of the depth-first search include the following:

- In scheduling jobs where a series of tasks is to be performed, and certain tasks must be completed before the next one begins.
- In solving problems such as mazes, which can be represented as a graph

Finding a way through a maze

A depth-first search can be used to find a way out of a maze. Junctions where there is a choice of route in the maze are represented as nodes on a graph.

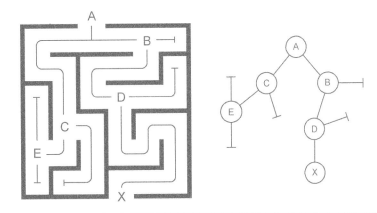

12-63

Q1: (a) Redraw the graph without showing the dead ends.

(b) State the properties of this graph that makes it a tree.

(c) Complete the table below to show how the graph would be represented using an adjacency matrix.

	A	B	C	D	E	X
A						
B						
C						
D						
E						
X						

Q2: Draw a graph representing the following maze. Show the dead ends on your graph.

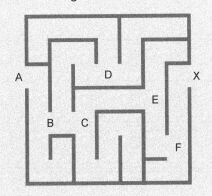

Applications of breadth-first search

Breadth-first searches are used to solve many real-life problems. For example:

- A major application of a breadth-first search is to find the *shortest* path between two points A and B, and this will be explained in detail in the next chapter. Finding the shortest path is important in, for example, GPS navigation systems and computer networks.

- Facebook. Each user profile is regarded as a node or vertex in the graph, and two nodes are connected if they are each other's friends.

- Web crawlers. A web crawler can analyse all the sites you can reach by following links randomly on a particular website.

Depth-first tree traversal

A tree is a special case of a graph, being defined as a connected, undirected graph with no cycles (see Chapter 39.)

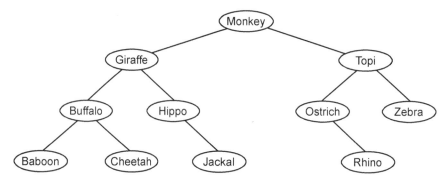

Remember that a depth –first traversal of a graph (and therefore, of a tree) goes as far down one path as possible, before backing up to the nearest root node and exploring that path as far as it goes. A depth-first traversal of this tree visits nodes in the order

Monkey, Giraffe, Buffalo, Baboon, Cheetah, Hippo, Jackal, Topi, Ostrich, Rhino, Zebra.

Q3: Write down the order of nodes visited in a pre-order traversal of the tree.

You should have discovered that the nodes are visited in the same order – in other words, a depth-first tree traversal is equivalent to a pre-order traversal.

Although it would be quite possible to do a depth-first tree traversal using the algorithm given above using the stack as a "helper" data structure, a much simpler algorithm is given in Chapter 39.

Breadth-first tree traversal

A breadth first traversal of the tree visits nodes in the order

Monkey, Giraffe, Topi, Buffalo, Hippo, Ostrich, Zebra, Baboon, Cheetah, Jackal, Rhino.

Q4: Write down the order of nodes visited in a post-order traversal of the tree.

They are not the same! The breadth-first traversal is best done using the algorithm for the breadth-first graph traversal, using a queue as the "helper" data structure.

12-63

Exercises

1. (a) Name the supporting data structure which is commonly used when traversing a graph

   (i) depth-first [1]

   (ii) breadth-first [1]

   (b) Show the order in which vertices in the following graph are visited, starting at A, using

   (i) depth-first traversal [3]

   (ii) breadth-first traversal [3]

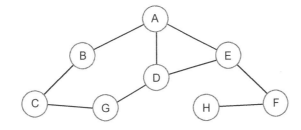

   (c) (i) Explain why the graph above is not a tree. Which edges would need to be removed for it to be a tree? [2]

   (ii) Show, by traversing the tree below using a pre-order traversal and writing the nodes in the order that they are visited, that a pre-order tree traversal is equivalent to a depth-first graph traversal. [2]

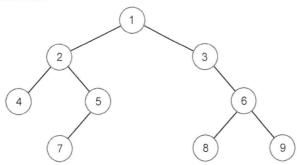

2. List the order in which nodes in the tree below will be visited using

   (a) a breadth-first traversal [3]

   (b) a post-order traversal. [3]

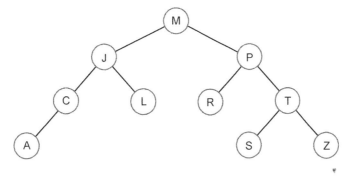

12-63

A-Level only

Chapter 64 – Optimisation algorithms

Objectives

- Ⓐ • Understand and be able to trace Dijkstra's shortest path algorithm
- Ⓐ • Be aware of applications of shortest path algorithm
- Ⓐ • Describe the A* algorithm

Optimisation problems

We increasingly rely on computers to find the optimum solution to a range of different problems. For example:

- scheduling aeroplanes and staff so that air crews always have the correct minimum rest time between flights

- finding the best move in a chess problem

- timetabling classes in schools and colleges

- finding the shortest path between two points – for building circuit boards, route planning, communications networks and many other applications

Finding the shortest path from A to B has numerous applications in everyday life and in computer-related problems. For example, if you visit a site like Google Maps to get directions from your current location to a particular destination, you probably want to know the shortest route. The software that finds it for you will use representations of street maps or roads as **graphs**, with estimated driving times or distances as **edge weights**.

Dijkstra's shortest path algorithm

Dijkstra (pronounced dike-stra) lived from 1930 to 2002. He was a Dutch computer scientist who received the Turing award in 1972 for fundamental contributions to developing programming languages. He wrote a paper in 1968 which was published under the heading "GO TO Statement Considered Harmful" and was an advocate of **structured programming**.

Dijkstra's algorithm is designed to find the shortest path between one particular start node and all other nodes in a weighted graph. This is similar to a breadth first search.

The weights could represent, for example, distances or time taken to travel between towns, or the cost of travel between airports.

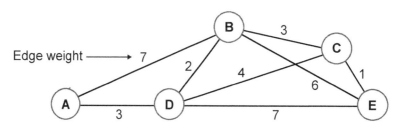

The algorithm

The algorithm works as follows:

```
Assign a temporary distance value to every node, starting with zero for
the initial node and infinity for every other node
Add all the vertices to a priority queue, sorted by current distance
(This puts the initial node at the front, the rest in random order.)
while the queue is not empty
    remove the vertex u from the front of the queue
    for each unvisited neighbour w of the current vertex u
        newDistance = distanceAtU + distanceFromUtoW
        if newDistance < distanceAtW then
            distanceAtW = newDistance
            change position of w in priority queue to reflect new
                                                  distance to w
        endif
    next w
endwhile
```

Example

In the figure below, A is the start node. A temporary distance value has been assigned to every node, starting with zero for the start node and infinity for every other node.

The priority queue is shown beside the graph, and it is kept in order of vertices with the shortest known distance from A. To start with, A is at the front, and the other nodes are in random order, in this case alphabetical.

The vertices are coloured.

- White vertices have not been visited and their distances remain at infinity.

- Pale blue vertices have been partially explored. A tentative distance to them has been found but all possible paths to them have not yet been explored, so this distance cannot be guaranteed to be the shortest one and they remain in the queue.

- Dark blue vertices have been removed from the queue and their minimum distance from A has been found. These vertices are described as having being visited.

Start at A, remove it from the front of the queue and shade it dark blue to show it has been visited

Node A has two neighbours B and D. Shade each of these pale blue to show they have been partially explored, and calculate new distance values for nodes B and D by taking the distance value at A (i.e. zero) and adding it to the edge weight between A and B, A and D.
Since all these values are less than infinity, update the distances at B and D. Distance at D is less than distance at B, so move D to the front of the priority queue.

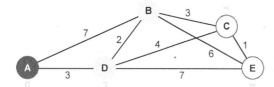

D = 3	B = 7	C = ∞	E = ∞	

Remove D from the front of the queue. Shade it dark blue to show it has been visited. Shade D's neighbours C and E pale blue to show they have been partially explored.

Now calculate new values for the unvisited neighbours of D, namely B, C and E. The distance between D and B is 2, and this is added to the edge weight between D and A. $3 + 2 = 5$ so the distance value at B is changed to the new lowest value, 5.

The current tentative distance ∞ at C is replaced with $3 + 4 = 7$, at E is replaced with $3 + 7 = 10$.

The order of nodes in the priority queue does not need to be changed since B, the node with the smallest current distance from A, is already at the front.

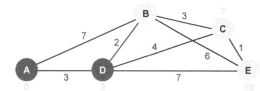

B = 5	C = 7	E = 10		

Remove B from the priority queue. Shade B dark blue to show it has been visited.

At B, the values at C and E are calculated as $5 + 3 = 8$ and $5 + 6 = 11$ respectively, but these are both greater than the tentative values already there, so these values are not changed.

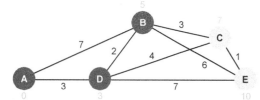

C = 7	E = 10			

Remove C from the queue and shade it dark blue to show it has been visited. The distance to E via C will be calculated as $7 + 1 = 8$. This is less than current tentative distance to E (10) so will replace it.

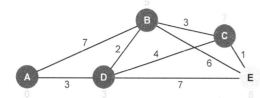

E = 8				

Remove E from the queue. It has no unvisited neighbours, so there are no new distances to calculate. Shade E dark blue.

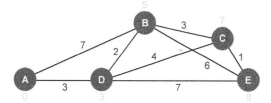

12-64

A-Level only

The queue is empty, all the nodes have now been visited so the algorithm ends.

We have found the shortest distance from A to every other node, and the shortest distance from A is marked in blue at each node.

Q1: Copy the graph below and use the method above to trace the shortest path from A to all other nodes. Write the shortest distance at each node.

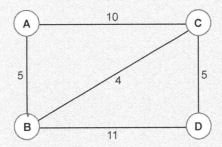

Q2: Use a similar method to trace the shortest path from A to all other nodes. Write the shortest distance at each node. What is the shortest distance from A to G?

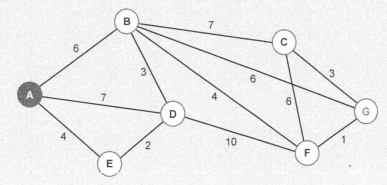

12-64

The A* algorithm

Dijkstra's algorithm is a special case of a more general **path-finding algorithm** called the **A* algorithm**. Dijkstra's algorithm has one **cost function**, which is the real cost value (e.g. distance) from the source node to every other node.

The A* algorithm has two cost functions:

1. $g(x)$ – as with Dijkstra's algorithm, this is the real cost from the source to a given node.

2. $h(x)$ – this is the approximate cost from node x to the goal node. It is a **heuristic function**, meaning that it is a good or adequate solution, but not necessarily the optimum one. This algorithm stipulates that the heuristic function should never overestimate the cost, therefore the real cost should be greater than or equal $h(x)$.

The total cost of each node is calculated as $f(x) = g(x) + h(x)$.

The A* algorithm focusses only on reaching the goal node, unlike Dijkstra's algorithm which finds the lowest cost or shortest path to every node. It is used, for example, in video games to enable characters to navigate the world.

Exercises

1. (a) What is the purpose of Djikstra's shortest path algorithm? [2]

   (b) Describe briefly **two** applications of the algorithm. [4]

   (c) The weighted graph (Figure 1) shows the distances between each of the graph's vertices.

   Copy Figure 1 and show the tentative distance from the starting node A allocated to each node after nodes B and D have been visited (dequeued and finished with) using Dijkstra's algorithm.

   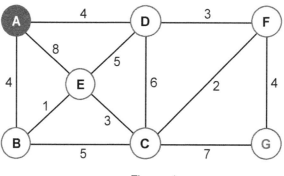

   Figure 1

   (d) A possible path from A to G is A→D→F→G.

   (i) Describe in a similar way, the shortest path from A to C. What is its length? [2]

   (ii) What is the shortest path from A to G? What is its length? [3]

2. The following graph shows distances between five cities. Djikstra's shortest path algorithm is used to find the shortest distance between Liverpool and each of the other cities. The algorithm is given below.

```
Assign a temporary distance value to every node, starting with zero
for the initial node and infinity for every other node

Add all the vertices to a priority queue, sorted by current
distance. (This puts the initial node at the front, the rest, which
all start with temporary distances of infinity, in random order.)

while the queue is not empty
    remove the vertex u from the front of the queue
    for each unvisited neighbour w of the current vertex u
        newDistance = distanceAtU + distanceFromUtoW
        if newDistance < distanceAtW then
            distanceAtW = newDistance
            change position of w in priority  queue to reflect new
                                                distance to w

        endif
    next w
endwhile
```

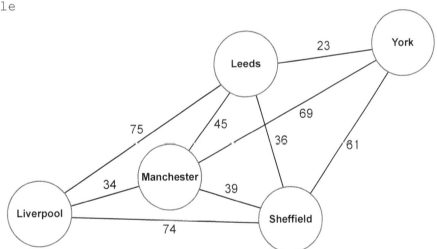

The following table represents the distances after the first statement in the algorithm is executed.

Liverpool	Leeds	Manchester	Sheffield	York
0	∞	∞	∞	∞

(a) Complete the following table after **one** iteration of the WHILE loop in the above algorithm. [3]

Liverpool	Leeds	Manchester	Sheffield	York

(b) Complete the table after the **second** iteration of the WHILE loop. [2]

Liverpool	Leeds	Manchester	Sheffield	York

Index

Index

Index

Index

CPSIA information can be obtained
at www.ICGtesting.com
Printed in the USA
BVHW02s1048180918
527830BV00022B/1244/P

9 781910 523056